ENDORSEM~~ENT~~

"If you have neglected Calvin's writings ~~~~ ~~~~ ~~are~~ too difficult or too dreary, this book will change your m~~~~. ~~I~~t is a compendium of his thought presented, as we might expect from these writers, clearly, engagingly, and with a devotional warmth that encourages us to know the God whom we worship."

—ALISTAIR BEGG
Senior pastor
Parkside Church
Chagrin Falls, Ohio

"Deep calls to deep, and Burk Parsons' rich and insightful work on John Calvin takes us both deep and wide into the heart of this extraordinary saint. Most of all, I'm grateful to God that a whole new generation of believers can now be introduced to one of the greatest theologians of all time. I highly recommend this book to all who are seeking a closer—and deeper—walk with our Savior!"

—JONI EARECKSON TADA
Founder, Joni and Friends
International Disability Center
Agoura Hills, California

"I personally have benefited in the reading of this work, and most heartily commend it. The value of this book is that it brings out something of John Calvin's own life and struggles, and then summarizes his doctrinal position, not just as an academic exercise, but in the true spirit of genuine Calvinism, which points men to Christ and justification by faith, producing godliness of life and true communion with God."

—DR. MORTON H. SMITH
Professor of systematic and biblical theology
Greenville Presbyterian Theological Seminary
Greenville, South Carolina

"On the five-hundredth anniversary of John Calvin's birth, it is utterly fitting that a book of essays should appear that is designed for ordinary Christians, not scholars. The scholars will have their conferences, of course, and rightly so, but here is a collection of essays that will inform and move ordinary readers to grasp something of the profound gift God gave to the church in the person and ministry—and especially the writings—of Calvin. Read this book, then find yourself drawn toward many profitable and stretching hours reading Calvin's *Institutes* and some of his many commentaries."

—D. A. CARSON
Research professor of New Testament
Trinity Evangelical Divinity School
Deerfield, Illinois

"To my knowledge, there never has been a collection of authors of any edited volume under whose ministry I would rather sit than these. What stands out is that they are humble, holy men of God. Most of them are too old—too seasoned—to care about scoring points. Their lives witness to the preciousness of Christ and the importance of purity. Expect no bombast. Expect humble, measured admiration and wise application. This is a good way to meet John Calvin: in the holy hearts of humble servants of Christ. The only better way would be to read the man himself."

—JOHN PIPER
Pastor for preaching and vision
Bethlehem Baptist Church
Minneapolis, Minnesota

"Calvinism often gets bad press, and John Calvin must rank among the least understood—and most misunderstood—of all the great leaders in church history. We badly need a fresh look at both, one that rightly reveals Calvin not as a doctrinal demagogue, but as a loving pastor, passionate evangelist, and sympathetic counselor, and above all as someone concerned to have all his thinking and living rendered in terms of obedience to God.

This is it! Twenty modern pastors, preachers, and authors have combined their knowledge and skills to produce a book that will inform and inspire countless readers for years to come. I know of nothing quite like it and I commend it enthusiastically and without reservation."

—JOHN BLANCHARD
Preacher, teacher, and apologist
Author, *Does God Believe in Atheists?*

"Reading Burk Parsons' new book, *John Calvin: A Heart for Devotion, Doctrine, and Doxology*, was like following a great chef on an early-morning trip to the farmer's market. Burk chose an incredible array of authors to speak to the most important themes of John Calvin's life, and the combination has resulted in a veritable feast of delicacies and delights. Surely this book will help introduce one of history's most gospel-centered men, Calvin, to a generation that wants to relegate him to dusty antiquity and dry orthodoxy. To read Calvin is to understand what a mind informed by the gospel and a heart enflamed with God's grace is supposed to look like! Thank you, chef Parsons!"

—SCOTTY SMITH
Senior pastor
Christ Community Church
Franklin, Tennessee

"There is a fresh breeze blowing in these pages. A new generation has discovered the riches of biblical truth to be found in John Calvin's work. Written in an inviting and accessible style, this book extends an invitation to all to come and learn as well. However, what they will learn will have far less to do with Calvin and far more to do with the centrality and greatness of the triune God whom he served. Calvin would have wanted it that way, and so do we."

—DAVID F. WELLS
Senior research professor
Gordon-Conwell Theological Seminary
South Hamilton, Massachusetts

"Virtually all of the great Reformers of the sixteenth century were students of the great church father Augustine. If we are to experience another renewal of the church, a renewal that many of us see as much needed today, I believe it will come through those who have been careful students of John Calvin. If you want to know why I say this or have any doubt that Calvin is all that important, then read this fine book. It presents a veritable kaleidoscope of perspectives on the many-sided greatness of this man and his work. I highly recommend it."

—G. I. WILLIAMSON
Pastor, editor
Author, *The Westminster Confession of Faith for Study Classes*

JAY E. ADAMS, ERIC J. ALEXANDER, THABITI
ANYABWILE, THOMAS K. ASCOL, JOEL R.
BEEKE, JERRY BRIDGES, SINCLAIR B.
FERGUSON, W. ROBERT GODFREY, D. G. HART,
MICHAEL HORTON, PHILLIP R. JOHNSON,
STEVEN J. LAWSON, JOHN MACARTHUR, KEITH
A. MATHISON, BURK PARSONS, RICHARD D.
PHILLIPS, HARRY L. REEDER, PHILIP
GRAHAM RYKEN, DEREK W. H. THOMAS

JOHN CALVIN
A HEART
FOR DEVOTION
DOCTRINE &
DOXOLOGY

EDITED BY BURK PARSONS
FOREWORD BY IAIN H. MURRAY

ʀR
Reformation Trust
PUBLISHING

A DIVISION OF LIGONIER MINISTRIES · ORLANDO, FLORIDA

John Calvin: A Heart for Devotion, Doctrine, and Doxology
© 2008 by Burk Parsons

Published by Reformation Trust
a division of Ligonier Ministries
400 Technology Park, Lake Mary, FL 32746
www.ligonier.org
www.reformationtrust.com

Printed in the United States of America

Cover design: Geoff Stevens
Interior design and typeset: Katherine Lloyd, The DESK, Colorado Springs, CO

Unless otherwise indicated, all Scripture quotations are from The Holy Bible, English Standard Version, copyright © 2001 by Crossway Bibles, a division of Good News Publishers. Used by permission. All rights reserved.

Library of Congress Cataloging-in-Publication Data
John Calvin : a heart for devotion, doctrine, and doxology / edited by Burk Parsons.
    p. cm.
 Includes bibliographical references and indexes.
 ISBN 978-1-56769-106-1
1. Calvin, Jean, 1509-1564. 2. Reformed Church--Doctrines. I. Parsons, Burk.
 BX9418.J6132 2008
 284'.2092--dc22

                                                            2008025945

DEDICATION

The contributors dedicate this book to R.C. Sproul, who has inspired a new generation of reformers to know, love, and proclaim the gospel of Jesus Christ.

Jay E. Adams

Eric J. Alexander

Thabiti M. Anyabwile

Tom Ascol

Joel R. Beeke

Jerry Bridges

Sinclair B. Ferguson

W. Robert Godfrey

D.G. Hart

Michael S. Horton

Steven J. Lawson

Jim Sutton

Keith Mathison

Iain H. Murray

B. Ryan

Richard D. Phillips

Harry F. Reeder III

Philip Ryken

Derek Thomas

TABLE OF CONTENTS

IAIN H. MURRAY

We may be sure that the man who wanted no stone to mark his grave would want no festivities to mark the anniversary of his birth. Why, then, the present volume? The answer is that it is the work of God that is to be remembered. In John Calvin's words, "God's loving-kindness to us was wonderful, when the pure Gospel emerged out of that dreadful darkness in which it had been buried for so many ages."[1] For him, the Reformation was a movement from heaven that turned attention from a man-centered religion to God; the message was "Call no man Master. Cease from man and attend to the Word of God." The hope of this book is that the memory of Calvin will aid in the recovery of God-centered Christianity today.

On the opening page of every edition of Calvin's *Institutes of the Christian Religion* stand the words that were the unifying motif of his life: "True and sound wisdom consists of two parts: the knowledge of God and of ourselves." So he first wrote in 1536. The next year, at the age of 28, he spoke of "true piety" as "a pure and true zeal which loves God altogether as Father, and reveres him truly as Lord, embraces his justice and dreads to offend him more than to die."[2] Through all the years that followed, the emphasis remained the same: "It is necessary always to begin with this principle—to know the God whom we worship."[3]

Calvin saw himself as a sinner who owed all that he was to God. It was God who "subdued" his mind to the knowledge of Christ; his call to Geneva was "as if God from heaven had laid his mighty hand upon me to arrest me"; and the subsequent ministry, in all its successes and setbacks, was to him an illustration of the truth, "Many are the plans in the mind of a man, but it is the purpose of the LORD that will stand" (Prov.

19:21). This text was equally true of the blessings and trials of his personal life. When he consoled a fellow pastor on the death of his wife, it was with the lesson he had first preached to himself seven years before: "We unjustly defraud God of his right, unless each of us lives and dies dependent on his sovereign pleasure. . . . Our principal motive of consolation consists in this, that by the admirable providence of God, the things we consider adverse, contribute to our salvation, and that we are separated in the world only that we may be once more reunited in his celestial kingdom."[4]

The piety that was recovered at the Reformation has sometimes been caricatured as a life of cold, austere obedience to God. Certainly Calvin taught, "Nothing pleases God but what he has commanded in his word; and the true principle of piety is the obedience which we ought to render to him alone."[5] But the caricature rests on ignorance of the connection between the love of God and the gratitude of believing hearts. To glorify this gracious God and not to displease Him are necessarily the desires of those whom He redeems. The words of a later hymn writer come straight from the gospel of the Reformation:

To see the law by Christ fulfilled
And hear his pardoning voice
Changes the slave into a child
And duty into choice.[6]

In reading Calvin, nothing challenges me more than the way in which the obedience due to God controlled his thinking and living. There were pastoral issues about which he knew how to be moderate and sensitive, but when issues concerned the glory of God, the worship of His name ("to be preferred to the safety of men and angels!"[7]), the purity of the church, and the truth of the gospel, he was resolute. For Calvin, to accept compromise when Scripture has spoken is to affront the divine majesty of the Author. What Scripture says, God says. We may assert this readily enough in our easygoing days, but for many in the sixteenth century (as for some at the present time), to act upon it meant being ready to die. Calvin never hid from those to whom he preached that believing the truth could well be their preparation for prison and martyrdom. Not without reason has it been said that Calvinism is a message for hard times.

It is the knowledge that a Christian is identified with the cause of God that raises this perspective from any shade of gloom. Nothing in the short term, or in death itself, can mean defeat: God must win. It is the vision of God that changes everything. Calvin writes, "We shall never be fit for the service of God, if we look not beyond this fleeting life."[8] He adds, "When any person has fixed his eyes on God, his heart will be invincible, and utterly incapable of being moved."[9]

This means that work done according to the will of God, and by His enabling, will be lasting work. All else will be found to be "wood, hay, straw" when "the Day will disclose it" (1 Cor. 3:12–13). The most useful Christian life, therefore, is the one lived near to God. To those who obey and follow when He calls, the promise is sure: "I chose you and appointed you that you should go and bear fruit and that your fruit should abide" (John 15:16). From these words, Calvin drew confidence: "The Church will last to the very end of the world; for the labour of the apostles yields fruit even in the present day, and our preaching is not for a single age only, but will enlarge the Church, so that new fruit will be seen to spring up after our death."[10]

"Lift your eyes and look to the heaven," says a Korean hymn; that is the direction in which our thought needs to be directed today. Our trifling concerns and our worldliness result from the poverty of our knowledge of God.

Jean Cadier, speaking of the need for deliverance from preoccupation with self, reports the following incident:

> I am thinking of the man who said to me a short time ago as he came out of a lecture, "I have been converted through reading the *Institutes.*" And when I asked him to tell me what exactly had

been the message which had effected this transformation in his life, he replied: "I learnt from reading Calvin that all the worries about health and about the uncertain future which had hitherto dominated my life were without much importance and that the only things that counted were obedience to the will of God and a care for His glory."[11]

As I think of the various authors of this book, and contrast their names with those of the comparative few leaders who were preaching and writing on these themes at the time of the last Calvin anniversary (the fourth centenary of his death in 1964), I see much to hearten us. Men have been raised up in the intervening years whose names, with few exceptions, were unknown in 1964. Since that time, also, a great number of Calvin's writings have become widely available and have found a new generation of readers across the world. We may say with Ezra, God has given us "a little reviving" (Ezra 9:8). Yet there are dangers for those who revere the memory of Calvin, and I will mention two that present themselves to me:

First, in our circles, piety and godliness are not the characteristics of Calvinistic belief to the extent that they ought to be. We believe that divine revelation has come to us in words and in propositions, and for these we must contend. But truth is only rightly believed to the extent that it is embodied in life. The gospel spread across Europe in the sixteenth century primarily through the witness of transformed people. To Christian women, facing martyrdom in Paris, Calvin wrote:

> How many thousands of women have there been who have spared neither blood nor their lives to maintain the name of Jesus Christ, and announce his reign! Has not God caused their martyrdom to fructify? . . . Have we not still before our eyes, examples of how God works daily by their testimony, and confounds his enemies, in such a manner that there is no preaching of such efficacy as the fortitude and perseverance they possess in confessing the name of Christ?[12]

Too often, in our time, beliefs associated with the name of Calvin have been identified with the lecture hall and the academy. Ford Lewis Battles, to whom we owe the best current translation of the *Institutes*, has written: "All the forces contrary to a truly Reformed faith that stood in the way in the sixteenth century have their late-twentieth-century counterpart. Lukewarm Nicodemites and learned scoffers are in the very bosom of the church, and—I may say—the seminaries."[13] I once had the misfortune to hear addresses on "the five points of Calvinism" delivered as though we were attending a chemistry lecture. In contrast, I am thankful that so many of the contributors to the present book are *preachers* first and foremost.

It is not by argument or teaching alone that the current scene can be reversed. "The kingdom of God does not consist in talk but in power" (1 Cor. 4:20). "I will supplicate our heavenly Father," Calvin writes to suffering Christians, "to fill you with the Holy Spirit."[14] There alone is the source of witness that is not in word only. The explanation of the Reformation lies in one short sentence of John Knox: "God gave his Holy Spirit to simple men in great abundance."[15]

Second, our example needs to be the best argument that belief in divine sovereignty does not weaken evangelistic preaching. There are prominent exceptions to the contrary—the names of some of them will be found in these pages—but in surveying the Christian scene at large, there is some justification for the idea that Calvinistic belief hinders evangelistic passion. Facing this perception, we would be mistaken to suppose we are free of blame. We have found it easier to be "teachers" and "defenders" of the truth than to be evangelists who are willing to die that men might be converted. Sometimes the impression can be given to other Christians that we regard "Calvinism" as co-terminus with Christianity and that we think all gospel preaching can be fitted into the five points. The five points are not to be depreciated, but God is incomprehensibly greater than our understanding, and there are other truths to be preached far beyond our capacity to harmonize.

Calvin cautions us here. In speaking of the indiscriminate invitations of Christ in John 5, he observes, "He is ready to give himself, provided that they are only willing to believe."[16] He can say that "nothing of all that God wishes to be saved shall perish"[17] and yet warn his hearers lest the opportunity of salvation "pass away from us."[18] He speaks of Christ's "great kindness" to Judas and affirms, "Christ does not lay Judas under the necessity of perishing."[19] If on occasions, when in controversy with opponents of Scripture, Calvin unduly presses the implications of a doctrine, he guards against that temptation in his general preaching and teaching. He does not hesitate to teach that God loves those who will not be saved;[20] indeed, he writes that God "wishes all men to be saved," and to the objection that God cannot wish what He has not ordained, it is enough for Calvin to confess: "Although God's will is simple, yet great variety is involved in it, as far as our senses are concerned. Besides, it is not surprising that our eyes should be blinded by intense light."[21] Our duty, he would say, is to adore the loftiness of God rather than investigate it.

Where Calvinistic truth is presented as though there is no love in God to sinners as sinners—that His only regard is for the elect—it is no wonder that evangelistic preaching falters. The preacher has to be possessed with a love for all or he will not represent the Savior in whose name he speaks. The men of Calvinistic belief who have stood out as evangelists and missionaries have always been examples of this. It was an eminent Welsh Calvinist, William Williams, Pantycelyn, who said, "Love is the greatest thing in religion, and if that is forgotten nothing can take its place."[22]

Dr. D. Martyn Lloyd-Jones, to whom, mainly, Britain owed the republication of the *Institutes* in 1949, used to advise us not to quote others unless we were sure we could not say it so well ourselves. Those who take up this book will soon notice that it is our inability to say it as well that lies behind the many fine quotations of Calvin in these pages. The lesson from that should not be lost. The best purpose will have been served if the reader comes to the conclusion, "I ought to be reading Calvin himself!" As Dr. J. I. Packer said when the recovery of the doctrines of grace was only beginning in England, "The student will find that Calvin makes richer and more straightforward reading than all his expositors."[23]

It would be a fine thing if we could all come to the decision that the Puritan leader John Cotton reached in the latter years of his ministry in Boston. Cotton Mather tells us that Cotton, on "being asked, why in his latter days he indulged *nocturnal studies* more than formerly, he pleasantly replied, 'Because I love to sweeten my mouth with a piece of Calvin before I go to sleep.'"[24]

None of us would regret taking up the same habit. Above all, it is to be fervently hoped that these pages will be used to do far more than to mark an anniversary. Our prayer is that they will fall into the hands of a young generation, called to the service of Christ, and that numbers of them will take up the apostolic resolution, "We will devote ourselves to prayer and to the ministry of the word" (Acts 6:4).

NOTES

[1] John Calvin, *Commentaries on the Book of the Prophet Daniel* (Grand Rapids: Eerdmans, 1948), 2:220.

[2] John Calvin, *Instruction in Faith*, trans. Paul T. Fuhrmann (Louisville, Ky.: Westminster John Knox Press, 1992), 22.

[3] John Calvin, *Commentaries on the Twelve Minor Prophets* (Edinburgh: Calvin Translation Society, 1849; repr. Grand Rapids: Baker, 2003), 5:500.

[4] John Calvin, *Letters of John Calvin*, ed. Jules Bonnet, trans. M. R. Gilbert (Philadelphia: Presbyterian Board of Education, 1858), 3:236.

[5] Calvin, *Commentaries on the Book of the Prophet Daniel*, 1:218.

[6] From the hymn "Love Constraining to Obedience," by William Cowper.

[7] John Calvin, *Calvin's Tracts* (Edinburgh: Calvin Translation Society, 1851), 3:260.

[8] Calvin, *Letters of John Calvin*, 3:128.

[9] John Calvin, *Commentary on the Gospel According to John* (Edinburgh: Calvin Translation Society, 1847; repr. Grand Rapids: Baker, 2003), 2:47.

[10] Ibid., 2:121.

[11] Jean Cadier, *The Man God Mastered*, trans. O.R. Johnston (London: Inter-Varsity Press, 1960), 178.

[12] Calvin, *Letters of John Calvin*, 3:365–366.

[13] John Calvin, *The Piety of John Calvin*, trans. and ed. Ford Lewis Battles (Grand Rapids; Baker, 1978), 25.

[14] Calvin, *Letters of John Calvin*, 3:232.

[15] John Knox, *Works of John Knox*, ed. David Laing (Edinburgh: James Thin, 1895), 1:31.

[16] Calvin, *Commentary on the Gospel According to John*, 1:261.

[17] Ibid., 1:407.

[18] Ibid., 1:305.

[19] Ibid., 2:72.

[20] See, for instance, Calvin on John 3:16 and *Sermons on Deuteronomy*, trans. Arthur Golding (1583; repr. Edinburgh: Banner of Truth Trust, 1987), 167.

[21] John Calvin, *Commentaries on the First Twenty Chapters of the Book of the Prophet Ezekiel* (Edinburgh: Calvin Translation Society, 1850; repr. Grand Rapids: Baker, 2003), 2:247. For more on this subject, see John Piper, "Are There Two Wills in God," in *The Grace of God, the Bondage of the Will*, eds. Thomas R. Schreiner and Bruce A. Ware, Vol. 1 (Grand Rapids: Baker, 1995).

[22] This theme is well handled in relation to Calvin by R. C. Reed, *The Gospel as Taught by Calvin* (repr. Grand Rapids: Baker, 1979). See also James McGuire, "A Kinder, Gentler Calvinism," in D. Steele, C. C. Thomas, and S. Lance Quinn, *The Five Points of Calvinism: Defined, Defended, and Documented* (Phillipsburg, N.J.: P&R, 2004), and Iain H. Murray, *Spurgeon* v. *Hyper-Calvinism* (Edinburgh: Banner of Truth Trust, 1995).

[23] Quoted in Cadier, *The Man God Mastered*, 187. For those looking for a starting point in the reading of Calvin himself, I would recommend J. Graham Miller, *Calvin's Wisdom, An Anthology Arranged Alphabetically* (Edinburgh: Banner of Truth Trust, 1992).

[24] Cotton Mather, *The Great Works of Christ in America* (repr. Edinburgh: Banner of Truth Trust, 1979), 1:274.

BURK PARSONS

John Calvin was a churchman for all ages. He was a Reformer, a pastor, and a revolutionary. He was a selfless husband, a devoted father, and a noble friend. But above all Calvin was a man whose mind was humbled and whose heart was mastered by the Lord God Almighty. His life's prayer—"I offer my heart to you, O Lord, promptly and sincerely"—was an unwavering declaration of surrender to the Lord, whom he sought to love with all of his heart, soul, mind, and strength. He saw himself first and foremost as a disciple of Jesus Christ, and he desired earnestly to be taught daily "in the school of Jesus Christ"[1] so that he might rightly know the Lord in order to "trust, invoke, praise, and love him."[2]

This, in essence, is also the purpose of this present volume—that the people of God might more fully trust, invoke, praise, and love the Lord. Calvin would have wanted readers to come away from this book not primarily with a greater knowledge of the life, ministry, and doctrine of the man John Calvin, but with a greater knowledge of all the doctrines of God and, what is more, with a greater knowledge and love of God Himself, leading to a life of sacrificial duty and overwhelming delight as citizens of His kingdom.

The pastors and teachers who have contributed to this volume in commemoration of Calvin's five-hundredth birthday have done so on account of their desire to honor the Lord by providing the church with an accessible book on the life, ministry, and doctrine of the man who was first and foremost a pastor to the people of God whom he served throughout his life.

Although many Christians throughout the world are somewhat familiar with Calvin's doctrines, most are unfamiliar with the man who was so passionately dedicated to prayer and the ministry of the Word. Given all that the Lord accomplished in him and through him, his legacy to Christians in the twenty-first century is one of devotional, doctrinal, and doxological surrender to the Lord. As such, we would do well to heed the words of Calvin's longtime friend and biographer, Theodore Beza, who penned the following shortly after Calvin's death: "Since it has pleased God that Calvin should continue to speak to us through his writings, which are so scholarly and full of godliness, it is up to future generations to go on listening to him until the end of the world, so that they might see our God as he truly is and live and reign with him for all eternity. Amen. (19 August 1564)."[3]

NOTES

[1] John Calvin, *Letters of John Calvin*, ed. Jules Bonnet, 4 vols. (Eugene, Ore: Wipf & Stock, 2007), July 20, 1558.

[2] John Calvin, *Institutes of the Christian Religion*, ed. John T. McNeill, trans. Ford Lewis Battles; Library of Christian Classics, XX–XXI (Philadelphia: Westminster John Knox, 1960), 1.14.22.

[3] Theodore Beza, *The Life of John Calvin* (1564; repr. Darlington, England: Evangelical Press, 1997), 140.

 Contributors

Jay E. Adams is a teacher, speaker, and author. A former professor at Westminster Seminary California and a retired pastor, Dr. Adams has authored more than one hundred books, many of which have been translated into other languages. Among his publications are *Compassionate Counseling*, *From Forgiven to Forgiving*, and *Encouragement Isn't Enough*.

Eric J. Alexander is a retired pastor of St. George's-Tron Church in Glasgow, Scotland, and a council member of Alliance of Confessing Evangelicals. He is a former president of the Universities and Colleges Christian Fellowship (UCCF) in Great Britain, and he served as chairman of the Scottish Council of the Overseas Missionary Fellowship. Rev. Alexander preaches and teaches at conferences and seminaries in Europe and the United States.

Thabiti Anyabwile is senior pastor of First Baptist Church in Grand Cayman, Cayman Islands. Rev. Anyabwile is a conference speaker and author of several books, including *The Decline of African American Theology: From Biblical Faith to Cultural Captivity*, *The Faithful Preacher: Recapturing the Vision of Three Pioneering African-American Pastors*, and the forthcoming *What Is a Healthy Church Member?*

Thomas K. Ascol is senior pastor of Grace Baptist Church in Cape Coral, Fla. He also serves as executive director of Founders Ministries and editor of *Founders Journal*. Dr. Ascol has written numerous articles and contributed to several books, including *Reclaiming the Gospel and Reforming Churches* and *A Puritan Speaks to Our Dying Nation*. He is also editor of the book *Dear Timothy: Letters on Pastoral Ministry*.

Joel R. Beeke is president and professor of systematic theology at Puritan Reformed Theological Seminary in Grand Rapids, Mich. He is also pastor of Heritage Netherlands Reformed Congregation and editorial director of Reformation Heritage Books. Dr. Beeke has authored more than fifteen hundred articles for various periodicals and reference works, and has written or edited fifty books, including *The Quest for Full Assurance, Meet the Puritans, Walking as He Walked,* and *Heirs with Christ: The Puritans on Adoption.*

Jerry Bridges has served with the Navigators since 1955. He speaks regularly at conferences and seminaries throughout the country and serves as a council member of the Alliance of Confessing Evangelicals. He is the author of several books, including *The Pursuit of Holiness, Trusting God, Transforming Grace,* and *Respectable Sins.*

Sinclair B. Ferguson is senior pastor of First Presbyterian Church in Columbia, S.C., and is distinguished visiting professor of systematic theology at Westminster Theological Seminary. Dr. Ferguson is also a council member of the Alliance of Confessing Evangelicals. He has written several books, including *In Christ Alone, The Holy Spirit, Taking the Christian Life Seriously,* and *The Sermon on the Mount.*

W. Robert Godfrey is president and professor of church history at Westminster Seminary California. He has taught at many colleges and seminaries, and frequently speaks at Christian conferences throughout the country. A council member of the Alliance of Confessing Evangelicals, Dr. Godfrey has written several books, including *An Unexpected Journey, Reformation Sketches,* and *Pleasing God in our Worship.*

D. G. Hart is director of academic programs at the Intercollegiate Studies Institute in Philadelphia, Pa. Previously he served as dean of academic affairs and professor of church history at Westminster Seminary California, where he remains an adjunct member of the faculty. Dr.

Hart has written several books, including *A Secular Faith: Why Christianity Favors the Separation of Church and State*, and has co-authored several others with John R. Muether, including *Seeking a Better Country: 300 Years of American Presbyterianism* and *With Reverence and Awe: Returning to the Basics of Reformed Worship.*

Michael Horton is J. Gresham Machen professor of apologetics and systematic theology at Westminster Seminary California. In addition to serving as editor in chief of *Modern Reformation* magazine and as host of the popular radio show *The White Horse Inn*, he is the author of numerous books, including *God of Promise: Introducing Covenant Theology, Too Good to Be True: Finding Hope in a World of Hype*, and *Covenant and Salvation.*

Phillip R. Johnson is executive director of Grace to You in Panorama City, Calif., and is a pastor at Grace Community Church. He has been closely associated with John MacArthur for nearly thirty years and edits most of Dr. MacArthur's books. Rev. Johnson may be best known for the Web sites he maintains, including The Spurgeon Archive and The Hall of Church History.

Steven J. Lawson is senior pastor of Christ Fellowship Baptist Church in Mobile, Ala., and serves on the ministerial board of Reformed Theological Seminary and on the board of directors of The Master's College and Seminary. Dr. Lawson has authored many books, including *Famine in the Land, Foundations of Grace*, and *The Expository Genius of John Calvin.*

John MacArthur has served as pastor-teacher of Grace Community Church in Sun Valley, Calif., for nearly forty years and is heard on more than two thousand radio outlets worldwide on the radio program *Grace to You.* He is president of The Master's College and Seminary and has written numerous books, including *Charismatic Chaos, Faith Works, The Gospel According to Jesus, Ashamed of the Gospel*, and *A Tale of Two Sons.*

He is also the author of the twenty-six-volume *MacArthur New Testament Commentary* series.

Keith A. Mathison is an associate editor of *Tabletalk* magazine in Orlando, Fla., and is associate editor of *The Reformation Study Bible* (ESV). Dr. Mathison is author of several books, including *Postmillennialism: An Eschatology of Hope, The Shape of Sola Scriptura, Given for You: Reclaiming Calvin's Doctrine of the Lord's Supper*, and *Dispensationalism: Rightly Dividing the People of God?*

Iain H. Murray is a co-founder of Banner of Truth Trust in Edinburgh, Scotland, and is minister emeritus of the Australian Presbyterian Church. Rev. Murray has authored many books, including *A Scottish Christian Heritage, Evangelicalism Divided, Jonathan Edwards: A New Biography*, and *The Puritan Hope.*

Burk Parsons serves as minister of congregational life at Saint Andrew's Chapel in Sanford, Fla., and is editor of *Tabletalk*, the monthly Bible-study magazine of Ligonier Ministries. Rev. Parsons is also editor of the book *Assured by God: Living in the Fullness of God's Grace.*

Richard D. Phillips is senior minister of Second Presbyterian Church in Greenville, S.C. He is also a council member of the Alliance of Confessing Evangelicals and is chairman of the Philadelphia Conference on Reformed Theology. Rev. Phillips' preaching is heard nationwide on the radio program *God's Living Word.* Among his twenty-one published books are his most recent titles, *What's So Great About the Doctrines of Grace?* and *Jesus the Evangelist.*

Harry L. Reeder is senior pastor of Briarwood Presbyterian Church in Birmingham, Ala. After completing his doctoral dissertation on "The Biblical Paradigm of Church Revitalization," he authored his first book, *From Embers to a Flame.* Dr. Reeder is devoted to the ministry of church revitalization, hosting conferences in the United States twice a year called "Embers to a Flame."

Philip Graham Ryken is senior pastor of Tenth Presbyterian Church in Philadelphia, Pa., and is a teacher for the Alliance of Confessing Evangelicals. Dr. Ryken is broadcast nationally on the radio program *Every Last Word.* He has written or edited more than twenty books, including *What Is the Christian Worldview?*, *City on a Hill: Recovering the Biblical Pattern for the Church in the 21st Century,* and Bible commentaries on Exodus, Jeremiah, Lamentations, 1 Timothy, and Galatians.

Derek W. H. Thomas is John Richards professor of practical and systematic theology at Reformed Theological Seminary in Jackson, Miss. He is also minister of teaching at First Presbyterian Church in Jackson and editorial director for The Alliance of Confessing Evangelicals. Among Dr. Thomas' many books are *God Strengthens: Ezekiel Properly Explained, Mining for Wisdom,* and *Praying the Saviour's Way.* Along with John W. Tweeddale, Dr. Thomas is co-editor of a forthcoming book on the life, ministry, and doctrine of John Calvin.

Chapter 1

THE HUMILITY
OF CALVIN'S CALVINISM

BURK PARSONS

As the surest source of destruction to men is to obey themselves, so the only haven of safety is to have no other will, no other wisdom, than to follow the Lord wherever he leads. Let this, then, be the first step, to abandon ourselves, and devote the whole energy of our minds to the service of God. By service, I mean not only that which consists in verbal obedience, but that by which the mind, divested of its own carnal feelings, implicitly obeys the call of the Spirit of God.[1]

—JOHN CALVIN

It has not been my habit to refer to myself as a Calvinist; if memory serves, I have never done so, primarily because I don't think John Calvin would want me to. In fact, whenever another Christian asks me what I am (with the seeming hope of determining my particular denominational affiliation), I respond simply, "I am a Christian." Nevertheless, if I were ever truly pressed on the matter of being a Calvinist, I suppose I would respond by saying, "Yes, I am a Calvinist because I am a Christian, and I am a Christian because I believe the gospel."

The nineteenth-century Baptist preacher Charles Haddon Spurgeon said it this way:

> I have my own private opinion that there is no such thing as preaching Christ and Him crucified, unless we preach what nowadays is called Calvinism. It is a nickname to call it Calvinism; Calvinism is the gospel, and nothing else. I do not believe we can preach the gospel, if we do not preach justification by faith, without works; nor unless we preach the sovereignty of God in His dispensation of grace; nor unless we exalt the electing, unchangeable, eternal, immutable, conquering love of Jehovah; nor do I think we can preach the gospel, unless we base it upon the special and particular redemption of His elect and chosen people which Christ wrought out upon the cross; nor can I comprehend a gospel which lets saints fall away after they are called, and suffers the children of God to be burned in the fires of damnation after having once believed in Jesus.[2]

A question remains, however, for many Calvinistically challenged Christians throughout the world: "What is a Calvinist?" For many, the answer is as simple as a simplistic adherence to the five points of Calvinism. That may be a helpful starting point for some, but I would suggest it may not be the best place to start for most Christians in their pursuit of the fundamentals of Calvinism according to Calvin.

I still remember my first contact with Calvinism. When I was a student in college, a good friend of mine gave me a copy of a monthly Bible-study magazine called *Tabletalk*. On the cover of that issue was a picture of an infant with the words "Total Depravity" stamped across the baby's smiling face. Shortly thereafter, I scheduled a meeting with my pastor and asked him whether he could explain what Calvinism is. His ten-second answer went something like this: "Calvinism is the doctrine that teaches that God picks those He wants and condemns those He doesn't want." He went on to talk about the biblical aberration of the doctrine and why I should stay as far as I could from Calvinism and Calvinists. He then explained how we must study the Word of God alone in order to discern truth from error: "If you study Calvinism," he admonished me "then you might become a Calvinist, but if you study the Word of God you will be able to combat any doctrine that is not biblical." Although his description of Calvinism was overwhelmingly deficient, his exhortation was exactly what I needed to hear.

I began to study everything I could get my hands on regarding Calvinism. For years, I went to every theology conference I could afford, I read every issue of *Tabletalk* cover to cover, and I studied every book or pamphlet I could find on the subject. More important, throughout that time I pored over Scripture, examining what it had to say about all things purportedly Calvinistic. Though I fought against Calvinism with all the free will I could muster, when it came right down to it, it wasn't books, conferences, or even well-edited magazines that fundamentally convinced me of Calvinism; it was the clear teaching of the Word of God that did it—through and through. In the end, I had spent all my resistance on something, and on Someone, I could not resist.

Still, my understanding of Calvinism was somewhat incomplete. Sure, I affirmed the five points of Calvinism, and I could even biblically explain and defend each of them; I could say a few things about Calvin himself; and I could provide a general answer to the question "What is a Calvinist?" But alas, I soon discovered, such things do not add up to the sum total of what it means to be a fully confirmed Calvinist.

THE HEART OF CALVINISM AND GOD'S GLORY IN IT

Since first hearing about Calvin and Calvinism, I have continued to examine what it means to be a true, dyed-in-the-wool Calvinist. Although my pursuit of Calvinism will be a lifelong task, during the past few years I have become increasingly concerned about how Calvinism is generally expressed by multitudes of my twenty-first-century Calvinist comrades.

I would suggest that there are many self-proclaimed Calvinists whose Calvinism runs only as deep as the five points, only as far as the last conference they attended, or perhaps only as long as the list of Calvinist theologians they can stack up against a similar list of non-Calvinists. They have perhaps found themselves prancing gleefully amid a valley of bright red tulips, but have not lifted their heads to behold the lush green forests and glorious mountains all around them.

Christopher Catherwood, in his book *Five Leading Reformers*, offers a word of warning to all Calvinists:

> We must be "Bible Calvinists" not "system Calvinists." We can all too easily get sucked into what we feel is a neat system of thought, and forget that we ought to make everything that we believe compatible with Scripture, even if that means jettisoning ideas that flow well in a purely logical sense but are nonetheless incompatible with what the Bible teaches. Although Calvin did not make that mistake himself, it is arguable that many of his followers have done so over the ensuing centuries—and I include myself, as a Calvinist, in that caution![3]

Although I would argue that "Bible Calvinism" necessarily, and rightly, engenders "system Calvinism," Catherwood's admonition is one we all should heed with care. Calvin was a Christian who first and foremost lived and breathed the living and active Word of God, and all true Calvinists must follow his example.[4] Calvin labored over his *Institutes of the Christian Religion*—which is unquestionably the most majestic volume in all of human history next to sacred Scripture[5]—in order to help those preparing for the pastoral ministry to study the Word of God and have "easy access to it and to advance in it without stumbling."[6]

According to Calvin, we are to be "daily taught in the school of Jesus Christ."[7] Thus, we must be students of Scripture if we are to possess right and sound doctrine: "Now in order that true religion may shine upon us, we ought to hold that it must take its beginning from heavenly doctrine and that no one can even get the slightest taste of right and sound doctrine unless he be a pupil of Scripture."[8] Elsewhere Calvin writes, "Let us not take it into our heads either to seek out God anywhere else than in his Sacred Word, or to think anything of him that is not prompted by his Word, or to speak anything that is not taken from that Word."[9] This, writes T. H. L. Parker, "is Calvin's theological programme—to build on the Scripture alone."[10]

The entirety of Calvin's ministry was established fundamentally on the Word of God. In accordance with the Reformation credo *ad fontes*, "to the sources" (particularly to the only infallible source), Calvin's *Institutes* was a summary of the Christian religion according to Scripture. This was Calvin's theological *modus operandi*, as Calvin scholar Ronald S. Wallace maintains: "We could, of course, argue cogently that the whole of his later teaching and outlook developed from the Bible. He insisted always that tradition must be constantly corrected by, and subordinated to, the teaching of Holy Scripture."[11]

Through the years, as I have spoken with fellow Reformed pastors throughout the world, I have often sensed their grief over the multitudes of so-called Calvinists who may have worked out some of the doctrinal difficulties of one point or another but have not even begun to grasp all the magnificent nuances of Calvin's Calvinism. Such Calvinism is engendered and shaped by Scripture alone—and that makes it a Calvinism that begins with God, teaches us about God, and directs our hearts and minds back to God according to the way He deserves, demands, and delights in our worship of Him and our obedience to Him.[12] This is the threefold foundation of Calvin's Calvinism: devotion, doctrine, and doxology—the heart's devotion to the biblical God, the mind's pursuit of the biblical doctrine of God, and the entire being's surrender to doxology.[13] Calvin writes, "The glory of God so shines in his word, that we ought to be so affected by it, whenever he speaks by his servants, as though he were near to us, face to face."[14]

THE HEART OF CALVIN
AND GOD'S SOVEREIGN MASTERY OF IT

So what is true Calvinism according to Calvin? In one sense, Calvinism is as systematically profound as Calvin's life's work, as historically extensive as all that has been deduced from Calvin's writings during the past five centuries, and, as Calvin would have it, as doctrinally narrow as the sixty-six books of sacred Scripture.[15] A true Calvinist is one who strives to think as Calvin thought and live as Calvin lived—insofar as Calvin thought and lived as our Lord Jesus Christ, in accordance with the Word of God.[16]

As Christians, we understand that we are not our own but have been bought with a price. By His saving grace, the Lord has taken hold of our hearts of stone, regenerated and conformed them into spiritually pliable hearts, and poured into them His love by the Holy Spirit who was given to us.[17] This was Calvin's perception of the Christian life:

If we, then, are not our own [cf. 1 Cor. 6:19] but the Lord's, it is clear what error we must flee, and whither we must direct all the acts of our life.

We are not our own: let not our reason nor our will, therefore, sway our plans and deeds. We are not our own: let us therefore not set it as our goal to seek what is expedient for us according to the flesh. We are not our own: in so far as we can, let us therefore forget ourselves and all that is ours.

Conversely, we are God's: let us therefore live for him and die for him. We are God's: let his wisdom and will therefore rule all our actions. We are God's: let all the parts of our life accordingly strive toward him as our only lawful goal [cf. Rom. 14:8; cf. 1 Cor. 6:19]. O, how much has that man profited who, having been taught that he is not his own, has taken away dominion and rule from his own reason that he may yield it to God! For, as consulting our self-interest is the pestilence that most effectively leads to our destruction, so the sole

6

haven of salvation is to be wise in nothing through ourselves but to follow the leading of the Lord alone.[18]

We are not our own; we belong to the Lord. That confession, in essence, is the heart of true Calvinism. Our salvation belongs to the Lord, from beginning to end (Ps. 3:8; Rev. 7:10). He has captivated our minds and has made His light to shine abroad in our hearts (2 Cor. 4:6; 10:5). Our whole being belongs to Him—heart, soul, mind, and strength. This is what Calvin proclaimed, and this is the foundation on which his life was established.

The Lord took hold of Calvin, and Calvin thus could not help but take away "dominion and rule from his own reason" and yield it to the Lord alone.[19] That is the glorious brilliance reflected by any study of Calvin. There was nothing in Calvin himself that was superhuman, super-theologian, or super-churchman. Calvin was a man whom God chose to call out of darkness and into His marvelous light so that he might go back into the darkness and shine brightly unto every generation of God's people until Christ returns.

In truth, any study of Calvin is actually just a study of God's work in the life of His servant in His kingdom. In the words of Calvin biographer Jean Cadier, Calvin was a man whom "God mastered."[20] In mastering him, the Lord used His servant to accomplish all that He had sovereignly purposed. In mastering his heart, the Lord left Calvin with no choice but to offer his heart to God promptly and sincerely. Although Calvin understood that "man's nature is a perpetual factory of idols,"[21] that the "mind begets an idol, and the hand gives it birth,"[22] and that man's heart is deceitfully wicked above all things (Jer. 17:9), he could do nothing but present his heart to God with outstretched hands, offering himself wholly to Him.[23]

In everything, Calvin, more than simply dedicating himself, offered himself sacrificially to the Lord: his family, his studies, his preaching—his entire ministry (Rom. 12:1–2). He was a man who ministered not for his own glory, but for the glory of God (Ps. 115); he was a man who preached not himself, but the Word of God (2 Tim. 4:1–2). According to Parker, Calvin "had a horror of those who preached their own ideas in place of the gospel of the Bible: 'When we enter the pulpit, it is not so that we may bring our own dreams and fancies with us.'"[24] Calvin was not concerned with offering to his congregation the quaint meditations of his own heart. Although it has become popular in many churches for the pastor to strive to "pour out his heart" to his congregation, such was not Calvin's aim in his preaching, for he had offered his heart to God alone. As a result, Calvin did not think it was profitable to share the ever-changing passions of his own heart, but to proclaim the heart of God in His never-changing Word. Calvin was not concerned that his congregants behold him but that they behold the Lord. This should be the aim of every pastor, and, if necessary, every pastor should place a placard behind his pulpit with the following words inscribed: "Sir, we wish to see Jesus" (John 12:21). Such was Calvin's aim in his preaching and in all his life.[25]

THE HUMILITY OF CALVIN AND GOD'S GLORIOUS MAJESTY OVER HIM

At the foundation of Calvinism according to Calvin is the reality that God is inherently holy and we are not.[26] Calvin's doctrinal explanation of the depravity of man was not formulated by a cursory comparative examination of the state of mankind in the sixteenth century; rather, his understanding of man's condition came as a result of his study of all the Bible has to say about the degenerate, humble existence of man after the fall and, in contradistinction, his study of the majestic holiness of God. In a section of his *Institutes* titled "True humility gives God alone the honor," Calvin writes of our humility and God's "loftiness" or "exaltation": "As our humility is his loftiness, so the confession of our humility has a ready remedy in his mercy."[27]

In his classic work *The Holiness of God*, R. C. Sproul recounts his conversion to God and the all-encompassing consequences of God's majestic holiness on his own life: "Suddenly I had a passion to know

God the Father. I wanted to know Him in His majesty, to know Him in His power, to know Him in His august holiness." He goes on to write, "I am convinced that [the holiness of God] is one of the most important ideas that a Christian can ever grapple with. It is basic to our whole understanding of God and of Christianity."[28] These were the kinds of questions Calvin wrestled with throughout his Christian life: What does it mean that God is holy? What are the implications of God's holiness for our study of doctrine? What are the implications of God's holiness for our lives?[29] Calvin writes:

> From what foundation may righteousness better arise than from the Scriptural warning that we must be made holy because our God is holy? . . . When we hear mention of our union with God, let us remember that holiness must be its bond; not because we come into communion with him by virtue of our holiness! Rather, we ought first to cleave unto him so that, infused with his holiness, we may follow whither he calls.[30]

We do not possess holiness inherently, Calvin explains; rather, it is the very holiness of God that overcomes us and enables us to follow the Lord. In his comments on Exodus 28, Calvin further explains this and describes the impurity of our own "holiness" as he considers Jesus' High Priestly Prayer, wherein He prayed, "And for their sake I consecrate myself, that they also may be sanctified in truth" (John 17:19):

> It is undoubtedly a remarkable passage, whereby we are taught that nothing proceeds from us pleasing to God except through the intervention of the grace of the Mediator; for here there is no reference to manifest and gross sins, the pardon of which it is clear that we can only obtain through Christ. . . . This is a harsh saying, and almost a paradox, that our very holinesses are so impure as to need pardon; but it must be borne in mind that nothing is so pure as not to contract some stain from us.[31]

Calvin's doctrine of God humbled him. He took no pride in his formulation of that doctrine, for he could not boast in a holiness that was not his to boast about.[32] Rather, he boasted only in the majesty and holiness of God. It was that holiness that made him aware of his naturally depraved condition and drove him in his struggle to think, speak, and live as Jesus did. Just as we fail daily in our endeavor to follow our Lord perfectly, so did Calvin; yet he was a man of constant repentance who was more critically aware of himself and his own frailties than anyone else could have been, even admitting toward the end of his life: "I am, and always have been a poor and timid scholar."[33] Such statements by Calvin were not deceitfully contrived by a mind held captive by false modesty; rather, they overflowed from a mind that had been captivated and a heart that had been humbled by God's majesty shining through His Word. As John Piper observes:

> So in his early twenties John Calvin experienced the miracle of having the blind eyes of his spirit opened by the spirit of God. And what he saw immediately and without any intervening chain of human reasoning, were two things, so interwoven that they would determine the rest of his life: The majesty of God and the Word of God. The Word mediated the majesty, and the majesty vindicated the Word.[34]

To his closest friends, Guillaume Farel and Pierre Viret, Calvin appeared to be a man of repentance and utter dependence on the Lord, "the wellspring of life."[35] In a sermon on 1 Timothy 3:16 and the apostle Paul's description of the mystery of godliness, we observe Calvin's attitude toward the miserable condition of our hearts and the majestic work of God in approaching us and conquering us:

> There is nothing but rottenness in us; nothing but sin and death. Then let the living God, the well-spring of life, the everlasting glory, and the infinite power, come; and not only approach to us and our

miseries, our wretchedness, our frailty, and to this bottomless pit of all iniquity that is in men; let not only the majesty of God come near this, but be joined to it, and made one with it, in the person of our Lord Jesus Christ![36]

We find no trace of despair or cynicism in Calvin; rather, we find a hope that does not disappoint because it is founded and focused on the majesty of God and His Word.[37] On this observation, Calvin's friend and first biographer, Theodore Beza, rightly asserts, "The reader who is truly seeking the glory of God will see this sense of majesty of which I am speaking permeating Calvin's writings."[38] Throughout his writings, Calvin admonishes readers to turn their attention from themselves to Scripture: "But I require only that, laying aside the disease of self-love and ambition, by which he is blinded and thinks more highly of himself than he ought [cf. Gal. 6:3], he rightly recognize himself in the faithful mirror of Scripture [cf. James 1:22–25]."[39]

With Calvin as our example in the endeavor of becoming discerning students and ready servants of the Word, we learn that the study of Scripture draws our arrogant hearts away from ourselves and unto the majesty of God in true faith. Concerning this often-neglected truth, Jonathan Edwards writes:

As we would therefore make the Holy Scriptures our rule, in judging of the nature of true religion, and judging of our own religious qualifications and state; it concerns us greatly to look at this humiliation, as one of the most essential things pertaining to true Christianity. [40]

In the footnote to this admonition, Edwards cites Calvin:

Calvin in his *Institutes of the Christian Religion*, Bk. II, ch. 2, no. 11, says, "A saying of Chrysostom's has always pleased me very much, that the foundation of our philosophy is humility (Chrysostom, *De profectu evangelli* 2 [MPG 51.312]). But that of Augustine pleases me even more: 'When a certain rhetorician was asked what was the chief rule in eloquence, he replied, "Delivery"; what was the second rule, "Delivery"; what was the third rule, "Delivery"; so if you ask me concerning the precepts of the Christian religion, first, second, third, and always I would answer, "Humility."'"[41]

Humility is the supreme virtue according to Calvin, not only in attitude but in all of life.[42] The Christian's humility should shine forth into the pompous darkness of this world. It is neither our eloquence nor our brilliance that directs men to God; rather, it is God who directs men to Himself through the seeming foolishness of preaching. Consequently, humility should conquer our minds and transform our hearts, arising from our study of God's majesty in His majestic Word.

In his book *The Expository Genius of John Calvin*, Steven J. Lawson observes the humility of Calvin in his preaching: "As a preacher, Calvin's primary aim was to communicate to the common person in the pew. He was not seeking to impress his congregation with his own brilliance, but to impact them with the awe-inspiring majesty of God."[43] In his life and ministry, Calvin preached Christ and Him crucified—He preached the gospel, in season and out of season.

Yet Calvin's estimation of himself and his own efforts was rather dismal, even at the end of his life. His only consolation was this: the fear of the Lord was in his heart. On Friday, April 28, 1564, four weeks before his death, Calvin, the 55-year-old pastor of St. Peter's Church in Geneva, stood before an assembly of ministers and elders in Geneva and offered words of farewell. Toward the end of his address, he acknowledged the following:

I have had many infirmities, which you have been obliged to bear with, and what is more, all I have done is worthless. The ungodly will seize on that, but I repeat that all that I have done has been worthless and that I am a miserable creature. But certainly I may say this: that I have meant for the best, that my vices have always displeased me, and that the root of the fear of the Lord has always been in my heart. You may say "he meant well" and I pray that my evil may be forgiven and that if there was anything good you may confirm yourselves by it and have it as an example.[44]

THE LEGACY OF CALVIN FOR TWENTY-FIRST-CENTURY CALVINISTS

In the daily service of shepherding Christ's flock, I often find myself turning to my spiritual forefathers for answers to the most difficult matters in the church's life and doctrine. Even though our forefathers are at home with the Lord, by our mutual faith they provide us with words of comfort, encouragement, and caution. As I reflect on the doctrinal, ecclesiastical, and personal hardships they faced, and take into account the Lord's sustaining work in their lives, I am humbled and challenged by their united voices, which seem to admonish us from the heavenlies, urging us to fight the good fight, to be faithful till the end, and to honor the Lord above all.

Among the many faithful voices from the past, there seems to be one that rises above them all. It is the voice of a man who desperately wanted us to hear not his own voice but the voice of God in His Word. It is precisely on account of the humility the Lord had instilled in the mind of Calvin that I am drawn to him. In fact, there is not a week that passes that I do not think about the example Calvin set forth for us and for Christians in every generation. And in life and ministry, as I have considered Calvin the man, I have observed the following things: Calvin was a man who died to himself and sought to take up his cross daily so that he might serve the Lord and the flock God had entrusted to him (Luke 9:23).[45] He was a man who did not think of himself more highly than he should have, but sought to esteem others better than himself (Rom. 12:3; Phil. 2:3).[46] He was a man who did not seek to please men first and foremost, but sought to please God ultimately and completely (Col. 1:10; 3:23).[47] He was a man who strove not to live for his own kingdom but for the kingdom of God (Matt 6:33; 21:43).[48] He was a man who sought to be faithful in the eyes of God, not successful in the eyes of the world (Rev. 2:10). He was a man who did not desire his own glory, but desired to seek the glory of God in all he did (1 Cor. 10:31; Col. 3:17).[49] He was a man who did not try to develop a system of theology that complemented the Word of God; rather, he strove to derive his theology from the Word of God for the right worship, enjoyment, and love of God.

Considering all of this, Calvin is among the greatest men of all time. However, his greatness, as B. B. Warfield recognized, was not in his service to himself but in his surrender to God: "Here we have the secret of Calvin's greatness and the source of his strength unveiled to us. No man ever had a profounder sense of God than he; no man ever more unreservedly surrendered himself to the Divine direction."[50] This is Calvin's greatness—his ultimate surrender to God. In this is Calvin's legacy for those of us who desire not simply to wear the five-pointed badge of Calvinism, but who desire to clothe ourselves in the humbling power of the gospel (1 Peter 5:5). Let us not be so easily satisfied with a simple insignia of a simplistic Calvinism; rather, let us drape ourselves with Calvin's Calvinism, a Christ-centered, Spirit-empowered, God-glorifying, gospel-driven Calvinism that shines so brilliantly that the deceitful darkness of sin would be conquered in our hearts so that, in turn, we might shine as the light of Jesus Christ to this dark world—for His kingdom and His glory.

NOTES

[1] John Calvin, *Institutes of the Christian Religion*, trans. by Henry Beveridge (Grand Rapids: Eerdmans, 1947), 3.7.1. (Henceforth, all citations from the *Institutes* are taken from the Battles edition; see endnote 4 below.)

2 From Charles Haddon Spurgeon's *A Defense of Calvinism*, quoted by J. I. Packer in his "Introductory Essay" to John Owen, *The Death of Death in the Death of Christ* (London: Banner of Truth, 1959), 10.

3 Christopher Catherwood, *Five Leading Reformers* (Fearn, Tain: Christian Focus, 2000) 104.

4 John Calvin, *Institutes of the Christian Religion*, ed. John T. McNeill; trans. Ford Lewis Battles; Library of Christian Classics, XX–XXI (Philadelphia: Westminster John Knox, 1960), 3.7.5.

5 Or, as John Murray called the *Institutes*: "the *opus magnum* of Christian Theology" (John Murray, "Introduction," in Calvin, *Institutes of the Christian Religion*, trans. Henry Beveridge, 1). Ford Lewis Battles, a translator of Calvin's *Institutes*, admonished his students as they commenced their study of the *Institutes*: "You are about to share in one of the classic experiences of Christian history . . . on the deceptively orderly and seemingly dispassionate pages that follow are imprinted one man's passionate responses to the call of Christ. If [you] keep ever before [you] that autobiographical character of the book, the whole man will speak to you in every truth" (Ford Lewis Battles, *Analysis of the Institutes* [Phillipsburg, N.J.: P&R, 2001], 14).

6 Calvin, *Institutes of the Christian Religion*, 4.

7 John Calvin, *Letters of John Calvin*, ed. Jules Bonnet, 4 vols. (Eugene, Ore.: Wipf & Stock, 2007), July 20, 1558.

8 Calvin, *Institutes of the Christian Religion*, 1.6.2.

9 Ibid., 1.13.21.

10 T. H. L. Parker, *Portrait of Calvin* (Philadelphia: Westminster, 1954), 52.

11 Ronald S. Wallace, *Calvin, Geneva, and the Reformation* (Eugene, Ore.: Wipf & Stock, 1998), 4.

12 Calvin, *Institutes of the Christian Religion*, 1.6.2: "All right knowledge of God is born of obedience." In his *Systematic Theology*, Louis Berkhof writes, "Thomas Aquinas expressed himself as follows: *Theologia a Deo docetur, Deum docet, et ad Deum ducit*" ("Theology is taught by God, teaches God, and leads unto God") (Louis Berkhof, *Systematic Theology* [Grand Rapids: Eerdmans, 1996], 390). The language of worshiping God according to the manner in which He "deserves, demands, and delights in" is borrowed from Dr. Scotty Smith of Christ Community Church in Franklin, Tenn.

13 See Wallace, *Calvin, Geneva, and the Reformation*, 210–218.

14 John Calvin, *Commentaries on the Twelve Minor Prophets* (Grand Rapids: Eerdmans, 1948–50), 4:343.

15 Calvin, *Institutes of the Christian Religion*, 1.7.1; 3.5.8.

16 Lester De Koster writes: "We know that Christianity is a multi-faceted thing. Only God knows in how many ways his spirit enriches the world. Calvin/Calvinism is one of them" (Lester De Koster, *Light for the City* [Grand Rapids: Eerdmans, 2004], x).

17 Cf. Jeremiah 31:33; Romans 5:5; Ezekiel 11:19.

[18] Calvin, *Institutes of the Christian Religion*, 3.7.1.

[19] Ibid.

[20] Jean Cadier, *Calvin: The Man God Mastered*, trans. O. R. Johnston (Grand Rapids: Eerdmans, 1960).

[21] Calvin, *Institutes of the Christian Religion*, 1.11.8.

[22] Ibid.

[23] Incidentally, in his list of qualifications for elder, the apostle Paul uses similar language, saying, "If anyone aspires to the office of overseer, he desires a noble task" (1 Tim. 3:1). The word *aspires* is a translation of the Greek word *oregomai*, which carries the idea of stretching out of one's self in order to touch or to grasp something, to reach after or desire something.

[24] Parker, *Portrait of Calvin*, 83.

[25] Steven J. Lawson, *The Expository Genius of John Calvin* (Orlando: Reformation Trust, 2007), 128–129.

[26] Calvin, *Institutes of the Christian Religion*, 3.6.2; 3.20.41.

[27] Ibid., 2.2.11.

[28] R. C. Sproul, *The Holiness of God* (Carol Stream, Ill.: Tyndale House, 1997), 12.

[29] For instance, on the matter of "imperfection and endeavor of the Christian life," Calvin writes, "the beginning of right living is spiritual, where the inner feeling of the mind is unfeignedly dedicated to God for the cultivation of holiness and righteousness" (Calvin, *Institutes of the Christian Religion*, 3.7.5).

[30] Ibid., 3.6.2.

[31] John Calvin, *Commentary on the Last Four Books of Moses, Arranged in the Form of a Harmony*, trans. C. W. Bingham (Grand Rapids: Baker, 1993), 202.

[32] Calvin, *Institutes of the Christian Religion*, 3.7.4.

[33] G. R. Potter and M. Greengrass, *John Calvin* (London: Edward Arnold, 1983), 172–173; translated from G. Baum, E. Caunitz, and E. Reuss, *Corpus Reformatorum* (*Opera Calvini*), 59 vols. (Braunschweig [Brunswick]: 1863–84), vol. 37, cols. 890–894.

[34] John Piper, *The Legacy of Sovereign Joy* (Wheaton, Ill.: Crossway, 2000), 127.

[35] Theodore Beza, *The Life of John Calvin* (Darlington, England: Evangelical Press, 1564, 1997), 12–13.

See also Richard Stauffer, *The Humanness of John Calvin*, trans. George Shriver (Nashville: Abingdon, 1971), 47–71.

[36] John Calvin, "The Mystery of Godliness," in *The Mystery of Godliness and Other Sermons* (Orlando: Soli Deo Gloria, 1999), 12–13.

[37] John Kromminga writes of Calvin: "He engages in searching examinations of human frailties, speaking plainly and without compromise about the depravity of man. But throughout he manifests also sturdy confidence in the grace of God which overcomes human sin" (John H. Kromminga, *Thine Is My Heart* [Grand Rapids: Reformation Heritage Books, 1958, 2006], Introduction).

[38] Beza, *The Life of John Calvin*, 140.

[39] Calvin, *Institutes of the Christian Religion*, 2.2.11.

[40] Jonathan Edwards, *Religious Affections*, ed. John E. Smith, in *The Works of Jonathan Edwards*, vol. 2 (New Haven: Yale Divinity Press, 1959), 314–315.

[41] Ibid., n1.

[42] Calvin writes, "The chief praise of Christians is self-renunciation" (John Calvin, *The Commentaries of John Calvin on the Second Epistle of Paul the Apostle to the Corinthians* [Grand Rapids: Baker, 2003], 2:233).

[43] Lawson, *The Expository Genius of John Calvin*, 85.

[44] Potter and Greengrass, *John Calvin*, 172–173.

[45] Calvin writes, "He who has denied himself has cut off the root of all evil, so as no longer to seek his own; he who has taken up his cross has prepared himself for all meekness and endurance" (Calvin, *Institutes of the Christian Religion*, 3.15.8).

[46] Ibid., 2.2.11; 2.2.25.

[47] Ibid., 3.14.7.

[48] Ibid., 3.15.5; 4.20.26.

[49] Piper writes, "I think this would be a fitting banner over all of John Calvin's life and work—zeal to illustrate the glory of God" (John Piper, "The Divine Majesty of the Word: John Calvin, The Man and His Preaching," *The Southern Baptist Journal of Theology*, 3/2 [Summer 1999], 40).

[50] B. B. Warfield, *Calvin and Calvinism* (Grand Rapids: Baker, 1932, 2000), 24.

Chapter 2

WHO WAS JOHN CALVIN?

DEREK W. H. THOMAS

Let us, then, unremittingly examine our faults, call ourselves back to humility. Thus nothing will remain in us to puff us up; but there will be much occasion to be cast down.[1]

—JOHN CALVIN

Theologian, pastor, preacher, correspondent, churchman, statesman—John Calvin was all of these and more. Proverbially, he was more than just the sum of his parts. Five hundred years later, he is still read, argued over, defended, even vilified. For some, his commentaries form the touchstone by which others are judged. For others, he remains "the unopposed dictator of Geneva."[2]

John Calvin was born some sixty miles north of Paris, at Noyon, Picardy, on July 10, 1509. The previous generations of his family had hailed from the nearby village of Pont-l'Evêque. His grandfather was either a boatman or a cooper (i.e., a barrel maker), and his father, Gérard, after migrating the few miles to Noyon, with its cathedral, two abbeys, and four city parishes, became the cathedral notary and *promoteur* (the equivalent ecclesiastical function of a civil prosecutor). He would climb the social ladder of ecclesiastical office, from notary to notary apostolic and notary fiscal until, in 1497, he was made *bourgeois*.

Gérard married an innkeeper's daughter, Jeanne Le Franc.

Jeanne's father, like Gérard, had recently been made *bourgeois*, but he also had been granted a seat on the city council and was by all accounts more financially secure. The marriage would last less than twenty years; Jeanne died in 1515, having given birth to at least five children, all sons: in addition to John, there was Charles (the eldest), Antoine and François, who both died young, and another Antoine, who was given the name of his deceased brother.[3] Three boys and two sisters survived into adulthood; the girls, Marie and her sister (whose name is not known), were the children born to Gérard and his second wife.

John could hardly have been more than 6 (perhaps 4 or 5) when his mother died. At 11 or 12, he was sent to Paris to attend the Collège de la Marche in preparation for his later entry to the University of Paris. There he studied "grammar," including Latin, under the instruction of one of the greatest Latin teachers of the period, Mathurin Cordier (to whom Calvin would later dedicate his commentary on 1 Thessalonians). From there, he went to the monastery school at Montaigu (a strict establishment designed to prepare young men for the priesthood). The school was situated on a street known for thieves and cutthroats, with open, stinking sewers; the food was sparse and coarse; and the discipline severe. Prayers began at 4 o'clock in the morning, followed by lectures until 6, when Mass was said. Then followed breakfast. From 8 until 10 o'clock came the *grande classe*, followed by discussion. Dinner at 11 was followed by Bible readings and prayers. At midday, students were questioned about their morning's work, then rested from 1 until 2. More classes were held from 3 until 5, followed by vespers. Between supper and its accompanying readings and bedtime at 8, further interrogations took place in the chapel. On two days of the week, an allowance was given for recreation.

PARIS, ORLÉANS, AND BOURGES

Montaigu served as a preparatory school for the University of Paris and the bachelor of arts degree, which would lead to the study of theology.

Clearly John was destined for the priesthood. But by 1525 or 1526, when he was 16 or 17, Martin Luther's impact on neighboring Germany was already gaining momentum and a "career" in the church must have looked less desirable to John's father (whose relationship with the church was becoming increasingly tense). Thus, after two unsuccessful attempts at gaining an ecclesiastical position for his son, Gérard sent John to Orléans for the study of law, followed in 1529 by a further move to the University of Bourges, where he would remain for eighteen months. It was at Bourges that John learned Greek (at a time when the study of Greek was deemed unfashionable). In addition, he taught rhetoric at an Augustinian convent and preached regularly in the stone pulpit of the local church. Some suggest that evangelical convictions were already in evidence in Calvin during this period (1530). Writing in his *Commentary on the Book of Psalms*, he would refer to his "sudden conversion."[4]

Following a brief return to Orléans in the fall of 1530, Calvin found himself in Paris again in the early spring of the following year. He had a notion of a quiet life spent in "literary ease." But his plans to return to Orléans were disrupted by the sudden death of his father in 1531. A letter Calvin wrote at this time portrayed a young man (he was 21) whose affection for his father, whom he had hardly seen in the previous ten years, was minimal. Whether Calvin had ever had any love for the study of law is debatable, but with his father out of the picture, Calvin returned briefly to Orléans and then to Paris to study classics and, among other disciplines, Hebrew. An outbreak of the plague forced the students and faculty to flee to the country, and we know little of his whereabouts until he re-emerged in 1532, having written what was in effect his doctoral thesis: a commentary on the Stoic philosopher Seneca titled *De Clementia* (*On Mercy*). His aim was that this work might steer him into the world of humanist scholarship and the quiet, academic life he desired.

On Nov. 1, 1533, Calvin's friend Nicolas Cop, the rector of the University of Paris, preached a barnstorming address to open the winter session. It was a plea for a modest reformation based on scriptural principles and after the manner of Luther. It caused something of a riot, and on Nov. 19, Cop was replaced. By December, an arrest order was given for Cop, but he could not be found. It was later suggested that Calvin himself had authored this address.[5] What is certain is that Calvin also disappeared from Paris during late November, having escaped from a bedroom window using sheets and disguising himself as a vinedresser. He would spend late 1533 and early 1534 in the south of France in the province of Saintonge, under the pseudonym Charles d'Espeville. He also spent some time in Orléans where he wrote the first draft of *Psychopannychia*, a book that did not see final publication until 1542.[6] It dealt mainly with the state of the soul after death and was an attack on the doctrine of soul sleep.

By May 1534, Calvin was back in the vicinity of Paris, though at some risk. On one occasion, he preached outside the city in a cave at Saint-Benoît, and he is known to have celebrated the Lord's Supper in the village of Crotelles.

Paris witnessed the *affaire de placards* during the night of Oct. 17–18, 1534. French Protestants were busily posting placards in major towns in defiance of the ritual of the Mass (one even appeared on the door of the king's bedroom). The king ordered the arrest of several hundred supporters of the "cursed Lutheran sect," and some were executed. Calvin was possibly implicated and left France (via Strasbourg) to settle in Basel, arriving in January 1535. There he took on another pseudonym, Martianus Lucianus. In a German-speaking city, Calvin settled among an increasing number of French exiles.

AN EXILE FROM FRANCE

Calvin was now converted and identifying himself openly with those who were leading the Reformation in Europe. His heart, which had been strongly devoted to the superstitions of the papacy, had experienced a "teachableness" (*docilitas*), a word that suggests a willingness to be subject to the teaching of Scripture. "For no man will ever be a good teacher," Calvin would write, "if he does not show that he himself is teachable (*docilis*), and is always ready to learn."[7] Was this the period of Calvin's "sudden conversion," as many think? Not all are agreed, and some have suggested Calvin's conversion took place before 1530, pointing out that the Latin for "sudden" can also be rendered "unexpectedly."[8]

The time in Basel would prove profitable for Calvin as an emerging writer. June 4, 1535, saw the publication of the French translation of the Bible by Olivetanus, for which Calvin wrote the Latin foreword. He also wrote a foreword to an edition of Chrysostom's sermons. Then, within fourteen months of coming to Basel, in March 1536, Calvin published his magnum opus: the first edition of the *Institutes of the Christian Religion*. It was a pocket-sized companion to theology, in 516 pages, expounding on the law, the Creed, the Lord's Prayer, the sacraments, and Christian liberty, all of which was designed to help the increasing number of Protestant Christians in his native France.[9]

Following a brief return to Paris (during a safer period), Calvin set his affairs in order, intending to leave the city for good and taking with him his bother Antoine and sister Marie. His plan was to go to Strasbourg to study, perhaps for the remainder of his life.

DETOURED TO GENEVA

Calvin's journey from Basel to Geneva is among the great tales of church history. His destination was Strasbourg, but a local war (between the forces of Francis I, the king of France, and Charles V, the Holy Roman emperor) prevented him from taking the most direct route, necessitating a detour for a night to Geneva. Entering the city, he was immediately recognized and taken to meet Guillaume Farel, who had led the Protestant cause in the city for the previous ten years. Farel, red-haired and with a temperament to match, threatened Calvin that if he dared leave the city and refuse to join him in the work of the

Reformation, God would curse him. Calvin, terrified and convicted, heeded Farel's pleas and, apart from a brief exile from 1538 until 1541, remained in Geneva until his death almost thirty years later.

Calvin's immediate goal in Geneva, a city of some ten thousand souls, was the establishment of a church that took seriously the claims of the Bible as to its form and government. This he did by establishing daily gatherings for psalm singing and expository preaching, monthly administrations of the Supper (Calvin's desire for a weekly celebration never gained the support of the city magistrates, without which it could not occur), and (most importantly) a church free to exercise its own authority over matters of discipline without the influence of the civil authorities or the undue influence of high-society Genevans (*Libertines*), who attacked Calvin as a Frenchman with ideas of grandeur above his station.

To some, including John Knox of Scotland, the city was the closest thing to heaven they had seen. For others, such as Michael Servetus, whose execution in 1553 (and Calvin's approval of it) is re-told with untiring frequency, found Geneva stifling. But Servetus was found guilty of heresy (anti-Trinitarianism) and of being a disturber of the peace (he had been warned not to enter Geneva), and would have fared equally badly in a Catholic city had he been caught in one. His execution is not an example of intolerant Calvinism, but of a layer of sixteenth-century civil jurisprudence in central Europe, where various lifestyles were considered untenable and punishable by law in a way that humanist societies of our own day would react to with apoplexy. He had been found guilty by a civil court of twenty-five men, and Calvin himself spent hours with Servetus, urging him to repent in order to avoid the inevitable sentence. Calvin's request for a less-painful execution (Servetus was burned) was refused. Arguably gentler Reformers, including Martin Bucer and Philip Melanchthon, fully approved of his death.

As early as January 1537, Farel and Calvin laid before the city council their Articles on the Organization of the Church and its Worship in Geneva. It was received, more or less, by the city's civil authorities (apart from the frequency of the Supper), but relations between the ministers and the civil authorities steadily deteriorated during 1537, so much so that by Easter of the following year, a quarrel over the use of unleavened bread in the Supper led to a call for the ministers to leave. On the Tuesday following Easter (following a near riot by an unruly mob in the city), Farel and Calvin were told to get out of the city immediately. The Reformer had been in Geneva barely eighteen months.

Farel settled in Basel and Calvin in Strasbourg. These were halcyon years for Calvin, for he ministered among exiles from his native France and was hugely productive in terms of church reform and writing projects: a French Psalter, a highly significant treatise on the Lord's Supper, and a new edition of the *Institutes*—revised, enlarged, and much more like the final product that would appear twenty years later in 1559. In addition, there were lectures (and later commentaries) on John's Gospel, 1 Corinthians, and Romans. And beyond all these accomplishments, Calvin found a wife.

IDELETTE DE BURE

Calvin's friends had urged him to marry in order to promote the Protestant understanding of marriage and family. Calvin set out his wish list: he made no mention of beauty, but he insisted a prospective bride must be chaste, sensible, economical, patient, and able and willing to take care of his health. Farel had just the woman in mind, but nothing came of it. Another "damsel of noble rank" was suggested, but even though a wedding was planned for March 10, 1540 (only two weeks later), Calvin remained a bachelor, saying that he would not consider marrying her "unless the Lord had entirely bereft me of my wits."[10] By August, however, he was a married man. He chose Idelette de Bure, the widow of a onetime Anabaptist who had joined Calvin's congregation in Strasbourg along with his wife and two children. In the spring of 1540, Idelette's husband died of the plague, and on August 6 of that year, she and Calvin married. The marriage proved to be a happy one and lasted until March 1549, when Idelette died after almost nine years of poor health. She had borne Calvin one son, whom they named Jacques, who died shortly after his birth.

Several years after evicting Calvin, the Geneva authorities changed their minds and asked Strasbourg to send Calvin back. There were attempts to reconcile as early as October 1540. Calvin initially was cool to the idea; on Oct. 24 of that year, Calvin wrote to Farel to say that he was not willing to return to Geneva. But, he added, "because I know that I am not my own master, I offer my heart as a true sacrifice to the Lord."[11] In the end, he did return, re-entering the city on Tuesday, Sept. 13, 1541. That Lord's Day, Calvin resumed his preaching respon-sibilities, picking up in the Scriptures at precisely the point where he had left off three and a half years earlier, "by which," he later reasoned, "I indicated that I had interrupted my office of preaching for a time rather than I had given it up entirely."[12]

GENEVA AGAIN

With his return came renewed authority to reform, and within two months a comprehensive reform of liturgy, ordination, and discipline known as the Ecclesiastical Ordinances (*Les Ordononnances ecclésias-tiques*) was passed into law. Within weeks, a committee of three (which included Calvin) was appointed to look into civil reform in the city. Such was Calvin's involvement that in 1543, he was relieved of all his preaching responsibilities (except for Sundays) so that he could give his attention to civil reform. And thus, for the next two decades, the basis of ministry in Geneva was set. Initially Calvin preached twice on Sunday and again on Monday, Wednesday, and Friday, but the strain proved too great, so until 1549, Calvin was refused permission to preach more than once a Sunday. Then Calvin's schedule increased again; in addition to two sermons on the Lord's Day, he preached every day of alternate weeks, averaging almost two hundred and fifty sermons a year. His style was consistent—he expounded the Bible in consecutive expository style, working through books of both the Old Testament (on weekdays) and the New Testament (on Sundays).

By 1546, opposition to Calvin had resurfaced as the *Libertines* fomented an armed riot against the French immigrants. In 1547, an anonymous note placed in the pulpit of St. Peter's Church threatened Calvin with death. Domestic issues also surfaced. Calvin's older brother, Charles, who had been ordained as a priest, had been accused of heresy and died excommunicate in 1537. Calvin's younger brother, Antoine, now lived in Geneva and did some clerical work for his brother. Antoine's marriage seemed to be in difficulty from the start. His wife, who had been accused of adultery on a previous occasion without proof, was eventually found guilty of relations with Calvin's household servant, and the marriage ended in divorce in 1557. His stepdaughter was also found guilty of adultery, and Calvin wrote of a period when he felt too ashamed to leave his house.

A monumental decision was taken in August 1549 by the deacons of the church in Geneva, when they appointed a stenographer, Denis Raguenier, to more or less take down in shorthand every word that Calvin spoke in public. Thus, over the next dozen years, 2,043 sermons were recorded and printed exactly as Calvin had given them. They remain among the most valuable documents of Reformation preaching extant today. After Raguenier's death in 1560 or 1561, others were appointed to continue this work until Calvin's death in 1564.[13]

Calvin was never far from theological criticism, and in 1551 the issue of predestination was center stage. Jérôme Bolsec had been banished from Geneva for denying it and Jean Trolliet had criticized Calvin publicly at a meal for holding to it. In 1553, relations between the church (the consistory) and the state (the Little Council) soured. On Sept. 1, Philibert Berthelier, who a year earlier had been denied access to the Lord's Supper by the consistory for being drunk, was granted permission to take the Supper by the council. A stand-off occurred that lasted for several months as Berthelier threatened to attend the Supper. The council eventually granted the consistory the right to excommunicate church members. Following the defeat of the *Libertines* in 1555, Calvin was able to devote his attention to the construction of a school to train young men for ministry and missionary work in the growing number of Reformed churches in Europe and overseas. The Academy of Geneva was inaugurated on June 5, 1559.[14] Apparently, the convocation included a sizeable representation of the syndics (Geneva's four ruling officials), members of the councils of Geneva, ministers, professors, and regents (teachers in a pre-university school) of the academy, as well as almost six hundred students. Calvin had been planning for this academy since 1541, and it had taken twenty years to realize the project.[15]

LAST DAYS

The final decade of Calvin's life in Geneva was one of much less conflict. During this period, he worked once more on the *Institutes*, publishing the final edition in 1559, which was four times the length of the first and almost completely revised and restructured. However, his health began to deteriorate, and in the winter of 1558-59 he was seriously ill. He recovered following the opening of the academy, but sickened again in 1564.[16]

On Feb. 26, 1564, Calvin gave his last lecture from a portion of Ezekiel 20. His final sermon had been given a few weeks earlier, on Feb. 6. He made visits to church meetings during the next few weeks, participating in the Lord's Supper on Easter Sunday (April 2). On April 25, Calvin dictated his will to a notary.[17] It gave expression to his belief that he had served the Lord as he had been given ability. Two days later, he bade farewell to the syndics and the members of the Little Council, they having come to his home for the purpose.[18] He died on May 27 and was buried the following day at 2 in the afternoon, "wrapped in a shroud and encased in a plain wooden coffin, without pomp or elaborate ceremony . . . his grave marked by a simple mound like that of his humbler associates in death," in accord with his own wishes.[19]

Calvin's life was over, but he left behind hundreds of sermons, commentaries on almost the whole Bible, a theology textbook that remains definitive, countless tracts and letters, and much more than these, a life lived wholeheartedly for God.

NOTES

1 John Calvin, *Institutes of the Christian Religion*, ed. John T. McNeill; trans. Ford Lewis Battles; Library of Christian Classics, XX–XXI (Philadelphia: Westminster John Knox, 1960), 3.7.4.

2 *The Oxford Dictionary of the Christian Church*, 2nd Ed., ed. F. L. Cross (Oxford: Oxford University Press, 1974), *s.v.*

3 See T. H. L. Parker, *John Calvin: A Biography* (Louisville, Ky.: Westminster John Knox, 2006), 18, and Williston Walker, *John Calvin: Revolutionary, Theologian, Pastor* (Ross-shire, U.K.: Christian Focus, 2005), 26–28.

4 Preface to *Commentary on the Book of Psalms*, trans. James Anderson (Edinburgh: Calvin Translation Society, 1845; repr. Grand Rapids: Baker, 2003), xl–xli. *Ioannis Calvini Opera Quae Supersunt Omnia* (hereafter CO), eds. Guilielmus Baum, Eduardus Cunitz, and Eduardus Reuss (Brunsvigae: Wiegandt & Appelhans, 1887), 31:22.

5 See Theodore Beza's revised biography of Calvin in 1575 for the first hint of this view. For an extensive discussion of this issue, see Alister E. McGrath, *A Life of John Calvin: A Study in the Shaping of Western Culture* (Oxford, England, and Cambridge, Mass.: Blackwell, 1990), 64–67.

6 The 1542 edition bore the title *Vivere apud Christum non dormire animis sanctos, qui in fide Christi decedent.* CO 5:165–232.

7 John Calvin, *The First Epistle of Paul to the Corinthians*, trans. John W. Fraser, eds. David W. Torrance and Thomas F. Torrance (Grand Rapids: Eerdmans, 1989), 303. CO 49:530.

8 For the earlier date of Calvin's conversion, see for example, "Appendix 2: Calvin's Conversion," by Parker in *John Calvin: A Biography*, 199–203, and W. de Greef, *The Writings of John Calvin: An Introductory Guide*, trans. Lyle D. Bierma (Grand Rapids: Baker, and Leicester, England: Apollos, 1993), 23. In support of the later date, see for example, Randall C. Zachman, *John Calvin as Teacher, Pastor and Theologian: The Shape of His Writings and Thought* (Grand Rapids: Baker Academic, 2006), 17–18, and François Wendel, *Calvin: Origins and Development of His Religious Thought*, trans. Philip Mairet (Durham, N.C.: The Labyrinth Press, 1950), 37–45. For a view that suggests too much has been made of this single reference to his "conversion," see the extensive discussion in Alexandre Ganoczy, *The Young Calvin*, trans. David Foxgrover and Wade Provo (Philadelphia: Westminster Press, 1966), 241–287.

9 It bore the grandiloquent title: *Basic Instruction* [Institution] *in the Christian religion comprising almost the whole sum of godliness and all that needs to be known in the doctrine of*

salvation. A newly published work very well worth reading by all who aspire to godliness [pietatis summam]. *The preface is to the most Christian King of France, offering to him this book as a confession of faith by the author, Jean Calvin of Noyon.* CO 1:6.

[10] CO 11:30. Cited in Parker, *John Calvin: A Biography*, 6.

[11] CO 11:99–110.

[12] CO 11, 365–366.

[13] In 1806, some of Calvin's unpublished sermons in the library at Geneva were sold to a public bookseller for lack of storage space, some of which have disappeared without trace.

[14] Charles Borgeaud, *Historie de 'Université de Genève*, vol. 1: *L'Académie de Calvin (1559–1978)* (Geneva, 1900), 1.

[15] Karin Maag, *Seminary or University? The Genevan Academy and Reformed Higher Education, 1560–1620* (Scolar Press, 1995), 8

[16] Calvin was to experience a considerable amount of sickness, including nephritis, gallstones, hemorrhoidal bleeding, headaches, and much more.

[17] CO 20:298–302

[18] CO 9:887–890

[19] Walker, *John Calvin*, 339.

 Chapter 3

CALVIN'S HEART FOR GOD

SINCLAIR B. FERGUSON

I call "piety" that reverence joined with love of God which the knowledge of his benefits induces. For until men recognize that they owe everything to God, that they are nourished by his fatherly care, that he is the Author of their every good, that they should seek nothing beyond him—they will never yield him willing service. Nay, unless they establish their complete happiness in him, they will never give themselves truly and sincerely to him.[1]

—JOHN CALVIN

John Calvin was one of the most reserved of Christian men, rarely disclosing in public the inner workings of his heart. Only occasionally did he lift the veil, as for example in his preface to his *Commentary on the Psalms.* Here he acknowledges himself to have been "of a disposition somewhat unpolished and bashful, which led me always to love the shade and retirement."[2]

How, then, did a reserved, studious, tightly wired young humanist scholar of the late 1520s and early 1530s became such a powerful force in the service of the gospel?

The simplest answer is found in a letter he wrote in 1564 to his friend and colleague Guillaume Farel: "It is enough that I live and die for Christ, who is to all his followers a gain both in life and death."[3] The echo of Paul's testimony is unmistakable: "For to me to live is Christ, and to die is gain" (Phil. 1:21). Hence the motto always associated with Calvin: "I offer my heart to you, Lord, promptly and sincerely (*Cor meum tibi offero, Domine, prompte et sincere*)."[4]

Calvin seems to have been conscious of two things that shaped him: God's sovereign renewal of his life and his progressive transformation into the likeness of Christ.

POWERFUL RENEWAL

Scripture teaches that renewal by the Holy Spirit involves the understanding, the will, and the affections. So it proved to be with Calvin:

> . . . since I was too obstinately devoted to the superstitions of Popery to be easily extricated from so profound an abyss of mire, God by a sudden conversion subdued and brought my mind to a teachable frame, which was more hardened in such matters than might have been expected from one at my early period of life. Having thus received some taste and knowledge of true godliness I was immediately inflamed with so intense a desire to make progress therein, that although I did not altogether leave off other studies, I yet pursued them with less ardor.[5]

The shape and burden of an individual's ministry often emerge from the influences and atmosphere in which his conversion took place. These seem at times to leave a permanent birthmark on an individual's life. This was true for Calvin. Whatever he means by the much-discussed phrase "by a sudden conversion (*subita conversione*)," the rich and emotive vocabulary he uses to describe that conversion provides us with a transcript of the principles that shaped his Christian life. His language here is strikingly different from that of contemporary evangelicalism. It is hard to imagine him speaking about "letting Jesus into my heart" or "praying to accept Jesus"; indeed, for Calvin, the movement of conversion is not "getting Christ in" but "getting into Christ."

In Calvin's conversion, two things stand out: First, his pre-conversion condition was marked by a "hardened" and resistant ("unteachable") mind, and, by implication, a distaste for true godliness (later reversed into an "inflamed . . . desire"). This, of course, was the informed biblical analysis of one who believed that the fallen human mind is "a perpetual factory of idols"[6] and therefore deeply resistant to the iconoclasm of grace.

Second, for Calvin, conversion to Christ meant not only a transition from condemnation to justification but from ignorance to knowledge and from arrogant rebellion to a humbled heart.[7] His mind was thus softened and brought "to a teachable frame." From this flowed powerful new affections. He now was "inflamed" with "intense . . . desire" to make progress in "true godliness." Thus, to have a heart for God meant to have a desire to grow in the "knowledge of the truth, which accords with godliness" (Titus 1:1).

PROGRESSIVE TRANSFORMATION

Calvin's description of the events that followed his "sudden" conversion gives us a further clue to his spiritual progress: "I was quite surprised to find that before a year had elapsed, all who had any desire after purer doctrine were continually coming to me to learn, although I myself was as yet but a mere novice and tyro."[8]

His distinctive genius, present virtually from his conversion, was a God-given ability to penetrate to the heart of the meaning of the text of Scripture. But these words also indicate in passing that his early progress was set in the context of an interconnected—and somewhat "underground"—fellowship of like-minded young men, first in Paris and thereafter throughout Europe. Such brotherhoods are often God's chief instruments in stimulating holy living and advancing the gospel.

Calvin had been a student in Paris in the aftermath of the Sorbonne doctors' scrutiny of Martin Luther's works. Out of that cauldron of spiritual unrest came a loose-knit group of younger men who became leaders of the new churches of the Reformation. It was from this school of prophets that Calvin emerged as the leading young theological scholar of his generation, evidenced by the publication of the first, and comparatively brief, edition of his *Institutes of the Christian Religion* in 1536. Its subtitle underlined the young Calvin's daring vision: *Summa Pietatis*,[9] or "the sum of piety." His goal from the first was not merely knowledge, but an understanding of the gospel that impacted the heart and the will, and in turn transformed lives.

This marriage of learning and piety marked the whole of Calvin's ministry and reflected his understanding of what it means to know Christ, to serve God, and to live in the power of the Spirit. "I call piety," he writes, "that reverence joined with the love of God which the knowledge of his benefits induces."[10] *Piety* has a family ring about it (devotion to one's father being its most common human expression). Alongside it in sheer frequency of use, Calvin employs another family term to describe the Christian life: *adoptio*—adoptive sonship. While he never made either concept a separate locus in the *Institutes*, together they virtually summarize what is involved in being a Christian and growing in likeness to Jesus Christ. Piety is an expression of adoption—reverence for God, living with a single eye to His glory. This is what the children of God are called to do and to be.[11]

A THEOLOGICAL TRANSCRIPT

Living the Christian life is a theme that runs throughout the *Institutes*, but it is the central theme of Book 3, which is titled: "The mode of obtaining the grace of Christ. The benefits it confers, and the effects resulting from it." Calvin's exposition has a distinctive (some have thought idiosyncratic) order, as a glance at the chapter headings will indicate. To some extent, this underlines the way in which his greatest work is simultaneously a trinitarian theology, an expression of the gospel, and a transcript of his own spiritual life.

Nowhere in Calvin's writings can we take his spiritual pulse more easily than in his exposition of the Christian life in *Institutes* 3.6–10. This material, in an earlier form, is the subject of a later chapter in the present volume, but its themes are germane to Calvin's own experience, and we cannot read his heart without some reference to them.[12]

CENTRALITY OF JESUS CHRIST

For Calvin, the gospel is not predestination or election, the sovereignty of God, or even the five points of doctrine with which his name is so often associated. These are aspects of the gospel, but the gospel is Jesus Christ Himself. That may seem a truism—who would think anything else? But this truth takes on fresh significance in Calvin's understanding.

By the time of the second (1539) and subsequent editions of the *Institutes*, Calvin's ongoing study of Scripture had brought a new depth to his understanding of the gospel (he completed his commentary on Romans in the same year). With this new understanding, he insisted that salvation and all its benefits not only come to us through Christ but are to be found exclusively in Christ. Union with Christ brings the believer into fellowship with Christ, crucified, resurrected, ascended, reigning, and returning.

Two considerations followed. First, Calvin realized that through faith in Christ all the blessings of the gospel were his. Second, he saw that his life must be rooted and grounded in fellowship with Christ. Perhaps it was the personal realization of this that led him to wax lyrical at the climax of his exposition of the christological section of the Apostles' Creed:

> We see that our whole salvation and all its parts are comprehended in Christ (Acts 4:12). We should therefore take care not

to derive the least portion of it from anywhere else. If we seek salvation, we are taught by the very name of Jesus that it is "of him" (1 Corinthians 1:30).

If we seek any other gifts of the Spirit, they will be found in his anointing. If we seek strength, it lies in his dominion; if purity, in his conception; if gentleness, it appears in his birth. . . . If we seek redemption, it lies in his passion; if acquittal, in his condemnation; if remission of the curse, in his cross (Galatians 3:13); if satisfaction, in his sacrifice; if purification, in his blood; if reconciliation, in his descent into hell; if mortification of the flesh, in his tomb; if newness of life, in his resurrection; if immortality, in the same; if inheritance of the Heavenly Kingdom, in his entrance into heaven; if protection, if security, if abundant supply of all blessings, in his Kingdom; if untroubled expectation of judgment, in the power given to him to judge.[13]

Calvin had made a great discovery, one that dominated both his theology and his life: if Christ is our Redeemer, then Christ was formed in the incarnation in order to deal precisely, perfectly, and fully with both the cause of our guilt and the consequences of our sin. Union with Christ was the means the Spirit used to bring this about.

LIKENESS TO CHRIST: GENTLE CALVIN, MEEK AND MILD?

One statement from Calvin's exposition of the Apostles' Creed can serve as a case study in his personal struggles for sanctification and the measure of progress he made: "If we seek . . . gentleness, it appears in his birth."[14]

This is the man who reputedly had been known by his fellow students as "The Accusative Case," the youth of tense and nervous disposition, conscious of a certain shortness of temper. But he realized that God had made provision for this in Christ—even to make John Calvin gentle. Intriguingly, the same theme reappears in the hymn attributed to him,

"I Greet Thee Who My Sure Redeemer Art,"[15] in which he wrote: "Thou hast the true and perfect gentleness. No harshness hast thou, and no bitterness."

This is the *ipsissima vox* ("the very voice," or the concept), if not the *ipsissima verba* ("the very words") of Calvin, wonderfully expressing that all that we lack is now ours in Jesus Christ. Calvin writes, "In short, since rich store of every kind of good abounds in him, let us drink our fill from this fountain, and from no other."[16]

How well Calvin drank of Christ with respect to personal gentleness and tenderness is indicated in several incidental ways:

1. In his restraint of personal malice to those who opposed him. Calvin could use strong language and regret it.[17] But Giovanni Diodati records how Johannes Eck was surprised, when he visited the Genevan Reformer, to have the door opened by a kind and modest-living Calvin himself, who refused with grace the offers of preferment in Rome if he would return to the fold.

2. In his empathy for those who suffered. His correspondence expresses his deep affection for his friends, but also his deep compassion for his brothers and sisters in Christ who were sick or bereaved. His extant letters to some of the young men he had schooled for martyrdom express a tender kindness mingled with fortitude that is deeply moving and impressive.

3. In his concern to show respect to others. On one occasion, his secretary, Charles de Jonvilliers, remonstrated with him to dictate his letters rather than write them in his own hand. Calvin was concerned lest the recipients of his letters should in any degree feel slighted that he himself was not the penman.

4. In his gracious attitude toward others. In his biography of Calvin, Theodore Beza, Calvin's colleague and successor, writes that Calvin never put "weak brethren to the blush."[18] There is something touching about Beza's comment. This Calvin had learned from the Christ who would not break a bruised reed or quench a faintly burning wick (Isa. 42:3). Thus Calvin concludes his exposition of that text with a comment

on ministry styles: "Following this example, the ministers of the gospel, who are his deputies, ought to show themselves to be meek, and to support the weak, and gently to lead them in the way, so as not to extinguish in them the feeblest sparks of piety, but, on the contrary, to kindle them with all their might."[19]

Clearly Calvin, "The Accusative Case," became in measure a Christlike pastor. Illustrations of other graces might be multiplied.

LIFE UNDER THE CROSS

"Howbeit, you must remember," Calvin wrote to a correspondent, "the cross of Jesus Christ will follow us."[20] He well understood that cross-bearing is central to the Christian life. Compulsory flight from persecution while in his mid-20s early introduced him to the implications of union with Christ: sharing in the death of Christ involves not only inward mortification (*mortificatio interna*) leading to sanctification, but also outward participation in sufferings (*mortificatio externa*), whether personal, or in the way of persecution and even martyrdom:

> For whomever the Lord has adopted and deemed worthy of his fellowship ought to prepare themselves for a hard, toilsome, and unquiet life, crammed with very many and various kinds of evils. It is the Heavenly Father's will thus to exercise them so as to put his own children to a definite test. Beginning with Christ, his firstborn, he follows his plan with all his children.[21]

This sentiment could be cited a hundred times from Calvin's writings.

These principles were written on a large scale in his own life as a gospel minister. Geneva was no sinecure. Effectively banished from the city in April 1538, Calvin wrote to his friend Pierre Viret when he was invited to return, "There is no place under heaven of which I can have a greater dread."[22] But return he did. Often vilified, he was sustained in his ministry precisely by the conviction that it is through tribulation that we enter the kingdom, and that God uses it to transform His children into the likeness of Christ.

Calvin also knew personal suffering. Married in 1540, he had lost his wife and his son Jacques before the end of the decade. The brevity of his comment to Viret on Jacques' death is starkly eloquent: "[God] is himself a Father, and knows what is best for his children."[23]

Beyond this, the closing years of his ministry were marked by a series of debilitating illnesses. He matter-of-factly describes one incident to his friend Heinrich Bullinger:

> At present, I am relieved from very acute suffering, having been delivered of a calculus [i.e., a "stone"] about the size of the kernel of a filbert [i.e., a hazelnut]. As the retention of urine was very painful to me, by the advice of my physician, I got upon horseback that the jolting might assist me in discharging the calculus. On my return home I was surprised to find that I emitted discolored blood instead of urine. The following day the calculus had forced its way from the bladder into the urethra. Hence still more excruciating tortures. For more than half an hour I endeavored to disengage myself from it by a violent agitation of my whole body. I gained nothing by that, but obtained a slight relief by fomentations with warm water. Meanwhile, the urinary canal was so much lacerated that copious discharges of blood flowed from it. It seems to me now that I begin to live anew for the last two days since I am delivered from these pains.

Remarkably, but somewhat typical of Calvin's sheer determination to focus on God's work, his next words are: "Of the state of France, I should have written to you with more details if I had been at leisure."[24]

What is the explanation for this pattern of divine working? Calvin explains in words that we may readily apply to him:

But even the most holy persons, however much they may recognize that they stand not through their own strength but through God's grace, are too sure of their own fortitude and constancy unless by the testing of the cross he bring them into a deeper knowledge of himself.[25]

LIVING FOR THE FUTURE

It is commonplace today in Reformed theology to recognize that the Christian lives "between the times"—already we are in Christ, but a yet more glorious future awaits us in the final consummation. There is, therefore, a "not yet" about our present Christian experience. Calvin well understood this, and he never dissolved the tension between the "already" and the "not yet." But he also stressed the importance for the present of a life-focus on the future.

Calvin sought, personally, to develop a balance of contempt for the present life with a deep gratitude for the blessings of God and a love and longing for the heavenly kingdom. The sense that the Lord would come and issue His final assessment on all and bring His elect to glory was a dominant motif for him. This, the theme of his chapter "Meditation on the Future Life,"[26] was a major element in the energy with which he lived in the face of the "not yet" of his own ailments and weakness. When he was seriously ill and confined to bed, his friends urged him to take some rest, but he replied, "Would you that the Lord, when He comes, should find me idle?"[27] By living in the light of the return of Christ and the coming judgment, Calvin became deeply conscious of the brevity of time and the length of eternity.

This sense of eternity overflowed from his life into his work. It was so characteristic of him that it flowed out naturally in his prayers at the conclusion of his lectures. Here we see the wonderful harmony of his biblical exposition, his understanding of the gospel, his concern to teach young men how to live for God's glory, and his personal piety. A fragment of one of these prayers, chosen almost randomly, fittingly summarizes this all-too-brief reflection on the heart for God that Calvin expressed in his learning and leadership:

> May we be prepared, whatever happens,
> rather to undergo a hundred deaths
> than to turn aside from the profession of true piety,
> in which we know our safety to be laid up.
> And may we so glorify thy name
> as to be partakers of that glory which has been acquired for us
> through the blood of thine only-begotten Son. Amen.[28]

NOTES

[1] John Calvin, *Institutes of the Christian Religion*, ed. John T. McNeill; trans. Ford Lewis Battles; Library of Christian Classics, XX–XXI (Philadelphia: Westminster John Knox, 1960), 1.2.1.

[2] John Calvin, *Commentary on the Book of Psalms*, trans. James Anderson (Edinburgh: Calvin Translation Society, 1845; repr. Grand Rapids: Baker, 2003), xli.

[3] John Calvin, *Letters of John Calvin*, ed. Jules Bonnet, trans. M. R. Gilbert (Philadelphia: Presbyterian Board of Education, 1858), 4:364. The letter was written on May 2, 1564. Calvin died on May 27.

[4] Cf. the language in his letter in August 1541 to Farel as he prepared to return to Geneva: "Had I the choice at my own disposal, nothing would be less agreeable to me than to follow your advice. But when I remember that I am not my own, I offer up my heart, presented as a sacrifice to the Lord." Calvin, *Letters of John Calvin*, 1:280–281.

[5] Calvin, *Commentary on the Book of Psalms*, xl.

[6] Calvin, *Institutes of the Christian Religion*, 1.11.8.

[7] Note in this connection his approval of a remark in one of Augustine's letters that the essence of the Christian life is humility. Ibid., 2.2.11.

[8] Calvin, *Commentary on the Book of Psalms*, xli.

[9] The title of the first edition was: *Christianae religionis institutio tota fere pietatis summam . . . complectens.*

[10] Calvin, *Institutes of the Christian Religion*, 1.2.1.

[11] Cf. the beautiful words in Calvin's French Catechism of 1537 describing piety as "a pure and true zeal which loves God altogether as Father and reveres him truly as Lord, embraces his justice and dreads to offend him more than to die" (John Calvin, *Instruction in Faith*, trans. Paul T. Fuhrmann [Louisville, Ky.: Westminster John Knox Press], 22).

The superabundance of Calvin's references to *pietas* is often masked by its translation in English versions as "godliness." Similarly, his intense focus on the Christian life as a life of adopted sons has been little recognized simply because he did not treat adoption as a separate locus for exposition in the *Institutes*.

[12] This material appeared in earlier form in the second edition of the *Institutes* in 1539 and was separately published in 1549 in an English translation by Thomas Broke under the title *The Life and Communicacion* [sic] *of a Christian Man*. It has often been republished as *The Golden Booklet of the Christian Life*.

[13] Calvin, *Institutes of the Christian Religion*, 2.16.19.

[14] Ibid.

[15] The hymn appeared in the Strasbourg Psalter of 1545. Calvin versified a number of psalms, but appears to have taken a low view of his gifts as a poet and his work did not reappear in the Genevan Psalter. Certainly the sentiment of this hymn is pure Calvin, whether penned by the Reformer himself or by someone deeply influenced by his teaching.

[16] Calvin, *Institutes of the Christian Religion*, 2.16.19.

[17] See Calvin's letter to Farel on Oct. 8, 1539, in which he describes his agonies with respect to this. Calvin, *Letters of John Calvin*, 1:151–157.

[18] Theodore Beza, *Life of Calvin*, in *Tracts and Treatises*, ed. and trans. Henry Beveridge (Edinburgh: 1844), 1:xcvii.

[19] John Calvin, *Commentary on Isaiah*, trans. William Pringle (Edinburgh: Calvin Translation Society, 1850; repr. Grand Rapids: Baker, 2003), 3:288.

[20] Calvin, *Letters of John Calvin*, 2:230.

[21] Calvin, *Institutes of the Christian Religion*, 3.8.1

[22] Calvin, *Letters of John Calvin*, 1:231.

[23] Ibid., 1:344.

[24] Ibid., 4:320–321. A letter to Farel in 1540 indicates that his sickness was long-standing, while simultaneously giving insight into the tension under which he lived. Ibid., 1:204ff.

[25] Calvin, *Institutes of the Christian Religion*, 3.8.2. Here Calvin's exposition of such passages as 2 Cor. 4:10–12 and Phil. 3:10 may be consulted with profit.

[26] Ibid., 3.9.

[27] Quoted in "Translator's Preface," in John Calvin, *Commentaries on the Book of Joshua*, trans. Henry Beveridge (Edinburgh: Calvin Translation Society, 1854; repr. Grand Rapids: Baker, 2003), vi.

[28] John Calvin, prayer after Lecture 16 on Daniel, *Commentaries on the Prophet Daniel*, trans. by Thomas Myers (Edinburgh: Calvin Translation Society, 1852; repr. Grand Rapids: Baker, 2003), 1:242.

Chapter 4

THE REFORMER
OF FAITH AND LIFE

D. G. HART

For when the whole church stands, as it were, before God's judgment seat, confesses itself guilty, and has its sole refuge in God's mercy, it is no common or light solace to have present there the ambassador of Christ, armed with the mandate of reconciliation, by whom it hears proclaimed its absolution.[1]

—JOHN CALVIN

J ohn Calvin did not set out to be a Reformer. Until 1536, when he turned 27 years old, Calvin had given every indication that he wanted to lead a life of contemplation dedicated to learning. He had first studied theology, but had switched to law at his father's insistence. His knack for languages and literature ideally suited him to the world of humanism, and his temperament bore all the marks of a scholar. Calvin's first book, a commentary on Seneca, published in 1532, revealed the direction of the aspiring scholar's maturing thought. It was a learned work that drew on the wisdom of antiquity to address matters of political import in Western Europe, particularly the tyranny of monarchs and the virtue of clemency.

This humanistic orientation was not inherently at odds with the Protestant Reformation. In fact, the Northern European expression of Renaissance humanism, most notably in the case of Desiderius Erasmus, regularly mixed the study and recovery of ancient authors with ecclesiastical reform. Thus, when Calvin converted from Roman Catholicism to the Protestant cause in late 1533 or early 1534, his religious pilgrimage was not at obvious odds with his scholarly ambitions. In fact, it actually enhanced them.

Soon after his repudiation of Rome, Calvin wrote the first edition of his *Institutes of the Christian Religion*. Not published until 1536, the book was a defense of Protestants who were being persecuted in France, and it served as a call for Christians to rally to the persecuted believers' cause. Still, Calvin's identification with Protestantism did not a Reformer make. What did, at least from Calvin's perspective, was an unplanned visit in 1536 to the city of Geneva, Switzerland.

Guillaume Farel had already started reforms in Geneva's churches, and Calvin's unexpected arrival caught the older Reformer's immediate attention. Here was an accomplished young scholar with impeccable skills who could greatly assist the cause of reform. Calvin was merely planning to pass through Geneva until the way was safe for him to go on to Strasbourg. But as Calvin himself later remarked, "God thrust me into the game."[2] Abandoning his plans to go to Strasbourg, he joined Farel in laboring to reform the Genevan church, but he remained uncertain that he had made the right decision. When the Geneva authorities in 1538 banished Calvin and Farel from the city for overstepping their bounds, Calvin was glad to be left free to resume his plan for further study and writing. This time he planned to reside in Basel. But Martin Bucer had other ideas and pled with Calvin to pastor the congregation of French-speaking exiles in Strasbourg. Calvin was reluctant. What convinced him to go to Strasbourg was Bucer's threat that "God will know how to find the rebellious servant, as he found Jonah."[3]

THE WORK OF REFORM

Of all the tasks that Calvin undertook as a Reformer, theology was arguably the easiest, for it was the one task that drew upon his natural talents
and interests. He was a proverbial machine in the production of doctrinal instruction and biblical exposition. In Geneva, where he spent the
bulk of his career, except for his three-year banishment in Strasbourg,
Calvin taught classes on the Bible three times a week and preached daily
every other week as part of his regular pastoral duties. Then, beginning
in 1540, Calvin began to write commentaries on books of the Bible;
these works were published and widely distributed. Likewise, his sermons were transcribed and published, and after 1557, he permitted his
class lectures to be set down for publication. His capacity for writing was
extraordinary. At one point, Calvin wrote a one hundred-page book
within a week's time. Even when he could not get out of bed because
of his many physical ailments, he dictated his thoughts for different
writings.

His diverse publications included expositions on the Lord's Supper,
advice to Protestants as far away as Poland, and controversial treatises
against the Council of Trent, the Anabaptists, anti-Trinitarians, astrol-
ogy, and ecclesiastical compromisers. His most successful short work
was *An Assessment of the Value Christianity Would Receive from an Inventory
of Relics* (1543).[4] By 1622, this work (an Erasmus-like lampoon of the literally incredible collections of saints' body parts by the Roman Catholic
Church at shrines throughout Europe) had gone through twenty editions. Based on this output, Calvin emerged before age 40 as the most
popular and widely read Reformed theologian. His French works were
translated into German, Italian, Spanish, English, Dutch, Czech, Polish,
and Latin.[5]

Of course, Calvin's *Institutes,* first published in 1536, contributed
most to his fame. The work started as a small exposition of the Lord's
Prayer, the Decalogue, and the Apostles' Creed; it also included sections

on the true and false sacraments and a section on the relations between church and state. However, the *Institutes* became a life-long project for Calvin. Subsequent editions followed in 1539, 1543, 1550, and 1559. In each edition, Calvin expanded and reworked the material on the basis of further study and changing circumstances in the church and society. By its last edition, the *Institutes* was more than five times the length of its original form, having grown from 85,000 to 450,000 words. It became the book that Protestantism's enemies used as the target for attack. The great sixteenth-century Roman Catholic polemicist Robert Bellarmine cited Calvin's *Institutes* more often in his *Disputations against the Heretics of Our Time* than the work of any other Protestant theologian, whether Lutheran or Reformed.[6]

Yet for all of Calvin's prodigious output as a theologian, he was every bit as engaged as an active and dutiful pastor and churchman. In fact, his work to reform the churches of Geneva was the primary cause for his dismissal from the city in 1538. Only a year after Farel had persuaded Calvin to take up the work of instructing Geneva's faithful in the Protestant doctrines, the young Frenchman initiated a church order that Geneva's pastors presented to the city's magistrates. It called for an immediate reform of the city's sacramental practice. The Lord's Supper was to be celebrated monthly. Church members were to be required, before being admitted to the table, to learn a brief outline of the Christian religion that Calvin had formulated. And the church was to establish a body of "persons of upright life" to determine those eligible for communion.[7] The city council accepted much of the proposed system of discipline, though not without animated debate and some resistance. The most objectionable piece of reform was the requirement that only examined believers might come to the table. The city council rejected this part of Calvin's polity. In response, the ministers refused to submit to the magistrates, not so much because of sacramental teaching but because of their conviction that the church should govern her own ordinances. When the ministers preached against the city's actions and refused to celebrate the Lord's Supper on

Easter Sunday, 1538, the magistrates told the pastors, Calvin included, to pack their bags.

Calvin received a second chance to carry out reforms of the Geneva church in 1541 when the city's officers realized the pastors who had complied with their policies were incapable of responding to the demands of a precarious religious situation. Rome had recently made overtures to Geneva to return to the fold, and Geneva recognized the need for Calvin to respond. His letter to Jacopo Sadoleto, the bishop of Carpentras, not only prevented Geneva from realigning with the papacy, it also helped to secure the leverage Calvin needed to push through the reforms he was advocating.

The Ecclesiastical Ordinances of 1541 drew upon Calvin's own reflections on biblical teaching about church offices. The document called for four offices in the church: ministers, teachers, elders, and deacons. It gave the sitting ministers, the city's magistrates, and the congregation each a role in the call of a pastor. It required parents to bring children to church for weekly catechism classes. It established weekly and quarterly meetings of the ministers for the sake of edification and mutual correction. And it appointed a body consisting of pastors and elders with the responsibility for carrying out church discipline. Although Calvin believed the power to excommunicate (the barring of unrepentant believers from the Lord's Table) belonged to the consistory (the body composed of pastors and elders), he knew the city council did not agree. The language of Calvin's Ecclesiastical Ordinances reflected that disagreement, and it gave both the church and the state a hand in excommunication.

The work of the consistory put into practice the reform of church life that Calvin proposed. In 1542 alone, the members of the consistory heard 320 cases. Half of these concerned such irregularities as people staying away from services and ignorance of the catechism. Others involved Genevans who had persisted in Roman Catholic devotional practices or dabbled in magic. In several instances, the consistory insisted that the offending parties acquire Bibles for use in the home or hire teachers who would offer instruction in the teachings of the church.

By 1550, the number of cases before the consistory had increased almost twofold (584); the jump stemmed from an expansion of subjects for the pastors and elders to oversee in the lives of their flocks. In addition to correcting the religious practices of the city's residents, the consistory sought to resolve family quarrels and domestic assaults, and to correct sexual impropriety. About one in twenty cases concerned misconduct, such as gambling, lewd dancing, and deceitful business practices. Almost as many instances of discipline addressed Genevans who had spoken disrespectfully of the city's pastors.

THE FRAGILITY OF REFORM

Church reforms in Geneva were not unanimously welcome. The city's native population had reservations about Calvin's efforts on several levels. One stemmed from the natural friction between those who had grown up in Geneva and the many immigrants coming to the city to escape religious persecution. Geneva accommodated many Protestant refugees; the largest number came from France, while the most influential came from England. At the same time, the new and exacting standards of church discipline broke with the relaxed codes of the pre-Reformation church. Thus, native Genevans had reason to believe that their city and its churches had been taken over by foreign elements. Because the ultimate responsibility for excommunication had yet to be officially resolved—whether it belonged to the church leaders or city magistrates—Geneva's older and longtime residents could express their resentment of the new church order by appealing to the city's governing body.

Harsh conflicts emerged in 1546 over the unlikely issue of superstitious names. A citizen and church member submitted his son for baptism and requested that he be given the name "Claude," the identification of a local saint. This was so objectionable to the officiating pastor that he assigned the name "Abraham," which initiated a protracted struggle between the church and the townspeople. While the city council sided with the church and passed a law forbidding the use of inappropriate names, those opposed to the church began to name their dogs Calvin and called the pastor "Cain." The situation only worsened.[8]

The leading opponent of ecclesiastical oversight was Philibert Berthelier. He originally had supported the Reformation, and in Lyon it was reported that he had even drawn his sword to defend Calvin's good name. But the tight control of the population was too much for him, and he later said he would not so much as clip his nail for Calvin. Unfortunately, Berthelier's behavior kept him under the consistory's eye. He had engaged in a sword fight while drunk and had broken off an engagement when he learned that his betrothed was less affluent than he thought. Not to help matters, he had assaulted several immigrants. Each of these infractions had taken him before the body of pastors and elders, with the result that he was barred from the Lord's Table. In 1553, when Berthelier wished to take communion, instead of going to the church's officers he went to the city council, the body that many believed had final authority over the church regarding excommunication. Because the council was dominated by a network of families hostile to Calvin, it granted Berthelier admission to the Lord's Table. In turn, Calvin and other ministers threatened to leave the city and replay the difficulties Geneva had faced between 1538 and 1541. Politics within Switzerland and relations with France prompted the city council to side with Calvin and to ask Berthelier not to present himself at the Lord's Table.[9]

For two more years the acrimony between anti-Calvin factions in the city and Geneva's pastors worsened, with flagrant displays of immorality meeting with stiff punishment. For instance, six residents were convicted and executed for sodomy. But the tide began to turn in 1555 when the townspeople favorable to Calvin were able to elect more pro-Calvin candidates to the city council, partly the result of more French immigrants being able to secure the status of citizen. Even so, a riot broke out in the spring of that year in which anti-Calvin Genevans ran through the streets crying for the execution of the Frenchmen. Though cooler heads prevailed, Calvin and city officials believed that a conspiracy was afloat to overturn the gains of the Reformation. An investigation of leading citizens ensued; twelve were found guilty and, according to city law, were sentenced to death because of their crimes. Two-thirds of the guilty found a way to leave the city, but the other four were executed.

In the words of one of Calvin's contemporaries, Nicholas Colladon: "The discovery of the conspiracy led to a great advance for God's Church, for the populace was rendered more obedient to the divine word, the holy reformation was better observed, and scandals were duly punished."[10] Even so, Calvin did hear from other Reformed pastors that the incident was hurting his reputation and costing Geneva valuable support from potential allies.

Although these political battles were not the only obstacles that Calvin faced—the case of Michael Servetus has gone down in infamy as an example of Calvinism's dark side—they were the most important for the daily life of the church in a city that was formerly known for its immorality and crime. The city's rate of illegitimate births plummeted, 30 percent of newborns received Old Testament names (compared with 3 percent before Calvin arrived), and profanity practically ceased.

These changes in city life coincided with an influx of Protestant exiles from Great Britain, escaping the terror of Mary Tudor (infamously known as Bloody Mary). Among the British immigrants was John Knox of Scotland, who called Geneva "the most perfect school of Christ . . . since the days of the Apostles."[11] What Knox observed as a flawless enterprise was the result of years of struggle, both personal and political, for Calvin and the other Reformed pastors.

THE MEANING OF REFORM

Knox's description of Geneva has inspired Protestants through the centuries to regard Calvinism as an activist faith with prodigious resources for social and political reform. In point of fact, because of the intimate connections between church and state in European society, a relationship that few questioned, the reform of one could not help but involve the reform of the other. This was especially true for the city of Geneva, a place that historians have described as a center of dissolute living. Townspeople had a variety of taverns and brothels from which to choose, and the pre-Reformation clergy and monks had a reputation for less-than-pious behavior. Meanwhile, the existence of a state church left almost no room for distinguishing between the churched and unchurched, as modern Christians have come to do. Calvin's efforts to reform the standards for fellowship at the Lord's Table could not help but have an effect on practically the entire city.

Nevertheless, as much as Calvin's reforms of the church had implications for the city of Geneva, his understanding of ecclesiastical discipline also distinguished between church and state in ways that the medieval church could not have anticipated. By insisting that the church alone had the power of excommunication, not the state, Calvin was reserving for the ministry a spiritual authority as opposed to the physical, or temporal, one possessed by the state. In fact, in the *Institutes*, in his discussion of the civil magistrate, Calvin distinguished clearly between the civil and ecclesiastical spheres, insisting that the former is concerned with "only . . . the establishment of civil justice and outward morality," while the latter "resides in the soul or inner man and pertains to eternal life."[12] He even calls it a "Jewish vanity" to confuse "Christ's spiritual Kingdom" with the civil government, because these are "things completely distinct."[13] This teaching was not simply a matter of expediency for the right ordering of the church and its affairs. Calvin also taught that Christ's kingdom was strictly "spiritual in nature."[14] Inasmuch as Christ's own rule is spiritual, "not earthly or carnal and hence subject to corruption," the church's authority needs to reflect this fundamental Christian reality.[15]

The relationship between church and state in Geneva, closely involved on the one hand and distinct on the other, helps to put into perspective the significance of Calvin as a Reformer. A variety of historians and social theorists have argued that Calvinism played a crucial role in transforming the West and creating the modern world. The Whig view of history, an outlook that attributed to Calvinism the success of the democratic and free societies of the Netherlands, Great Britain, and the United States of America, contrasted the liberating and demystifying qualities of Calvin's reforms with the tyrannical and superstitious habits of Roman Catholicism. Especially influential in this regard was Max Weber's argument that Calvinism nurtured a kind of piety that encouraged the virtues and habits necessary for the growth and spread of capitalism.

Philip Benedict, in his book, *Christ's Churches Purely Reformed*, a splendid account of Calvinism's origins and history, argues that the interpretations of Calvin's influence on the West miss that Reformed Christianity was first and foremost a religious phenomenon. It was crucial to a time in the West when "confessional principles and attachments became structural elements in European society."[16] Calvinism offered "ordinary Christians motivation and models for forming alternatives to the established church" and convinced rulers and their theological advisers to be faithful to the Bible. As such, Calvinism's deepest imperative on believers, pastors, and magistrates alike was to "profess Christ's teachings purely, not to obey the text of any human document."[17] If Calvin's reforms played a pivotal role in the history of the West, they did so not as organizing principles that shaped political and economic developments, but rather because of their demands that individual believers and congregations conform their lives to God's Word.

NOTES

[1] John Calvin, *Institutes of the Christian Religion*, ed. John T. McNeill; trans. Ford Lewis Battles; Library of Christian Classics, XX–XXI (Philadelphia: Westminster John Knox, 1960), 3.4.14.

[2] John T. McNeill, *The History and Character of Calvinism* (New York: Oxford University Press, 1954), 131.

[3] Ibid., 144.

[4] Published in *Selected Works of John Calvin: Tracts and Letters*, trans. and ed. Henry Beveridge (repr. Grand Rapids: Baker, 1983).

[5] Philip Benedict, *Christ's Churches Purely Reformed: A Social History of Calvinism* (New Haven: Yale University Press, 2002), 91.

[6] Ibid., 92–93.

[7] Ibid., 94.

[8] Ibid., 99.

[9] Ibid., 100.

[10] Ibid., 102.

[11] Ibid., 108.

[12] Calvin, *Institutes of the Christian Religion*, 4.20.1.

[13] Ibid.

[14] Ibid., 2.15.3.

[15] Ibid., 2.15.4.

[16] Benedict, *Christ's Churches Purely Reformed*, 543.

[17] Ibid., 545.

Chapter 5

THE CHURCHMAN
OF THE REFORMATION

HARRY L. REEDER

*The pastor ought to have two voices: one, for gathering the sheep;
and another, for warding off and driving away wolves and thieves.
The Scripture supplies him with the means of doing both.*[1]

—JOHN CALVIN

After Calvin's conversion and success consequential to the publication of his *Institutes of the Christian Religion* in 1536, he became convinced he could best serve the Lord by retiring to solitude and producing literary works expounding upon the theological issues of the Reformation and encouraging the expansion of the Protestant church. But God said "No" through the fiery, red-haired missionary to Geneva, Guillaume Farel.

Calvin had decided on Strasbourg as a place conducive to his desire to write. A raging war providentially detoured him to Geneva for what he supposed would be a single night's stay en route to Strasbourg. Farel, hearing of Calvin's presence, found him and implored him to remain in Geneva to lead the church that had formally embraced Protestantism that year. Farel was convinced that there was much to be done for the

55

Reformation in Geneva and that Calvin was God's man to do it. Initially, Calvin was unmoved by Farel's passion and vision. Farel's response of a vehement imprecatory curse upon Calvin's desired life of retirement, including a request that God's wrath and judgment would fall on him if he rejected the call to Geneva, resulted in a sleepless night for Calvin and a changed heart. He set aside his personal desires and became pastor of St. Peter's Church in Geneva.

Calvin's decision to remain in Geneva ultimately produced the preeminent churchman of the Reformation. Martin Luther, whom Calvin admired, had helped to wrest the church away from the grip of Roman Catholic heresy, superstition, and immorality, and the Reformers certainly displayed an amazing devotion to the church. But it was Calvin who brought the Reformation to the life of the church by restoring biblical faithfulness and apostolic simplicity. His pastoral ministry in Geneva demonstrated the importance and fruit of faithful pastoral leadership. It led to the training of countless pastors and church planters. It advanced the church not just in Geneva, but throughout Europe, Great Britain, Scotland, and eventually the Americas. And it resulted in the publication of literature of great theological significance. Thus, the Lord granted Calvin his desire to write and publish far beyond his original expectations. Why? Because Calvin had made the Lord the delight of his life: "Delight yourself in the Lord and He will give you the desires of your heart" (Ps. 37:4).

Calvin's personal motto read, "I offer my heart to you, Lord, promptly and sincerely," but this was more than a slogan—it was Calvin's life, the life of a churchman serving as pastor of St. Peter's Church in Geneva. He was unalterably committed to God and His glory, passionately desirous for the preeminence of Christ, and confidently reliant upon the Holy Spirit.

Calvin's pastoral ministry can best be comprehended by examining his commitments as a leader, preacher, teacher, writer, shepherd, and evangelist-missionary.

CALVIN AS PASTOR

Calvin was a pastor for twenty-seven years, or exactly half of his life. He served three pastorates in but two churches—St. Peter's in Geneva and a church of French exiles in Strasbourg. He began his first pastorate at St. Peter's in 1536. In January 1537, Calvin and Farel took a proposal to Geneva's governing Little Council to reform the life and practice of the city's churches. The proposal called for monthly communion, division of the city into parishes, and requiring the citizenry to adopt a catechism/creed previously written by Farel.

After a stormy two years of opposition, Calvin and Farel were banished from Geneva on April 23, 1538. The crisis moment came when Calvin, while "fencing the table" on Easter Sunday, refused to use the liturgy legislated by the civil authorities and denied communion to prominent Geneva citizens engaged in public immorality.

Farel left Geneva and took up a pastorate in Neuchatel, remaining there for the life of his ministry. Calvin eventually accepted an invitation from Martin Bucer and moved to Strasbourg, his desired destination before his stop in Geneva. Calvin's short pastorate in Strasbourg was, by his own testimony, the happiest period of his life. There he was mentored by Bucer, whom he considered his father in the faith, and became the pastor of the French immigrant/exile church, with freedom to write theological publications. He became an honored civic leader and established friendships with many Reformers, including Ulrich Zwingli and Philip Melanchthon. In 1540, he married the widow of an Anabaptist, Idelette de Bure, and adopted her two children. His writing projects included a commentary on Romans, an enlarged edition of the *Institutes of the Christian Religion,* and perhaps the greatest apologetic for the Reformation, *A Reply to Sadoleto.*

These marvelous years were interrupted by a letter from the authorities of Geneva, which invited him to return as pastor of St. Peter's and leader of the church in Geneva. Calvin was married, happy, doing what he loved, and enjoying the able leadership of Bucer and ample opportunity for scholarly writing. Beyond that, Strasbourg had become a center for the Reformation. Still, on Sept. 1, 1541, being convinced the call was from God, Calvin submitted and left his idyllic pastoral ministry to return to Geneva, fully aware of the inevitable challenges, dangers, and persecutions. As he left Strasbourg, his state of mind and heart, as well as his expectations, were revealed in his letters. To Pierre Viret, his dear friend and fellow pastor, he wrote: "I now go to Geneva. There is no place under heaven that I am more afraid of."[2] To Farel, he wrote: "I would rather die a thousand deaths than to take the cross of this calling."[3]

When he arrived in Geneva on Sept. 13, all seemed glorious. He was given a sufficient salary and a generous budget for hospitality because of his commitment to open his home to the multitudes who would come to seek time with him. A house on Canon Street near St. Peter's was provided, along with the expenses to move his family from Strasbourg. A high pulpit was installed in St. Peter's and provision was made for a fur-trimmed black velvet pulpit robe. A two-horse carriage was purchased for the comfort of his wife and children. Furthermore, the Geneva authorities affirmed their irrevocable commitment to Calvin by publicly declaring, "Be it resolved to keep John Calvin here always."[4]

Calvin's restoration to St. Peter's began his third pastorate. It was to be marked by significant battles, ecclesiastical strife, spiritual warfare, intense illnesses, and even physical persecution from 1541 to 1555. Thankfully, this period would be followed by a concluding era of productive ministry from 1555 until his death May 27, 1564. These final years, though challenging, allowed Calvin to concentrate on the spiritual vitality of his congregation and the missionary expansion of the gospel and the Protestant church.

CALVIN AS PASTOR/LEADER

In Strasbourg, Calvin learned to make fewer changes, selecting those that would provide the greatest impact for effective pastoral ministry. In

Geneva, he accomplished change by producing a document called the Ecclesiastical Ordinances of the Church of Geneva. This historic document became a foundational guide for sixteenth-century Reformed churches, and its effects continue to bless the church to this very day.

In this historic document, Calvin resisted the temptation to redesign the church and followed the Reformation pattern of returning the church to its biblical design and apostolic simplicity. He was convinced the church had a sufficient designer, Jesus Christ, and an effective design, which was delineated in Scripture and displayed in the church of the first century. Clearly, Calvin would abhor the efforts of today's church leaders to "redesign" the church. He was aware that the Lord does not call us to pray for church designers, since the designer of the church is Christ, but to pray for "builders and laborers" to faithfully build on "the foundation of the apostles and the prophets, Christ Jesus himself being the cornerstone" (Eph. 2:20).

The Ecclesiastical Ordinances addressed church government, leadership, and membership. Notably, it initiated what today we call the "separation of church and state." Calvin embraced the idea of three biblically ordained and interdependent yet non-hierarchical spheres of life—the family, the state, and the church. The Ordinances initiated changes designed to affirm this biblical concept. Finally, the Ordinances developed a practical plan for the life and ministry of the church, including the three marks of the church—the ministry of prayer and the Word, the faithful administration of the sacraments, and church discipline.

One key element in the Ordinances was the establishment of a biblical infrastructure for the government of the church through four offices: pastor, teacher, elder, and deacon:

• *The pastor.* The pastor was to be an ordained elder committed to the preaching and teaching of God's Word, to intercessory prayer, and to oversight of the administration of the sacraments of baptism and the Lord's Supper. In addition, the pastor was to guide and minister alongside the elders to shepherd the flock and, in Calvin's words, "make fraternal corrections."[5] Entrance into the office of pastor was by way of examination—first, an examination of doctrine and theology, and second, an examination of personal conduct, marriage, family, and community reputation. The formal training of pastors was done through the Geneva Academy, while the practical training was achieved through apprenticeship. By July 1542, Calvin had trained four pastors, who in turn were training others, instituting a process that eventually would produce countless pastors and missionaries for the church. Pastors were required to meet weekly for discussion and prayer, and quarterly in a presbytery, called the Consistory of Geneva, to address matters of church purity and discipline.

• *The teacher/doctor.* The teachers of the church were required to focus upon the academic training of pastors, provide regular theological lectures, and guard the doctrinal purity of the church. The Geneva Academy was staffed by teachers/doctors who provided ministerial training and universal public education designed to promote Christian citizenship and vocation.

• *The elder.* The elders were to be ordained laymen set apart to give oversight to the church by guiding and shepherding the flock while engaging in consistent intercessory prayer and, when necessary, implementing church discipline. They were to meet the qualifications of 1 Timothy 3:1–7 and Titus 1:5–9. Initially, twelve elders joined the pastors to form the Consistory of Geneva.

• *The deacon.* Calvin divided the office of deacon into two orders. One order managed the resources of the church and gave administrative oversight. The second order cared for the sick and needy, and led the church in the ministry of mercy. The examination of deacons was guided by the qualifications delineated in Acts 6:1–7 and 1 Timothy 3:8–13. The mercy deacons established a charity hospital, a traveler's hospital, and eventually a plague hospital. They also secured physicians, surgeons, and nurses for each parish and provided medical care for the poor.

Through the Ordinances, Calvin divided the city into three parishes. Each parish was organized around one of the three churches of Geneva: St. Peter's, St. Gervais, and Rive. In 1541, the population of Geneva was twelve thousand, which placed three thousand to five thousand people under the care of each parish. Each church was to administer the Lord's Supper four times a year in concert so that monthly Communion was available to the citizens of Geneva. The Communion schedule also included Christmas, Easter, Pentecost, and the first Sunday of September. A catechism was developed to evangelize and disciple the citizens; it was administered weekly with special classes for children. Marriages could be scheduled on any day except Communion Sunday. Matrimonial issues were addressed by the pastors, with the assistance of the elders. Funerals were to avoid any vestiges of superstition, focusing instead on gospel communication and providing thoughtful encouragement to the bereaved family.

CALVIN AS PASTOR/PREACHER

On Sept. 16, 1541, Calvin returned to the pulpit of St. Peter's after his three-year exile in Strasbourg. An expectant and overflowing congregation assembled. What would he say? How would he address through this first sermon the injustices that had been perpetrated upon him, the lessons God had taught him, and the contemporary issues of Geneva? Ascending the newly constructed high pulpit, he opened the Word of God and began expounding the next verse in the text he had been preaching prior to his banishment. This extraordinary action clearly announced to all assembled that the church was to forget what lay in the past and press ahead. But it simultaneously affirmed Calvin's pastoral commitment to the primacy of preaching in general and the importance of expository preaching in particular.

Initially, Calvin preached three times each Lord's Day, twice at St. Peter's and once in a weekly rotation of St. Gervais and Rive. Daily worship was offered in all three churches. Therefore, his preaching schedule required five sermons each week and twenty each month.

Calvin's habit was to preach expositional sermons from the New Testament on Sunday and from the Old Testament on weekdays. His preaching was normally extemporaneous, yet it was noted to be not only intellectually challenging but passionate, practical, and easily comprehended by the common man, resulting in an extraordinary level of biblical literacy throughout Geneva.

Eventually, a secretary was hired to record Calvin's sermons for posterity. The inscribed sermons were sold by the pound for scrap paper after the French Revolution, but were rescued and yielded a treasury of forty-four volumes.

Thus, the man who had renounced his personal desires to produce scholarly theological works to enter the pastorate produced, through his preaching and teaching, a staggering volume of theological publications. The pulpit of St. Peter's became the fountainhead of Reformation theological publications guiding the Protestant church, feeding hungry Christians, and training innumerable pastors, leaders, and theologians to the present day.

CALVIN AS PASTOR/TEACHER

Calvin was the quintessential Reformation man. His commitment to education rooted in the church and expressed pastorally was perhaps one of the most profound aspects of his life and ministry as a churchman.

As an educator, Calvin regularly discipled the Consistory of Geneva, as well as hundreds who came from all over Europe. His catechism, written for both citizens and children, and its implementation revealed not only Calvin's heart for the transformed mind, but also his commitment to evangelize and educate the next generation. He was a proponent for providing public education for the entire citizenry of Geneva, including boys and girls implemented through gender-distinctive schools.

Prior to establishing the Academy of Geneva, Calvin consulted his close pastoral confidant, Viret, about the Lausanne Academy, and then

Johann Sturm concerning the curriculum of the Strasbourg Academy. The Geneva Academy was divided into two levels. One level was a college devoted to public education and the other a seminary devoted to the training of future ministers. Eventually, the Academy grew to more than twelve thousand college students and three hundred seminarians. It was led by Calvin with a recruited faculty of noted scholars, such as Theodore Beza, Francois Hotman, Viret, and others. As Calvin's health failed toward the end of his life, he secured approval to install Beza as superintendent. The Academy, which charged no tuition, attracted immigrants and produced many noteworthy pastors, missionaries, and scholars. Its impact was felt throughout Europe in the professional vocations of law, politics, medicine, and education, while the seminary produced pastors who transformed the religious landscape of Europe with effective ministries such as that of John Knox in Scotland.

David Hall, a contemporary biographer of Calvin, has documented the effort of Thomas Jefferson in 1795 to purchase the Geneva Academy and relocate it to America.[6] The effort failed. Therefore, Jefferson founded what is today the University of Virginia. It is noteworthy that more than two hundred years after Calvin's death, the Geneva Academy was still considered a premier institution of education.

CALVIN AS PASTOR/WRITER

By and large, the greatest theological publications from Pentecost to the first half of the nineteenth century were by pastors. There were two reasons. The first was that the church and its leaders expected and desired pastors to focus upon the prayerful study of God's Word for effective preaching and teaching. The second was the desire among pastors to multiply the blessing of God's Word preached by publishing sermons in written form. The invention of the printing press providentially presented an enormous asset for the breadth of this endeavor. All these factors combined to make Calvin the unchallenged and premier example of the pastor/writer. His ministry became a fountainhead of homiletic discourses, commentaries, devotionals, and theological treatises and tracts.

Calvin's masterpiece was the *Institutes of the Christian Religion*, first produced in 1536 with an attached letter of appeal to Francis I, king of France, requesting the cessation of persecution against French Protestants. This book, popularly known as Calvin's *Institutes* or simply the *Institutes*, was both a defense of the core theological issues of the Reformation and a body of divinity for the Christian and the church. As a work in progress, it developed through five editions over twenty-five years.

One neglected but rich aspect of Calvin's writing ministry was the enormous number of letters and notes produced from his study, home, and even his sickbed. Calvin's letters of encouragement and instruction to the pastors and persecuted believers throughout Europe and England revealed his heart for the Lord's servants to prosper in ministry and persevere under persecution. They also demonstrated an unwavering commitment to establish the Reformed church through prayer and leaders who were saturated with God's Word, and who therefore were able to respond, even in martyrdom, with love and truth.

Calvin's love of music, particularly in worship, resulted in the publication of the Geneva Psalter of 1562, which used the metrical psalms of *Marot's Hymn Book* set to new tunes. These upbeat tunes were referred to sarcastically as "Geneva jigs."[7]

Not surprisingly, Geneva became a publishing center, producing countless books by multiple authors. So profound were these books that any volume published in Geneva or by Calvin was banned in France. Other than the *Institutes*, perhaps the most noteworthy project was the Geneva Bible, which contained notes and insights addressing issues of life, government, vocation, and ethics. This became the Bible of the Reformation, instructing and inspiring God's people and authors such as William Shakespeare, who frequently quoted from it. This Bible was carried by Colonists who founded America.

CALVIN AS PASTOR/SHEPHERD

The public perception of Calvin to this day is that of a brilliant and intense but hard man. Calvin was certainly brilliant and intense, and he could be firm in battle if convinced of its necessity, but his heart as a pastor/shepherd has unfortunately been obscured and neglected. For this reason, J. D. Benoit, in the book *John Calvin, Contemporary Prophet*, writes, "Though he may be first thought of as a theologian, he was even more a pastor of souls."[8]

The Ecclesiastical Ordinances required every family to report to the church through the pastors and elders anyone who was sick within three days. Calvin's three reasons for this requirement were distinctly pastoral. First, the sick needed personal and pastoral comfort. Second, the family of the sick needed encouragement and pastoral guidance. Third, if the sickness resulted in death, the believer needed to be shepherded into glory, but if the one dying was not a believer, then every effort had to be expended to lead him or her to salvation.

During Calvin's ministry, Geneva was terrorized by the plague on five occasions. During the first outbreak, in 1542, Calvin personally led visitations into plague-infected homes. Knowing that this effort likely carried a death sentence, the city fathers intervened to stop him because of their conviction that his leadership was indispensable. The pastors continued this heroic effort under Calvin's guidance, and they recounted the joy of multiple conversions. Many pastors lost their lives in this cause. Unknown to many, Calvin privately continued his own pastoral care in Geneva and other cities where the plague raged. Calvin's pastoral heart, already evidenced by the provision of hospitals for both citizens and immigrants, was further revealed as he collected the necessary resources to establish a separate hospital for plague victims. When believers died, he preached poignant funeral homilies with passion and personal concern.

The depth of Calvin's heart as a shepherd is also revealed through his letters. He penned innumerable letters of comfort and consolation to suffering believers in Geneva and Europe. An excerpt from one letter to a pastor whose family had been ravaged by the plague shows the profundity of his pastoral concerns: "Your messenger came to me bearing your letter. I was hit with a fresh fear and at the same time overwhelmed with a deep sorrow. Actually, yesterday someone told me that he had been stricken with the plague. So I was not simply worried about the grave danger he was in, I was staggered, I was already weeping for him as if he were already dead. I love him so much yet my grief did not arise as much from my love for him as for my general concern for the church."[9]

Without a doubt, Calvin's sweet, faithful, and loving wife, Idelette, not only enhanced Calvin's ministry as a pastor/shepherd but amazingly expanded it. Calvin and Idelette not only opened their home on Canon Street for extended periods to family members, but to hundreds of the poor, immigrants, and students, all of whom received care and love in their small but accommodating house.

Calvin also demonstrated intense concern for the numerous believers who were being martyred for the cause of Christ, particularly in his beloved France. The *Institutes* originally was prompted by his desire to encourage the tortured and persecuted, and to persuade King Francis I to cease supporting the atrocities of anti-Protestant activists. The indescribable cruelties inflicted upon the faithful struck deeply at his heart and motivated him to intervene on behalf of the tortured and dying. Calvin's well-known intervention on behalf of the Waldensians encouraged their heroic witness for Christ in what became the French Huguenot Church.

Calvin's heart for the church beyond Geneva was revealed not only by his overt ministry to the plague-ridden and the persecuted, but also through his tireless efforts to promote unity among the Reformers. Although he personally did not embrace a bishopric system of church government, he was more than willing to work with Lutherans and the Church of England to achieve unity, as revealed through his communications with Luther and Thomas Cranmer. This persistent desire, though never achieved in Europe, did lead to an amazing unification of the Reformed Church in Switzerland. Calvin, in concert with Farel and Viret, entered into nine years of prayerful negotiations and laborious dialogue with Henry Bullinger of Zurich, culminating in the 1549 Consensus Tigurinus. Consequentially the churches of Zurich, Lausanne, Bern, Basel, and Geneva, along with connecting parish churches, united in a doctrinal confession. Calvin's boundless joy for this public agreement was expressed on numerous occasions and through multiple publications.

Calvin's personal relationships with Luther, Melanchthon, Bucer, Cranmer, and, of course, Knox, to identify only a few, also reveal the depth of his shepherd's heart for his colleagues. These Reformers personally testified to Calvin's ministry as a pastor of pastors and shepherd of shepherds, as he encouraged and instructed them through challenging predicaments and joined them in praising God for glorious victories.

CALVIN AS PASTOR/EVANGELIST/MISSIONARY

Most are aware of the stereotypical charge that Calvinists are concerned only about doctrine and are indifferent to evangelism and missions. It is further charged that Calvinism is actually counterproductive to the missionary/evangelistic enterprise. Not only is that historically untrue, as revealed by examining the roster of great evangelistic pastors and missionaries who were avowed Calvinists (i.e., George Whitefield, Charles H. Spurgeon, William Carey, David Brainerd, Jonathan Edwards, etc.), it is patently untrue of Calvin himself.

Calvin's passion as a pastor/evangelist was revealed in multiple venues. Calvin persistently evangelized the children of Geneva through catechism classes and the Geneva Academy. Moreover, he trained preachers to appeal for men and women to follow Christ. The visitation of the sick prescribed an evangelistic inquiry. Even a cursory examination of Calvin's sermons readily reveals an unquenchable zeal for men and women to be converted to Christ.

But what about missions? In the Registry of the Venerable Company of Pastors, it is recorded that eighty-eight missionaries had been sent out from Geneva. In actually, there were probably more than one hundred, and most of them were trained directly under Calvin. But missions work also went on at a more informal level. Geneva became a magnet for persecuted believers, and many of these immigrants were discipled and eventually returned to their own countries as effective missionaries and evangelists.

As the troubled times in Calvin's pastoral ministry subsided, the opportunity for intentional missionary expansion and church planting ripened. The blessing of God upon the missionary endeavors of Calvin and the Geneva churches from 1555 to 1562 was extraordinary—more than one hundred underground churches were planted in France by 1560. By 1562, the number had increased to 2,150, producing more than three million members. Some of these churches had congregations numbering in the thousands. The pastor of Montpelier informed Calvin by letter that "our church, thanks to the Lord, has so grown and so continues to grow every day that we are preaching three sermons every Sunday to more than 5 to 6 thousand people."[10] Another letter from the pastor of Toulouse declared "our church continues to grow to the astonishing number of 8 to 9 thousand souls."[11] Calvin's beloved France, through his ministry, was invaded by more than thirteen hundred Geneva-trained missionaries. This effort, coupled with Calvin's support of the Waldensians, produced a French Huguenot Church that almost triumphed over the Catholic Counter-Reformation in France.

Calvin did not evangelize and plant churches in France alone. Geneva-trained missionaries planted churches in Italy, the Netherlands, Hungary, Poland, Germany, England, Scotland, and the independent states of the Rhineland. Even more astonishing was an initiative that sent missionaries to Brazil. Calvin's commitment to evangelism and missions was not theoretical, but as in every other area of his life and ministry, a matter of zealous action and passionate commitment.

PASTOR TO PASTOR

On May 27, 1564, Beza, Calvin's handpicked and publicly affirmed successor, wrote concerning Calvin's death: "On that day with the setting sun the brightest light that was in the world for the guidance of God's church was taken back to heaven."[12] What an epitaph for a churchman and pastor!

Calvin carried out his pastoral ministry tirelessly through leading, preaching, teaching, writing, shepherding, and evangelizing. It flowed from a man called of God to be a pastor of pastors, of the persecuted, and of the Reformers. His pastoral ministry impacted entire nations, even nations yet to exist, such as the United States of America. Amazingly, this world-transforming pastoral ministry flowed from a man whose chief character trait was submission. He submitted to his father's command to matriculate at the University of Paris and then to change his studies from theology to law, a subject he disdained. He submitted to the call of God through Farel and became the pastor of St. Peter's in Geneva. He submitted to the entreaty of Bucer to become a pastor and leader in Strasbourg. Even though fearful and reticent, he submitted to God's providence and returned to Geneva and St. Peter's. Willingly, he submitted to the persecution of his adversaries as they named their dogs Calvin, sent him life-threatening notes, and sought to intimidate him by sending mobs to his church and home. He patiently submitted to lifelong excruciating physical sufferings exacerbated by the demands of the pastorate. Observers in Geneva and his own letters record multiple attacks of kidney stones, hemorrhages of blood coughed up while preaching, multiple ailments of a diseased gastrointestinal system that produced extended periods of bedridden pain, and chronic hemorrhoids. His diet was severely limited to minimize his pain.

That Calvin freely poured out his life upon the altar of pastoral ministry was, ultimately, the result of submission to Christ, his Lord, a submission nurtured by the joy of salvation by grace and propelled by the majesty of his preeminent Savior. This world-changing and history-transforming ministry flowed from a candle-lit study, where a man on his knees devoured the pages of Scripture, carried the burden of the needs of others, and faithfully served his Lord and Savior. Who was this man? He was John Calvin, churchman.

NOTES

[1] John Calvin, *Commentaries on the Epistles to Timothy, Titus, and Philemon*, trans. William Pringle (repr. Grand Rapids: Baker, 1979), 296

[2] John T. McNeill, *The History and Character of Calvinism* (New York: Oxford University Press, 1970), 158.

[3] Ibid.

[4] Ibid., 160.

[5] Ibid., 161.

[6] David W. Hall, *A Heart Promptly Offered: The Revolutionary Leadership of John Calvin* (Nashville: Cumberland House, 2006).

[7] Ibid.

[8] J. D. Benoit, "Pastoral Care of the Prophet," in *John Calvin, Contemporary Prophet,* ed. Jacob T. Hoogstra (Grand Rapids: Baker, 1959).

[9] Richard Stauffer, *The Humanness of John Calvin* (Nashville: Abingdon, 1971), 69.

[10] Frank James, "Calvin the Evangelist," *Reformed Quarterly*, Vol. 19, No. 2/3 (2001).

[11] Ibid.

[12] Philip Schaff, *History of the Christian Church* (Grand Rapids: Eerdmans, 1958), 8:823.

Chapter 6

THE PREACHER
OF GOD'S WORD

STEVEN J. LAWSON

A rule is prescribed to all God's servants that they bring not their own inventions, but simply deliver, as from hand to hand, what they have received from God.[1]

—JOHN CALVIN

Towering above the rooftops of the Old Town of Geneva rises the magnificent St. Peter's Church, the famed house of worship where John Calvin ministered during the heady days of the Reformation. Inside, the vaulted ceiling rises to a majestic height, spanning the entire length of the sanctuary. A feeling of transcendence fills the souls of those who enter. This former Roman Catholic bastion was transformed in 1536 into a Protestant fortress for biblical truth, becoming the epicenter of the Reformed world.

Atop a massive column encircled by a spiral staircase rests Calvin's pulpit. It was here, high above the stone floor of the sanctuary, that the Genevan Reformer stood Sunday by Sunday, even day by day, to proclaim the Word of God. This pulpit became a throne from which God's Word ruled, governing the hearts of those who joined the history-altering effort to reform the church.

Five hundred years after his birth, Calvin remains, arguably, the most influential preacher of God's Word that the world has ever witnessed. No man before him or since has been so prodigious in his handling of sacred Scripture. Calvin was many things—a world-class theologian, a revered exegete, a renowned teacher, an ecclesiastical statesman, an influential Reformer, and more. But as James Montgomery Boice notes, "Calvin was pre-eminently a preacher, and as a preacher he saw himself primarily as a Bible teacher."[2] Elsewhere Boice writes:

> Calvin had no weapon but the Bible. From the very first, his emphasis had been on Bible teaching. Calvin preached from the Bible every day, and under the power of that preaching the city began to be transformed. As the people of Geneva acquired knowledge of God's Word and were changed by it, the city became, as John Knox called it later, a New Jerusalem.[3]

Given that Calvin's preaching was so prolific, certain questions beg to be addressed: What kind of preacher was this remarkable man? How did he approach his sacred duty of expositing the Word of God? What were the distinctive features of his famed pulpit? I believe we can point to ten distinguishing marks of Calvin's preaching.

FOCUSING ON SCRIPTURE

First, *Calvin's preaching was biblical in its substance*. The Reformer stood firmly on the chief cornerstone of the Reformation—*sola Scriptura* ("Scripture alone"). He believed the minister's chief mandate was to preach the Word of God. Calvin writes that ministers' "whole task is limited to the ministry of God's Word; their whole wisdom to the knowledge of His Word; their whole eloquence, to its proclamation."[4] J. H. Merle D'Aubigné, the revered historian of the Reformation, notes, "In Calvin's view, everything that had not for its foundation the Word of God was futile and ephemeral boast; and the man who did not lean on

Scripture ought to be deprived of his title of honor."[5] The preacher, Calvin believed, has nothing to say apart from Scripture.

Restricting himself to Scripture, Calvin writes, "When we enter the pulpit, it is not so that we may bring our own dreams and fancies with us."[6] The Genevan Reformer was convinced that "as soon as men depart, even in the smallest degree from God's Word, they cannot preach anything but falsehoods, vanities, impostures, errors, and deceits."[7] Calvin asserts, "A rule is prescribed to all God's servants that they bring not their own inventions, but simply deliver, as from hand to hand, what they have received from God."[8] When the Bible speaks, he believed, God speaks. This was the unshakable foundation of Calvin's preaching—the faithful exposition of Scripture.

PREACHING THROUGH ENTIRE BOOKS

Second, *Calvin's preaching was sequential in its pattern.* For the duration of his ministry, Calvin's approach was to preach systematically through entire books of the Bible. "Sunday after Sunday, day after day, Calvin climbed up the steps into the pulpit," T. H. L. Parker writes. "There he patiently led his congregation verse by verse through book after book of the Bible."[9] Calvin preached from the New Testament on Sunday mornings, from the New Testament or the Psalms on Sunday afternoons, and from the Old Testament every morning of the week, every other week. In this consecutive fashion, Calvin preached through most of the books of the Scriptures.

These expositions were protracted series, often lasting more than a year. During his Genevan pastorate, Calvin preached through the following Old Testament books: Genesis (123 sermons), Deuteronomy (201), Judges (a short series), 1 Samuel (107), 2 Samuel (87), 1 Kings (various sermons), Job (159), individual psalms (72), Psalm 119 (22), Isaiah (353), Jeremiah (91), Lamentations (25), Ezekiel (175), Daniel (47), Hosea (65), Joel (17), Amos (43), Obadiah (5), Jonah (6), Micah (28), Nahum (not recorded), and Zephaniah (17). For the most part, these Old Testament sermons were preached at 6 in the morning (7 during the winter months) each weekday, every other week, at St. Peter's Church.

In addition, Calvin preached through much of the New Testament, expounding its fullness and richness. During his ministry at Strasbourg, Calvin preached through the Gospel of John and Romans. In Geneva, he preached on a harmony of the Gospels (65 sermons, concluding when he died), Acts (189), 1 Corinthians (110), 2 Corinthians (66), Galatians (43), Ephesians (48), 1 and 2 Thessalonians (46), 1 Timothy (55), 2 Timothy (31), and Titus (17). This kind of exposition gave breadth to Calvin's preaching. No doctrine was left untaught, no sin unexposed, no promise undelivered.

BEGINNING IN A DIRECT MANNER

Third, *Calvin's preaching was direct in its message.* When expounding Scripture, Calvin was remarkably straightforward and to the point. He did not launch his message with a captivating story, a compelling quote, or a personal anecdote. Instead, Calvin immediately drew his listeners into the biblical text. The focus of the message was always Scripture, and he spoke what needed to be said with an economy of words. There were no wasted statements. Theodore Beza writes, "Every word weighed a pound."[10]

For the most part, Calvin began each message by reviewing his previous sermon. He then established the context of his passage, introducing the congregation to the thinking of the biblical author and the original recipients. Calvin next showed how the particular text fit into the building argument of the entire book. After disclosing his stated proposition for the sermon, Calvin proceeded directly to his text, expounding it phrase by phrase. Parker writes, "Clause by clause, verse by verse, the congregation was led through the epistle or the prophecy or the narrative."[11]

PREACHING IN A "LIVELY" FASHION

Fourth, *Calvin's preaching was extemporaneous in its delivery*. When Calvin stepped into his pulpit, he did not bring with him a written manuscript or any sermon notes. The Reformer made a conscious choice to preach *extempore*, that is, spontaneously. He wanted his sermons to have a natural and passionate delivery that was energetic and engaging, and he believed spontaneous preaching was best suited to achieve those ends.

The Reformer once said, "It appears to me that there is very little preaching of a lively kind in the Kingdom; but that the greater part deliver it by way of reading from a written discourse."[12] Therefore, relying on the Holy Spirit, he stood before the people with only an open Bible. He preached from a Hebrew Bible when expounding the Old Testament and from a Greek Bible when preaching the New Testament. For his exposition, he drew on his thorough study of the passage and relied on his rigorous preparation for his other ministry assignments, especially his classroom lecturing and commentary writing. The sermon came together as he preached.

Here is the genius of Calvin at work. Without any visual aids or even a sermon outline to guide his thoughts, with only an open Bible in the original language, his sermons nonetheless achieved a natural flow. He did not deliver stiff, academic treatments of the Scriptures. Rather, his sermons were warmhearted presentations of the truth. But his preaching was also fervent. The preacher must speak, he said, "in a way that shows he is not pretending."[13] This Calvin did—he was blood-earnest in his preaching.

EXCAVATING THE BIBLICAL TEXT

Fifth, *Calvin's preaching was exegetical in its approach*. Calvin insisted that the words of Scripture must be interpreted in their particular historical backgrounds, original languages, grammatical structures, and biblical contexts. Philip Schaff notes that Calvin affirmed "the sound and fundamental hermeneutical principle that the biblical authors, like all sensible writers, wished to convey to their readers one definite thought in words which they could understand."[14] Calvin believed that the discerning of the author's meaning was the expositor's first duty. He writes, "Since it is almost his [the interpreter's] only task to unfold the mind of the writer whom he has undertaken to expound, he misses his mark, or at least strays outside his limits, by the extent to which he leads his readers away from the meaning of his author."[15] Therefore, as Calvin preached, he moved "sentence by sentence, sometimes even word by word, explaining what each part means."[16]

In this exegetical practice, Calvin insisted on the *sensus literalis*, the literal sense of the biblical text. "The true meaning of Scripture is the natural and obvious meaning,"[17] he writes, adding, "The important thing is that the Scripture should be understood and explained; how it is explained is secondary."[18] Calvin declares, "I have felt nothing to be of more importance than a literal interpretation of the biblical text."[19]

Calvin held to the analogy of faith, the idea that the Bible speaks with one voice, never contradicting itself—*sacra Scriptura sui interpres*, or "Scripture interprets Scripture." So in his interpretation, he appealed to the full breadth of Scripture for light and support. Thus, he carefully consulted and cited cross-references, yet without deviating from the central thrust of the text he was preaching.

SPEAKING TO THE COMMON MAN

Sixth, *Calvin's preaching was accessible in its simplicity.* As a preacher, Calvin's primary aim was not to communicate to other theologians, but to reach the common person in the pew. He wanted people to become familiar with the Bible and to "make it a personal matter, not just a collection of historical ideas."[20] To that end, this brilliant man intentionally chose to employ simple words and understandable language.

"Preachers must be like fathers," he writes, "dividing bread into small pieces to feed their children."[21]

As Parker explains, the Reformer's vocabulary was "nearly always familiar and easy."[22] He adds, "The word that Calvin used to describe what he regarded as the most suitable style for the preacher is *familiere*,"[23] meaning a familiar or personal form of speaking. Further describing Calvin's simple style, Boice writes: "There is little rhetorical flourish. His words are straightforward, the sentences simple."[24] As Calvin preached, he spoke "very deliberately,"[25] making it easy, as one observer notes, "to write down all that he says."[26] The result was that Calvin's towering intellect lay "concealed, behind [his] deceptively simple explanations of his author's meaning."[27]

Occasionally, Calvin would explain the meaning of a word more carefully, but without ever giving the Hebrew or Greek original. Yet Calvin did not hesitate to use the language of the Bible. "Calvin's terminology . . . hardly moves outside the Bible," Parker observes. "Common words are 'justify,' 'elect,' 'redeem,' 'sin,' 'repentance,' 'grace,' 'prayer,' 'judgment'—in fact, all the familiar language of the Old and New Testaments."[28]

PASTORING THE LORD'S FLOCK

Seventh, *Calvin's preaching was pastoral in its tone.* The Genevan Reformer never lost sight of the fact that he was a pastor. Thus, he warmly applied Scripture with loving exhortation to shepherd his flock. He preached with the intent of prompting and encouraging his sheep to follow the Word.

Calvin often used first-person plural pronouns—"us," "we," and "our"—as he exhorted his congregation. For example, he said: "Let us learn, therefore, not to become drunk on our foolish hopes. Rather, let us hope in God and in God's promises, and we will never be deceived."[29] By doing so, he humbly included himself in the need to act upon biblical truth. In this way, he avoided preaching down to his listeners.

Nevertheless, Calvin did not hesitate to call his listeners to self-examination as he applied biblical truth. For example, he proclaimed: "We must all, therefore, examine our lives, not against one of God's precepts but against the whole law. Can any of us truly say that we are blameless?"[30] Sharp admonishment also distinguished Calvin's preaching. When he was aware that members of his flock were flirting with sin, he openly attacked it. Calvin warned his congregation, asserting: "This vice reigns today far more than it ever did in Micah's time. Indeed, much more! True, many are content to have the gospel preached, provided it does not touch them, or make them uncomfortable."[31] Such loving reproof was an essential part of his pastoral duty.

FENDING OFF RAVENOUS WOLVES

Eighth, *Calvin's preaching was polemic in its defense of the truth*. For Calvin, preaching necessitated an apologetic defense of the faith. He believed that preachers must guard the truth, so systematic exposition required confronting the Devil's lies in all their deceptive forms. He writes, "To assert the truth is only one half of the office of teaching . . . except all the fallacies of the devil be also dissipated."[32]

From his pulpit, Calvin, as a staunch guardian of the truth, took every opportunity to uphold sound doctrine and to refute all who contradicted it. He openly rebuked the false teachers of his day, especially the pope. For instance, he said: "The Roman Catholic Church today continues the same kind of idolatrous practices that were common amongst the heathen, but in the name of the apostles and of the virgin Mary. The only things that have changed are the names of the idols! But superstition is as wicked and detestable today as it was amongst the first idolaters!"[33]

When preaching, the Reformer writes, "The pastor ought to have two voices: one, for gathering the sheep; and another, for warding off . . . wolves."[34] To be sure, Calvin used a stern voice to fend off the ravenous wolves. In defending the gospel, Calvin minced no words.

CALLING OUT TO LOST SINNERS

Ninth, *Calvin's preaching was passionate in its outreach.* There is a sad misconception today that because Calvin believed in predestination, he was not evangelistic. The persistent myth is that he did not have a passion to reach lost souls for Christ. Nothing could be further from the truth. Calvin possessed a great passion to reach lost souls. For that reason, he preached the gospel with heart-stirring persuasion, passionately pleading with errant sinners to cast themselves on God's mercy.

As he concluded his sermons, Calvin often gave a pressing appeal to the lost. Hear Calvin's own words as he preached Galatians 2:15–16:

> We cannot rest until the Lord Jesus Christ has saved us. See, therefore, how good it is for us to be heavy laden, that is to say, to hate our sins and to be in such anguish over them that we feel surrounded by the pains of death, so that we seek God in order that He might ease us of our burdens. We must, however, seek Him in the knowledge that we cannot obtain salvation, full or in part, unless it is granted to us as a gift.[35]

He then urged his listeners to be "saved through faith . . . [for we must] give ourselves to Him wholly and completely."[36] Clearly Calvin was a true evangelist.

MAGNIFYING THE GLORY OF GOD

Tenth, *Calvin's preaching was doxological in its conclusion.* All of Calvin's sermons were God-centered throughout, but his closing appeals were especially heartfelt and passionate. He simply could not step down from his pulpit without lifting up the Lord and urging his listeners to yield to His absolute supremacy. They must humble themselves under the mighty hand of God.

As he concluded, Calvin regularly exhorted his congregation: "Let us fall before the majesty of our great God." Whatever his text, these fervent words called for the unconditional submission of his listeners.

Calvin always concluded with a God-exalting prayer. His intent was to elevate his congregation to the throne of God. These concluding intercessions were vertical in their thrust, pointing his listeners upward to God. They unveiled the glorious majesty of the heavenly Father as he left his people *coram Deo*—before the face of God.

FIVE HUNDRED YEARS LATER

As we mark the five hundredth year since Calvin's birth, we must conclude that he remains "one of the most influential preachers in the history of Christian thought."[37] Arguably the greatest theologian and commentator the church has ever known, he nevertheless was primarily a preacher. This magisterial Reformer gave himself to the exposition of the Word as perhaps no one else in history.

May God raise up a new generation of expositors like Calvin. May we experience a new Reformation in our day. And may we see, once more, the illuminating power of the Word preached in this midnight hour of history.

NOTES

[1] John Calvin, *Commentaries on the Book of the Prophet Jeremiah and the Lamentations*, trans. John Owen (repr. Grand Rapids: Baker, 1979), 1:43.

[2] James Montgomery Boice, foreword to John Calvin, *Sermons on Psalm 119 by John Calvin* (1580; repr. Aububon, N.J.: Old Paths Publications, 1996), viii.

[3] James Montgomery Boice, *Whatever Happened to the Gospel of Grace? Rediscovering the Doctrines that Shook the World* (Wheaton, Ill.: Crossway, 2001), 83–84.

[4] John Calvin, *Institutes of the Christian Religion* (1536 edition), trans. Ford Lewis Battles (Grand Rapids: Eerdmans, 1975), 195.

[5] J. H. Merle D'Aubigné, *History of the Reformation in Europe in the Time of Calvin* (1880; repr. Harrisonburg, Va.: Sprinkle, 2000), 7:85.

6   Quoted in T. H. L. Parker, *Portrait of Calvin* (Philadelphia: Westminster Press, 1954), 83.

7   Calvin, *Commentaries on the Book of the Prophet Jeremiah and the Lamentations*, 2:226–227.

8   Ibid., 1:43.

9   T. H. L. Parker, *Calvin's Preaching* (Louisville, Ky.: Westminster John Knox Press, 1992), 39.

10   Theodore Beza, quoted in Leroy Nixon, *John Calvin, Expository Preacher* (Grand Rapids: Eerdmans, 1950), 31.

11   Parker, *Calvin's Preaching*, 90.

12   John Calvin, *Letters of John Calvin* (1855–1857; repr. Edinburgh, Scotland: Banner of Truth Trust, 1980), 95.

13   Quoted in Parker, *Calvin's Preaching*, 115.

14   Philip Schaff, *History of the Christian Church* (1910; repr. Grand Rapids: Eerdmans, 1984), 8:532.

15   John Calvin, *The Epistle of Paul the Apostle to the Romans*, ed. David W. Torrance and Thomas F. Torrance (Grand Rapids: Eerdmans, 1973), 1.

16   Boice, foreword to Calvin, *Sermons on Psalm 119 by John Calvin*, ix.

17   John Calvin, *John Calvin's Sermons on Galatians*, trans. Kathy Childress (Edinburgh: Banner of Truth Trust, 1997), 136.

18   Quoted in T. H. L. Parker, *Calvin's New Testament Commentaries* (Grand Rapids: Eerdmans, 1971), 50.

19   General introduction in *Calvin: Commentaries*, ed. John Baillie, John T. McNeill, Henry P. Van Dusen (London and Philadelphia: S.C.M. and Westminster, 1958), 359.

20   Parker, *Calvin's Preaching*, 139.

21   Quoted by Joel R. Beeke in "John Calvin, Teacher and Practitioner of Evangelism," *Reformation and Revival*, 10:4 (Fall 2001), 69.

22   Parker, *Calvin's Preaching*, 141–142.

23   Ibid., 139.

24   Boice, foreword to Calvin, *Sermons on Psalm 119 by John Calvin*, x.

25   Publisher's introduction, "John Calvin and His Sermons on Ephesians," in John Calvin, *Sermons on the Epistle to the Ephesians* (1562; repr. Edinburgh: Banner of Truth Trust, 1998), ix.

26   Ibid.

27   Parker, *Calvin's Preaching*, 87.

28   Ibid., 141.

29   John Calvin, *Sermons on the Book of Micah*, trans. and ed. Benjamin Wirt Farley (Phillipsburg, N.J.: P&R, 2003), 84.

30   Calvin, *John Calvin's Sermons on Galatians*, 264.

31   Calvin, *Sermons on the Book of Micah*, 101.

32   Quoted in J. Graham Miller, *Calvin's Wisdom: An Anthology Arranged Alphabetically by a Grateful Reader* (Edinburgh: Banner of Truth Trust, 1992), 252.

[33] Calvin, *John Calvin's Sermons on Galatians*, 3.

[34] John Calvin, *Commentaries on the Epistles to Timothy, Titus, and Philemon*, trans. William Pringle (repr. Grand Rapids: Baker, 1979), 296.

[35] Calvin, *John Calvin's Sermons on Galatians*, 186.

[36] Ibid.

[37] Donald K. McKim, *The Cambridge Companion to John Calvin* (Cambridge: Cambridge University Press, 2004), 121.

Chapter 7

THE COUNSELOR
TO THE AFFLICTED

W. ROBERT GODFREY

Now, where solace is promised in affliction, especially where the deliverance of the church is described, the banner of trust and hope in Christ himself is prefigured.[1]

—JOHN CALVIN

To the extent that people remember John Calvin today, he is thought of first as a great theologian and second as a great biblical scholar. When most people think of him, "counselor" is probably not a role that comes readily to mind.

Calvin certainly deserves recognition for his theological and exegetical work. But Calvin saw himself preeminently as a pastor, and all his efforts ultimately served the needs of pastoral ministry. And as a pastor, he often offered advice and counsel to those who had spiritual, emotional, or physical needs. Those who knew him well counted him a faithful and helpful pastor and friend in their various circumstances of life.

In many ways, Calvin's counsel rested on his doctrine of providence. The profound nature of his understanding of God's providence was the foundation of the character of his counsel to troubled Christians.

Calvin presents a systematic exposition of his doctrine of providence in his *Institutes of the Christian Religion*, especially in book 1, chapters 16 and 17. But his presentation of the doctrine also unfolds in his study of the book of Psalms. There he addresses the subject of providence just as thoroughly and perhaps somewhat more personally and experientially. The psalms were very important to Calvin in his own life, and he returned to them again and again in his ministry.

In 1557, Calvin published his large commentary on the book of Psalms. In the English translation, this commentary runs to five substantial volumes. This commentary reflects a life lived with the Psalter. He loved the psalms: he knew them, studied them, wrote on them, preached them, and sang them.

Calvin believed that the value of the Psalter was not just for himself but for all Christians because the psalms teach all to know and honor God: "There is no other book in which we are more perfectly taught the right manner of praising God, or in which we are more powerfully stirred up to the performance of this religious exercise."[2] In other words, the Psalter shows how Christians are to offer praise and prayer to God amid all the various circumstances of life.

He was drawn to the book of Psalms, as he makes clear in his preface to the commentary, because of his strong identification with the emotions David expressed in these poems. Calvin saw the book as "an anatomy of all the parts of the soul, for," he writes, "there is not an emotion of which any one can be conscious that is not here represented as in a mirror. Or rather, the fears, doubts, hopes, cares, perplexities, in short, all the distracting emotions with which the minds of men are wont to be agitated."[3]

For Calvin, the Psalter in particular teaches the vital lesson that the Christian will suffer for his Lord in this life: "They will principally teach and train us to bear the cross."[4] But in our sufferings, the psalms also provide encouragement, teaching "true believers with their whole hearts confidently to look to him for help in all their necessities."[5]

FIVE THEMES ABOUT PROVIDENCE

In the course of his commentary, Calvin gave strong expression to various aspects of his doctrine of providence. Five themes about providence recur in his exposition of the book of Psalms.

First, he recognizes God's power as the active governor of the world:

> He gives us to understand by this word, that heaven is not a palace in which God remains idle and indulges in pleasures, as the Epicureans dream, but a royal court, from which he exercises his government over all parts of the world. If he has erected his throne, therefore, in the sanctuary of heaven, in order to govern the universe, it follows that he in no wise neglects the affairs of earth, but governs them with the highest reason and wisdom.[6]

Second, he declares that this active power should lead all creatures to honor God as God: "As God by his providence preserves the world, the power of his government is alike extended to all, so that he ought to be worshipped by all."[7]

Third, he teaches that in His governance of the world God always acts as the loving Father of His people:

> By *the face of God*, must be meant the fatherly care and providence which he extends to his people. So numerous are the dangers which surround us, that we could not stand a single moment, if his eye did not watch over our preservation. But the true security for a happy life lies in being persuaded that we are under divine government.[8]

This fatherly care of God does not mean that His people will not suffer:

We are here warned that the guardianship of God does not secure us from being sometimes exercised with the cross and afflictions, and that therefore the faithful ought not to promise themselves a delicate and easy life in this world, it being enough for them not to be abandoned of God when they stand in need of his help. Their heavenly Father, it is true, loves them most tenderly, but he will have them awakened by the cross, lest they should give themselves too much to the pleasures of the flesh. If, therefore, we embrace this doctrine, although we may happen to be oppressed by the tyranny of the wicked, we will wait patiently till God either break their sceptre, or shake it out of their hands.[9]

Fourth, Calvin affirms that confidence in providence causes Christians to grow in faith in Christ and confidence in living for Him:

Besides, the joy here mentioned arises from this, that there is nothing more calculated to increase our faith, than the knowledge of the providence of God; because without it, we would be harassed with doubts and fears, being uncertain whether or not the world was governed by chance. For this reason, it follows that those who aim at the subversion of this doctrine, depriving the children of God of true comfort, and vexing their minds by unsettling their faith, forge for themselves a hell upon earth. For what can be more awfully tormenting than to be constantly racked with doubt and anxiety? And we will never be able to arrive at a calm state of mind until we are taught to repose with implicit confidence in the providence of God.[10]

Fifth, Calvin teaches that knowing that God directs all things leads His people to more frequent and heartfelt prayer:

Were they to reflect on the judgments of God, they would at once perceive that there was nothing like chance or fortune in the government of the world. Moreover, until men are persuaded that all their troubles come upon them by the appointment of God, it will never come into their minds to supplicate him for deliverance.[11]

In his preface to his commentary on the book of Psalms, Calvin made a most remarkable statement about providence that went to the very heart and soul of the religion he embraced and counseled others to embrace. He writes that knowing the Psalter teaches Christians to suffer for God so that "we renounce the guidance of our own affections, and submit ourselves entirely to God, leaving him to govern us, and to dispose our life according to his will, so that the afflictions which are the bitterest and most severe to our nature, become sweet to us, because they proceed from him."[12]

The bitterest afflictions of this life are sweet when Christians know that they come from God, serve His purposes, and ultimately contribute to their good. Calvin had a truly astounding daily confidence in God and His ways, and he encouraged the same confidence in his followers.

COMFORT FOR A GRIEVING FATHER

For the historian, the record of Calvin's actual counsel is limited. The character of his commentaries and his sermons certainly points to his pastoral concern, but the conversations he must have had with those in need are not preserved for us. His letters are the best source we have for the counsel Calvin offered.

Calvin carried on a very extensive correspondence throughout his ministry, writing to people and churches he knew and even to those he did not know. He answered theological questions, offered advice to troubled churches, encouraged pastors and friends, and wrote letters of consolation to those in distress. Those letters, numbering more than twelve hundred, preserved a clear picture of the character and extent of the counsel that Calvin gave to those in need. The many letters of counsel that Calvin wrote were applications of his doctrine of providence to the various circumstances and struggles of life.

While he wrote on many matters, two examples can give a sense of his advice and help. The first is a letter of consolation to a father on the death of his son. In April 1541, Calvin wrote a long letter of condolence to Monsieur de Richebourg on the death of his son Louis. Louis had been a student whom Calvin had known well in Strasbourg.

Calvin begins the letter expressing his intense grief and showing that faith in God does not mean a fatalistic or unemotional response to the sadness of life:

> When I first received the intelligence of the death . . . of your son Louis, I was so utterly overpowered that for many days I was fit for nothing but to grieve; and albeit I was somehow upheld before the Lord by those aids wherewith he sustains our souls in affliction, among men, however, I was almost a nonentity.[13]

He then speaks of finding comfort, writing, "My heart was refreshed in prayer and private meditations, which are suggested by His word."[14]

Calvin records his reactions to the death and the source of his comfort to encourage de Richebourg: "I desire to communicate to you the remedies I took advantage of, and those which were of greatest benefit."[15] In particular, Calvin reminds the grieving father of the biblical truth of God's fatherly providence, "that determinate counsel, whereby he not only foresees, decrees, and executes nothing but what is just and upright in itself, but also nothing but what is good and wholesome for us."[16] Calvin then applies that doctrine to de Richebourg's loss:

> Nevertheless, the faithful have a sufficient alleviation of their sorrows in the special providence of God, and the all-sufficiency of his provision, whatsoever may happen. For there is nothing which is more dispiriting to us than while we vex and annoy ourselves with this sort of question—Why is it not otherwise with us? . . . It is God, therefore, who has sought back from you your son, whom he had committed to you to be educated, on the condition, that

he might always be his own. And, therefore, he took him away, because it was both of advantage to him to leave this world, and by this bereavement to humble you, or to make trial of your patience. If you do not understand the advantage of this, without delay, first of all, setting aside every other object of consideration, ask of God that he may show you. Should it be his will to exercise you still farther, by concealing it from you, submit to that will, that you may become wiser than the weakness of your own understanding can ever attain to.[17]

Calvin encourages the father with assurance about the piety of Louis: "That, however, which we rate most highly in him was, that he had drunk so largely into the principles of piety, that he had not merely correct and true understanding of religion, but had also been faithfully imbued with the unfeigned fear and reverence of God."[18] In light of that piety, Calvin assures the grieving father of the promise of heaven for his son: "Nor can you consider yourself to have lost him, whom you will recover in the blessed resurrection in the kingdom of God."[19]

Calvin concludes his consolation by reflecting on the reality and legitimacy of human emotions, but also on the need to control them:

Neither do I insist upon your laying aside all grief. Nor, in the school of Christ, do we learn any such philosophy as requires us to put off that common humanity with which God has endowed us, that, being men, we should be turned to stones. These considerations reach only so far as this, that you do set bounds, and, as it were, temper even your most reasonable sadness; that, having shed those tears which were due to nature and fatherly affection, you by no means give way to senseless wailing. Nor do I by any means interfere because I am distrustful of your prudence, firmness, or high-mindedness; but only lest I might here be wanting and come short in my duty to you.[20]

This letter shows Calvin the young pastor seeking to be comprehensive in his grief counseling. It is full of thoughtful direction and encouragement.

ENCOURAGEMENT TO A PERSECUTED SAINT

The second example of Calvin's counsel is drawn from several letters he wrote to a man facing persecution. Mathieu Dimonet, a Reformed Christian from Lyon, was arrested on Jan. 9, 1553, and martyred on July 15 of that year. Shortly after his arrest, Calvin wrote to encourage him. Calvin comments that Dimonet had not long been Reformed, but that God had "bestowed such strength and steadfastness" on him that many had remarked on his devotion to Christ. [21] Calvin acknowledges the difficulty of Dimonet's plight: "I feel indeed by the sympathy I have for you (as I ought) that Satan ceases not to give you new alarms; but you must have recourse to him who has made so good a beginning, praying to him to complete his own work."[22] Calvin then assures him of God's care for His own people:

> You need not be daunted, seeing that God has promised to equip his own according as they are assaulted by Satan. Only commit yourself to him, distrusting all in yourself, and hope that he only will suffice to sustain you. Further, you have to take heed chiefly to two things: first, what the side is you defend, and next, what crown is promised to those who continue steadfast in the Gospel.[23]

Calvin writes that Dimonet's future is uncertain, but that even if he faces death, God's love and provision are certain:

> We do not know as yet what he has determined to do concerning you, but there is nothing better for you than to sacrifice your life to him, being ready to part with it whenever he wills, and yet hoping that he will preserve it, in so far as he knows it to be profitable for

your salvation. And although this be difficult to the flesh, yet it is the true happiness of his faithful ones; and you must pray that it may please this gracious God so to imprint it upon your heart that it may never be effaced therefrom. For our part, we also shall pray that he would make you feel his power, and vouchsafe you the full assurance that you are under his keeping; that he bridles the rage of your enemies, and in every way manifests himself as your God and Father.[24]

On July 7, 1553, Calvin wrote again to Dimonet and others imprisoned with him in Lyon to assure them that God had promised them strength for what they must endure. Calvin writes, "Be then assured, that God who manifests himself in time of need, and perfects his strength in our weakness, will not leave you unprovided with that which will powerfully magnify his name."[25]

Calvin acknowledges that according to human reasoning their suffering is wrong, but he urges them to be confident in God and his purposes:

It is strange, indeed, to human reason, that the children of God should be so surfeited with afflictions, while the wicked disport themselves in delights; but even more so, that the slaves of Satan should tread us under foot, as we say, and triumph over us. However, we have wherewith to comfort ourselves in all our miseries, looking for that happy issue which is promised to us, that he will not only deliver us by his angels, but will himself wipe away the tears from our eyes. And thus we have good right to despise the pride of these poor blinded men, who to their own ruin lift up their rage against heaven; and although we are not at present in your condition, yet we do not on that account leave off fighting together with you by prayer, by anxiety and tender compassion, as fellow-members, seeing that it has pleased our heavenly Father, of his infinite goodness, to unite us into one body, under his Son, our head. Whereupon

I shall beseech him, that he would vouchsafe you this grace, that being stayed upon him, you may in nowise waver, but rather grow in strength; that he would keep you under his protection, and give you such assurance of it that you may be able to despise all that is of the world.[26]

These two examples are only a brief sample of Calvin's work of counseling as a faithful pastor. He sought always to minister the truth and comfort of God's Word to the children of God. His counsel had both a tough realism and a sensitive compassion to it. He faced the miseries and struggles of this life straightforwardly, and he pointed Christians to God's fatherly care both in this life and in the life to come. Above all, he encouraged Christians to look to Christ as the one who deserves the Father's love, and he assured them that while weeping may last for the night, joy comes in the morning.

NOTES

[1] John Calvin, *Institutes of the Christian Religion*, ed. John T. McNeill; trans. Ford Lewis Battles; Library of Christian Classics, XX–XXI (Philadelphia: Westminster John Knox, 1960), 2.6.3.

[2] John Calvin, *Commentary on the Book of Psalms*, trans. James Anderson (Edinburgh: Calvin Translation Society, 1845; repr. Grand Rapids: Baker, 2003), 1:xxxviii-xxxix.

[3] Ibid., 1:xxxvii.

[4] Ibid., 1:xxxix.

[5] Ibid.

[6] Ibid., 1:549.

[7] Ibid., 1:401.

[8] Ibid., 2:416.

[9] Ibid., 5:92.

[10] Ibid., 4:265.

[11] Ibid., 4:252.

[12] Ibid., 1:xxxix.

[13] John Calvin, *Selected Works of John Calvin*, ed. by H. Beveridge and J. Bonnet (Grand Rapids: Baker, 1983), 4:246.

[14] Ibid., 4:247.

[15] Ibid.

[16] Ibid., 4:248.

[17] Ibid., 4:249.

[18] Ibid., 4:250.

[19] Ibid., 4:251.

[20] Ibid., 4:253.

[21] Ibid., 5:384.

[22] Ibid., 5:385.

[23] Ibid.

[24] Ibid., 5:386.

[25] Ibid., 5:412.

[26] Ibid., 5:413.

Chapter 8

THE WRITER FOR
THE PEOPLE OF GOD

PHILLIP R. JOHNSON

*Yet nothing shall ever hinder me from openly avowing what I have
learned from the Word of God; for nothing but what is useful is
taught in the school of this master. It is my only guide, and to acqui-
esce in its plain doctrines shall be my constant rule of wisdom.*[1]

—JOHN CALVIN

John Calvin excelled in every ministerial duty he ever set his hand
to. He stood out in his own generation for the sheer power of his
preaching and his amazing command of Scripture. His skill as an
exegete and biblical commentator surpassed anyone the church had
ever seen. His proficiency as a teacher of theology was likewise superior
to all who had gone before him. His influence as a discipler of young
men bore fruit that is still multiplying today. He was renowned for his
competence as a church leader, his forcefulness as an apologist for the
truth, and his remarkable ability to educate and motivate others. In the
words of William Cunningham, "Calvin was by far the greatest of the
Reformers with respect to the talents he possessed, the influence he
exerted, and the services he rendered in the establishment and diffu-
sion of important truth."[2]

But of all Calvin's extraordinary gifts, his aptitude as a writer is the one that most amplified all the others and secured Calvin's position in history. Calvin was a prolific, almost obsessive, writer. Practically everything he ever did by way of teaching, preaching, or debate was set down in writing and subsequently published—his sermons, his commentaries, his views on theology, his polemical exchanges over disputed points of doctrine and practice, and a large volume of his personal correspondence. No other mind in that generation is quite so well documented, and it is thanks largely to Calvin's own industriousness as a writer that we have that invaluable record.

A VAST LITERARY LEGACY

It is a remarkable fact that the first major theological work Calvin ever published was the book that would become the centerpiece of his vast literary legacy—the most important, best known, and most influential of all his books.[3] He titled it *Institutes of the Christian Religion*. Its first edition was published in 1536, when Calvin was only 27 years old. The book became a huge success right away, earning Calvin immediate respect and name recognition among Protestants in France and Switzerland—and beyond. Over the course of the next few decades, the *Institutes* became an important doctrinal compass for the Protestant movement worldwide. No doubt the widespread success and lasting influence of that volume impressed Calvin with the value of publishing his ideas, because from that point on, he never stopped writing.

Calvin's collected works fill fifty-nine large volumes in the *Corpus Reformatorum*, a 101-volume set of crucial Reformation-era works.[4] But as Robert Reymond points out, "even these do not exhaust Calvin's total literary output; twelve more volumes under the title *Supplementa Calviniana* . . . are available."[5]

Calvin was not Protestant Christianity's most prolific author. That honor would probably go to Charles H. Spurgeon (if the criterion were a simple tally of words published) or to Cotton Mather (if we counted only the number of books written). But Calvin surely would win hands down if we were to weigh the depth, profundity, importance, scholarship, ingenuity, and long-term impact of each author's collected works. Spurgeon and Mather themselves both declared their indebtedness to Calvin and regarded him as something of a model, and the same goes for practically every important Protestant theologian and Bible commentator from Calvin's own generation until now. No other Protestant luminary from his time to the present comes close to him in terms of his far-reaching significance as an author.

From the initial publication of the first edition of the *Institutes* until Calvin's death in May 1564, only twenty-eight years and two months elapsed. Thus, those seventy-one encyclopedic volumes of Calvin's published writings were written at a pace of two and a half thick volumes every year—equal to two full works the size of the *Institutes* (in its massive final edition).

In his most prolific years, Calvin published as many as half a million words.[6] That would be a nearly impossible pace for someone who did nothing but write—especially someone trying to produce serious biblical and theological material with the depth and diversity we have in Calvin's writings. But we must remember that Calvin was also a pastor, a theology professor, and an adviser to Geneva's city officials. He simultaneously carried a heavy workload of study, teaching, and pastoral work—including weddings, baptisms, consistory meetings, and a full load of personal instruction and counseling with members of his flock—not to mention various civic and diplomatic duties made necessary by the Genevan city council's dependency on him for moral and spiritual advice. Any of those things would make concentration on writing an extremely difficult discipline. All of them combined would seem to make the task of writing book-length commentaries and theological treatises impossible.

"A DRIVEN MAN"

How, we might ask, could one man—known for the frailty of his physical constitution and his frequent infirmities—possibly produce such a large body of truly important written work in so short a time? It is clear he was a remarkable man, possessing extraordinary gifts and enough mental stamina to make up ten times over for what he lacked in physical strength.

Calvin was famous for his work ethic, of course. His belief in the importance of hard work was not merely an academic notion, but something he practiced—redeeming the time through labor and industry, and eschewing idleness even in his leisure hours. Commenting on John 9:4 ("We must work the works of him who sent me while it is day; night is coming, when no one can work"), Calvin said, "When we see that a short time of life is allotted to us we should be ashamed of lazing in idleness."[7] He himself was never idle, often lecturing to students quite literally from his sickbed.

In the words of biographer William Bouwsma, Calvin "was a driven man, driven by external demands but above all by powerful impulses within himself. We might now call him an over-achiever; he was never satisfied with his own performance, always contrasting the petty done with the undone vast. As a young man, he was already lamenting his 'habitual sloth.'"[8]

Despite what we might assume from Calvin's prodigious output, writing was a particular strain on him. He wrote to Heinrich Bullinger, "I am so exhausted by constant writing that often, almost broken by fatigue, I hate writing letters."[9] Calvin therefore did not personally, manually write down and edit everything of his that ultimately found its way into print. He relied heavily on amanuenses—literary assistants who wrote by dictation and carefully edited Calvin's content for style, grammar, logical flow, and so on. These unsung heroes' names are lost to history, but they were no doubt young men chosen from among Calvin's finest, most literate students. Calvin himself explained how they turned his sermons and lectures into published works: "I do not have much time for writing, but [a scribe] takes everything down as I dictate and afterwards arranges it at home. I read it over, and if anywhere he has not understood my meaning, I restore it."[10]

In later years, Calvin's commentaries were assembled by committees of literary assistants, who did the editing themselves, sometimes entirely without Calvin's input or review. Thankfully, Calvin's editorial assistants seemed wary of overworking his material, choosing often to leave things that might better have been changed than to edit too heavily. In some of the later commentaries, therefore, the signs of transcription from the lecture format are all too evident. The lecture on Jeremiah 30:1–7, for example, ends with the words, "There will be no Lecture tomorrow on account of the Consistory."[11] The end of Calvin's lecture on Jeremiah 1:8–12 is even more abrupt, literally ending where he was interrupted midsentence by the chiming of the church bell: "It then follows,—but as the clock strikes, I cannot proceed farther today."[12]

Despite such cosmetic flaws, Calvin's published works remain as important, as rich with insight, and as useful as they have always been. They all rank among the finest biblical and theological works ever produced. No theologian can possibly afford to neglect his *Institutes*; no pastor or serious student of Scripture should ever overlook Calvin's commentaries; no theology professor should miss the lessons contained in his lectures; indeed, no Christian should fail to get to know Calvin personally through a generous sampling of the Reformer's own writings.

CALVIN'S INSTITUTES

A brief survey of Calvin's writings must begin with his most famous and lasting work. As we have seen, that work was also practically his first. Published before Calvin's name was well known beyond the circle of his personal acquaintance, the first edition of the *Institutes* (1536) comprised 111 pages in six large chapters. Calvin roughly followed the Apostles' Creed in the way he organized his content.

He seems to have begun writing the book largely for his own benefit. Its original purpose was simply to help organize and explain the major ideas of Protestant doctrine in a logical and easy-to-grasp fashion.[13] He apparently began the work in France but completed the bulk of it while in Basel, Switzerland, to which he had fled in 1535 when persecution of Protestants made his position in France precarious.

France's king at the time, Francis I, was torn by competing political motives and therefore somewhat ambivalent about what to do with the Protestants in his country. He himself was Roman Catholic, but was rival to Charles V, emperor of the Holy Roman Empire. Therefore, out of sheer political expediency, Francis had made an informal alliance against Charles with Sulieman the Magnificent, Islamic emperor of the Ottoman Empire. Of course, Francis also needed the support of the German princes (all devoted to the Protestant cause). So he initially regarded Protestants in France as politically useful and showed a great deal of tolerance for their movement at its start.

But then a Protestant printer had some placards made attacking the Roman Catholic Mass, and they were secretly placed in strategic places throughout central France. One of the notices was affixed to the king's own bedroom door. According to one story, a copy was even placed in a box on his dressing table. Francis interpreted these events as part of a plot against him, and he turned against the Protestants. In fact, in a public expression of outrage over the placards, immediate, widespread persecution erupted among the French populace against Protestants. Because Francis felt personally attacked by the placing of the placards, he approved the persecution. People were beaten, imprisoned, and cruelly tortured—and some were burned to death, including several acquaintances of Calvin.

That was the persecution that drove Calvin to Switzerland, and it also provoked him to finish and publish his *Institutes* much earlier than he had planned. King Francis quickly issued a public letter, charging the French Protestant movement with anarchy and sedition. It needed to be answered, and what better way to answer than with a simple, systematic explanation of what Protestants *actually* believed? Calvin's preface to the work, therefore, was a dedicatory open letter to Francis I, appealing to the king for justice on behalf of French Protestants.

The book immediately gained Calvin respect, support, and followers among Protestants worldwide. It was a scholarly work, yet clear, concise, and compelling. It was also a perfect answer to the persecutors of Protestantism, because it was dispassionate, meticulous in its reasoning, and thoroughly biblical—neither accusatory nor overtly defensive, but a positive affirmation of Protestant belief. It dispelled many popular misunderstandings and won converts to the Protestant cause all over Europe.

Calvin's devotion to the authority of Scripture is probably the work's most distinctive and persuasive feature. He frequently appealed to the church fathers' writings to demonstrate that he was setting forth no new ideas about what the Bible meant. But he was not reluctant to dissent from the fathers and demonstrate clearly where their opinions were at odds with Scripture when those occasions arose. Because Scripture was so prominently highlighted throughout the work as Calvin's supreme authority—and given Calvin's remarkable knowledge of the Bible—anyone who would dispute him must do it biblically. But almost five hundred years later, none of the essential features of his soteriology, his bibliology, his Christology, or his theology proper has ever been successfully discredited on purely biblical grounds.

Calvin lived another twenty-eight years after the first publication of the *Institutes,* and he republished the work in several revised editions, including the first French edition in 1541. His final Latin edition was published in 1559 (five years before his death), and his own French translation of that final edition came out the following year.[14]

Remarkably, even though the book went through these many revisions and editions in its author's lifetime, the primary changes were additions. Until the day he died, Calvin held to the same fundamental doctrinal positions spelled out in the original 1536 edition. As Cunningham observes, "The first edition, produced at that early age, contained the substance of the whole system of doctrine which has since been commonly associated with his name."[15]

CALVIN'S COMMENTARIES

Calvin's doctrine is a fine balance of exegetical and systematic theology. His exegetical skill—his care, thoroughness, and precision in handling Scripture—is most evident in his commentaries. Amazingly, he wrote full commentaries on twenty-four of the thirty-nine books in the Old Testament and all of the New Testament books except 2 and 3 John and Revelation. Even today, the commentaries are rewarding to read and full of rich insight, and by virtue of what they are and what they aim to accomplish, they are more accessible to the average layman than most of his other writings.

Some critics have imagined that they see numerous contradictions between Calvin's *Institutes* and his commentaries, but on close inspection these invariably turn out to be differences in emphasis, determined by whatever text Calvin is commenting on in its native context. For example, Calvin's famous remarks on John 3:16 are often singled out by Arminians as contradictory to fundamental Calvinist soteriology—especially the doctrines of election and effectual calling. Calvin writes:

> Christ brought life, because the Heavenly Father loves the human race, and wishes that they should not perish. . . . And he has employed the universal term *whosoever*, both to invite all indiscriminately to partake of life, and to cut off every excuse from unbelievers. Such is also the import of the term *World*, which he formerly used; for though nothing will be found in the world that is worthy of the

favor of God, yet he shows himself to be reconciled to the whole world, when he invites all men without exception to the faith of Christ, which is nothing else than an entrance into life.[16]

In reality, nothing in those comments is the least bit incompatible with Calvin's views on salvation or the doctrine he lays out in the *Institutes*. Calvin affirmed *both* the doctrine of election and the indiscriminate proposal of reconciliation in the gospel message. Like most strains of Calvinism even today, Calvin saw no conflict between the truths of God's sovereign election, His well-meant proposal of mercy to all sinners, the sinner's own duty to repent and believe, and the truth that sinners are so depraved none can or will respond to the gospel apart from God's enabling grace.

Half a century ago, a helpful review of Calvin's commentaries in a theological journal gave this sound advice:

The commentaries complement the *Institutes*. Many of the controversies which have racked and sometimes splintered the Reformed Churches could have been avoided if the commentaries had been studied as assiduously as the *Institutes*. The student who knows only the *Institutes* does not have a complete picture of the theology of the French reformer. Questions such as inspiration, natural theology, and predestination are dealt with in another way in the exegetical works of Calvin, This is not to say that there is any contradiction between the *Institutes* and the commentaries. They must be taken together, however, to get a clear understanding of Calvin's theology.[17]

The commentaries are at once warm and pastoral, powerful and lucid, sumptuous and scholarly. They are a remarkable achievement, and if this had been Calvin's only contribution to the literature of the Reformation, his reputation as the greatest biblical thinker among the leading Reformers would have been secured.

CALVIN'S SERMONS AND LECTURES

Calvin's sermons reveal the perfect blend of a persuasive mind and a pastoral heart. We have little knowledge of Calvin's mannerisms or vocal inflection, but his words alone convey the amazing power of his preaching.

Calvin himself distinguished between his lectures and his sermons. The lectures were scholarly orations delivered regularly in the auditorium next to St. Peter's Church in Geneva, and many of them were later edited for publication—at first by him, but in later years by his editorial assistants. The sermons were preached for the benefit of Calvin's congregation, laypeople of every class and literacy level. For this reason, the sermons were deliberately simple, more hortatory, and full of the preacher's passion. Both the lectures and sermons are instructive and worth reading for their distinctive merits.

The preservation of the sermons in published form was not Calvin's idea and was not a project he was particularly enthusiastic about. But beginning in 1549, some of Calvin's more well-to-do parishioners decided his sermons needed to be recorded by stenographers and published for the benefit of readers who found Calvin's other works too challenging.

As a result, we have a wonderful window into Calvin's pastoral philosophy. He preached to all segments of his audience, never favoring one over the other, and frequently referring to issues that were of immediate concern to the community—political, moral, and societal matters. Although city magistrates sat in the front row when Calvin preached, he never adapted his sermons to please them. In the words of one author, for those magistrates, "Calvin's sermons had an uncomfortable unpredictability," and sometimes his preaching exacerbated tensions between factions rather than smoothing over all disagreements.[18]

Much of the dynamism of these messages still comes through in the English versions. I encourage preachers to read Calvin's sermons on a regular basis that they might absorb some of the pastoral passion he exuded in his preaching.

CALVIN'S LETTERS

Calvin's most underrated body of work was his letters—long epistles, in many cases. Some four thousand of them have been published, comprising eleven large volumes in the *Corpus Reformatorum*. Modern editions of Calvin's letters are hard to come by, but the Banner of Truth Trust published a small paperback collection in 1980 that includes some of the finest examples of Calvin's correspondence.[19]

As noted previously, Calvin grew fatigued with the duty of answering so much correspondence, but he stayed at the task nonetheless. Occasionally, he employed the pseudonym "Charles d'Espeville" in his polemic letters (including his personal exchange with Servetus), but it was no secret to Servetus (or to other intended recipients) who the real author was. Church historian Philip Schaff refers to Calvin's pen name as "well-known."[20]

Most of Calvin's letters convey the great tenderness of his pastor's heart—especially when he wrote to admonish or correct someone who was in error. The tone of the letters belies the modern caricature of Calvin as a stern, fire-breathing, doctrinaire authoritarian. Still, his passion for the truth, his vast knowledge of Scripture and church history, and his meticulous logic are perpetually evident. There are occasional touches of emotion, ranging from frustration to humor, and throughout we get the sense of a man who (while consistently plainspoken) was never aloof or unapproachable but always sociable, affectionate, and cordial. The letters give us the best and most intimate sense of Calvin as a man.

I will close this chapter with one of my favorite examples of Calvin's personal correspondence, a portion of a letter he wrote to Laelius Socinus, an Italian who became enthralled with the Reformation but then abandoned both Catholic and Reformation principles. Socinus became the chief architect of the heresy that bears his name: Socinianism. His theology (such as it was) consisted of a particularly pernicious blend of skepticism and humanistic values, posing as Christianity but denying practically everything distinctive about the faith. Socinus was, in short, a theological liberal, and his system laid the foundation for deism, Unitarianism, and a host of similar variations, ranging from process theology and open theism to the pure skepticism of the so-called "Jesus Seminar."

Like many of today's "Emergent" and post-evangelical writers, Socinus preferred to question everything rather than assert anything definitively. He lived for a time in Wittenberg, Germany, and while there, wrote to Calvin with a list of questions, which apparently were nothing more than thinly disguised protests against Calvin's teaching.

Calvin's reply is full of good advice for many professing Christians in these postmodern times who like to toy with skepticism:

> Certainly no one can be more averse to paradox than I am, and in subtleties I find no delight at all. Yet nothing shall ever hinder me from openly avowing what I have learned from the Word of God; for nothing but what is useful is taught in the school of this master. It is my only guide, and to acquiesce in its plain doctrines shall be my constant rule of wisdom. Would that you also, my dear Laelius, would learn to regulate your powers with the same moderation! You have no reason to expect a reply from me so long as you bring forward those monstrous questions. If you are gratified by float-ing among those airy speculations, permit me, I beseech you, an humble disciple of Christ, to meditate on those things which tend towards the building up of my faith. And indeed I shall hereafter follow out my wishes in silence, that you may not be troubled by me. And in truth I am very greatly grieved that the fine talents with which God has endowed you, should be occupied not only with what is vain and fruitless, but that they should also be injured by pernicious figments. What I warned you of long ago, I must again

seriously repeat, that unless you correct in time this itching after investigation, it is to be feared you will bring upon yourself severe suffering. I should be cruel towards you did I treat with a show of indulgence what I believe to be a very dangerous error. I should prefer, accordingly, offending you a little at present by my severity, rather than allow you to indulge unchecked in the fascinating allurements of curiosity. The time will come, I hope, when you will rejoice in having been so violently admonished. Adieu, brother very highly esteemed by me; and if this rebuke is harsher than it ought to be, ascribe it to my love to you.[21]

NOTES

[1] Philip Schaff, *History of the Christian Church, Vol. VIII: Modern Christianity: The Swiss Reformation* (repr. Grand Rapids: Eerdmans, 1949–50), 128.

[2] William Cunningham, *The Reformers and the Theology of the Reformation* (repr. Edinburgh: Banner of Truth Trust, 1967), 292.

[3] Calvin's first published work (in 1532) was an edition of Seneca's *De Clementia* with Calvin's commentary on Seneca's philosophy. That was basically a secular treatise. Calvin's first religious work, titled *Psychopannychia*, was a refutation of the doctrine of soul sleep, which some early Anabaptists were promoting in France at the time. *Psychopannychia* was written in 1534 but not published until 1542, six years after the first edition of the *Institutes*.

[4] Karl Gottlieb Bretschneider, et al., eds., *Corpus Reformatorum*, 101 vols. (Halle: Schwetske, 1863–1900). The Calvin works comprise Series 2 of that massive collection, *Ioannis Calvini, Opera Quae Supersunt Omnia*, vols. 29–87.

[5] Robert Reymond, *John Calvin: His Life and Influence* (Ross-shire, U.K.: Christian Focus, 2004), 13n. Reymond's brief work on Calvin, 152 pages adapted from a series of lectures given in 2002 at Coral Ridge Presbyterian Church in Fort Lauderdale, Fla., is the finest brief introductory overview of Calvin's life and influence available. In the book's opening words, Reymond introduces the Reformer as "John Calvin, Author"—pointing out that Calvin's writing ministry was of preeminent importance in all the aspects of his life and work.

[6] Andrew Pettegree, *Reformation and the Culture of Persuasion* (New York: Cambridge University Press, 2005), 23.

[7] John Calvin, *The Gospel According to St. John*, ed. David W. Torrance and Thomas F. Torrance; trans. T. H. L. Parker (Grand Rapids: Eerdmans, 1961), 240.

8 William J. Bouwsma, *John Calvin: A Sixteenth-Century Portrait* (New York: Oxford University Press, 1988), 29–30.

9 Feb. 17, 1551, letter to Heinrich Bullinger. Cited in ibid., 30.

10 March 7, 1550, letter to Francisco de Enzinas (Dryander). Cited in ibid., 29.

11 John Calvin, *Commentaries on the Book of the Prophet Jeremiah and the Lamentations*, ed. John Owen (repr. Grand Rapids: Baker, 1963), 4:11.

12 Ibid., 1:51.

13 Calvin explains his original design for the work in his own words in the opening paragraph of the book's dedication to King Francis I of France.

14 For a comprehensive survey of the various editions of the *Institutes*, see B. B. Warfield, "On the Literary History of Calvin's Institutes," in John Calvin, *Institutes of the Christian Religion*, trans. John Allen (Philadelphia: Presbyterian Board of Christian Education, 1936), xxx–xxxi.

15 Cunningham, *The Reformers and the Theology of the Reformation*, 294.

16 John Calvin, *Commentary on the Gospel according to John*, trans. William Pringle (repr. Grand Rapids: Baker, 1963), 1:123–125.

17 Walter G. Hards, "Calvin's Commentaries," *Theology Today* (April 1959), 16:1:123–124.

18 Pettegree, *Reformation and the Culture of Persuasion*, 23–24.

19 John Calvin, *Letters of John Calvin* (Edinburgh: Banner of Truth Trust, 1980).

20 Schaff, *History of the Christian Church, Vol. VIII: Modern Christianity: The Swiss Reformation*, 328.

21 Ibid., 128–129.

Chapter 9

THE SUPREMACY
OF JESUS CHRIST

ERIC J. ALEXANDER

*No matter how many strong enemies plot to overthrow the church,
they do not have sufficient strength to prevail over God's immutable decree by which he appointed his Son eternal King.*[1]

—JOHN CALVIN

It is interesting, and I think significant, that scholars searching
for a one-word description of John Calvin's theology, preaching,
and thinking have been drawn, in many cases, to the word *Christocentric*.[2] It infers that, in all his concerns, Calvin allowed nothing and
no one to displace the Lord Jesus Christ from His supreme place in
every sphere. And that was not only how Calvin thought, wrote, and
preached, it was how he lived and prayed. For the sake of complete-
ness, some scholars would prefer to substitute the word *theocentric*, or at
least add it to *Christocentric*. To be described as both would have been
Calvin's deepest wish.

There is no doubt that Calvin has been misunderstood and maligned
in a remarkable way and, curious beyond understanding, especially
within the professing Christian church. J. I. Packer gives his judgment
that "the amount of misrepresentation to which Calvin's theology has

been subjected has been enough to prove his doctrine of total depravity several times over!"[3]

If Calvin's critics would only read his works, they would come to a very different conclusion. There are two main sources from which Calvin may be read. One is his *Institutes of the Christian Religion.* It consists of eighty chapters, four books, and more than one thousand pages. Packer calls it "a systematic masterpiece, one that has carved out a permanent niche for itself among the greatest Christian books."[4] The other source is Calvin's commentaries on the Bible.[5] Neither source offers dull or difficult reading.

These works offer innumerable insights for the reader. But they also reveal conclusively that Calvin was a humble, godly, and Christlike man, one who gloried in nothing so much as in the person and work of Jesus Christ, to whom he was entirely devoted.

Calvin's desire to exalt Christ to a place of unique supremacy is displayed in his commentaries on the New Testament. Even a superficial acquaintance with them reveals how accurate the word *Christocentric* is to describe the gospel he preached and the emphasis he discerned in New Testament theology. In those commentaries, he wrote:

- There is no part in our salvation that may not be found in Christ (Acts).
- The whole gospel is contained in Christ (Romans).
- All the blessings of God come to us through Christ (Romans).
- Christ is the beginning, middle, and end—nothing is or can be found apart from Him (Colossians).
- There is nothing necessary for salvation that faith finds apart from Christ (the General Epistles).

Sinclair B. Ferguson has well summed up the supremacy of Christ in Calvin's theology in these words: "Everything lacking in us is given to us by Christ; everything sinful in us is imputed to Christ; and all judgment merited by us is borne by Christ."[6]

There are innumerable ways in which Calvin's desire to exalt Jesus Christ to a place of unique supremacy stands out. In the remainder of this chapter, however, I will confine myself to one of them, namely, his teaching on the work of Christ as Mediator through His threefold office of Prophet, Priest, and King.

Paul Wells has written that "John Calvin is undoubtedly the greatest theologian of 'mediation through Christ.'"[7] He adds, "It was Calvin who developed the threefold office of Christ as prophet, priest and king as a way of presenting the different facets of the accomplishment of salvation."[8] Of course, the Old Testament is the seedbed of the three mediatorial offices, each of which anticipates its fullness in Christ. By name and by God's activity on His behalf, He is "the Anointed One."

THE OFFICE OF CHRIST AS PROPHET

When we begin to understand the full scope of the work of Christ as Mediator, we readily share Calvin's sense of the greatness and glory that belong to Christ. Calvin writes, "The work to be performed by the mediator was of no common description: being to restore us to the divine favor so as to make us, instead of sons of men, sons of God; instead of heirs of hell, heirs of a heavenly kingdom. Who could do this, unless the Son of God should also become the Son of Man, and so receive what is ours as to transfer to us what is His, making that which is His by nature to become ours by grace."[9]

The classic event in which Christ was commissioned and revealed as a Prophet was His anointing and baptism. Calvin comments, "The voice which thundered from heaven, 'This is my beloved Son, hear him,' gave him a special privilege above all teachers. Then from him, as head, this unction is diffused through the members, as Joel has foretold, 'Your sons and your daughters shall prophesy.'"[10]

At the beginning of His ministry, Christ announced His prophetic calling when, in the synagogue and during worship, He was handed the scroll of the prophet Isaiah. It is significant that He read a messianic passage: "The Spirit of the Lord is upon me, because he has anointed me to proclaim good news to the poor. He has sent me to proclaim liberty to the captives and recovering of sight to the blind, to set at liberty those who are oppressed, to proclaim the year of the Lord's favor" (Luke 4:17–19). When He had rolled up the scroll, He returned it to the attendant and sat down. Then, with the eyes of all in the synagogue fixed on Him, He said, "Today, this Scripture has been fulfilled in your hearing" (Luke 4:21), and the people marveled at the gracious words that were coming from His mouth. Calvin explains:

> The purpose of this prophetical dignity in Christ is to teach us that in the doctrine which he delivered is substantially included a wisdom which is perfect in all its parts. Outside of him there is nothing worth knowing, and those who by faith apprehend his true character possess the boundless immensity of heavenly blessings.[11]

An important application of Christ's prophetic office in Calvin's life was his utter commitment to the teaching and preaching of the text of Holy Scripture. His exposition of the greater part of the Bible has left the Christian church since the Reformation with a treasure beyond assessment. But more vital still was his absolute submission to the final authority of Scripture. In his comment on Isaiah's vision in chapter 6, Calvin says, "I do not venture to make any assertion where Scripture is silent."[12] Likewise, he reaches a conclusion in a discussion on judgment with this delightful statement: "Our wisdom ought to consist in embracing with gentle docility, and without any exception, all that is delivered in the sacred Scriptures."[13]

Christ's position as our anointed and appointed Teacher has profound implications for our attitude toward Scripture. To divorce the absolute supremacy of Christ from the absolute supremacy of Scripture (to which He firmly held) would, for Calvin, be preposterous and impossible. Indeed, he describes Scripture as "Christ's royal scepter,"[14] implying that Christ rules us with it. Thus, Calvin frequently concludes, "*Ad verbum est veniendum*" ("You must come to the Word").[15]

THE OFFICE OF CHRIST AS PRIEST

The second of the three offices for which Christ is anointed is that of Priest. A priest is one appointed by God to act for others in matters related to God. In other words, He is a mediator between God and man. The Old Testament made ample preparation for this concept, and the epistle to the Hebrews develops this idea intensively. Calvin explains the priest's task in the most solemn words: "His function is that he might 'procure the favor of God for us.' But because a deserved curse obstructs the entrance and God in His character of Judge is hostile to us, expiation must necessarily intervene, that as a priest chosen to appease the wrath of God, he may reinstate us in his favor."[16]

The unique aspect of Christ's Priesthood is that He is not only Priest but victim—not only the subject of the work of intercession, but the means of it, too. He not only presents an offering, He becomes an offering, and He thereby deals with men for God and with God for men.

There were three fatal disabilities in the Old Testament priesthood. First, the priest had sins of his own that cried out for atonement. However, being imperfect, he could not atone for himself, much less another. Second, "It is impossible for the blood of bulls and goats to take away sins" (Heb. 10:4). That blood taught the way of salvation through the death of a spotless Lamb, but it could not and did not confer the reality of salvation. Third, the sacrifices of the priest were continuous, happening daily in the temple. The Old Testament priest's work was never finished.

Calvin contrasts all this with the perfection of Christ's Priesthood as described in Hebrews 9:12–14. He writes, "And the apostle . . . explains the whole matter in the Epistle to the Hebrews, showing that without shedding of blood, there is no forgiveness (Hebrews 9:22). . . . The whole burden of condemnation of which we were relieved was laid on Him."[17]

However, Calvin calls our attention to further implications of Christ's Priesthood. His Priesthood is permanent and eternal, not temporary or confined to His incarnate state. He appears at the right hand of the Father in the present time, seated to signify His completed work on the cross, and yet active as our Advocate and Intercessor. Calvin writes:

> Faith perceives that his seat beside the Father is not without great advantage to us. Having entered the temple not made with hands, he constantly appears as our advocate and intercessor in the presence of the Father; directs attention to his own righteousness, so as to turn it away from our sins; so reconciles him to us, as by his intercession to pave for us a way of access to his throne, presenting it to miserable sinners, to whom it would otherwise be an object of dread, as replete with grace and mercy.[18]

Calvin refers to numerous examples of Christ's intercession in the Gospels, one of them being Christ's personal assurance to the apostle Peter that, in the face of satanic attack, Peter may reckon upon the intercession of Christ on his behalf. But the principal example is Christ's great intercessory prayer in John 17. The ultimate value of this prayer is that Jesus assures His disciples that He is the great Intercessor for them, not only in this world, but even when He ascends to the right hand of the Father. On account of the fact that believers have access to the Father, we ourselves have a priestly ministry of prayer as well.[19]

THE OFFICE OF CHRIST AS KING

Christ's kingly office, of course, also has close connection with His priestly work of offering a sufficient sacrifice on the cross, so much so that Calvin says, "Christ's kingdom is inseparable from His priesthood."[20]

That kingdom is not yet consummated, but it has been inaugurated through Christ's triumph over sin and Satan at the cross. It is this marvelous picture of *Christus Victor* ("Christ, the Victor") that Calvin gives us when commenting on Colossians 2:14–15: "Hence it is not without cause that Paul magnificently celebrates the triumph which Christ obtained upon the cross, as if the cross, the symbol of ignominy, had been converted into a triumphal chariot."[21]

This kingdom is already established in one sense. As R. C. Sproul has written: "It is a present reality. It is now invisible to the world. But Christ has already ascended. . . . At this very moment He reigns as the King of kings and Lord of lords. . . . The kings of this world and all secular governments may ignore this reality, but they cannot undo it."[22]

Yet there is in this life always a "not yet" in our thinking about the kingdom. We not only glory in the invisible inauguration of the kingdom, we anticipate with joy unspeakable that day when the invisible will become visible and every knee will bow before the "heir of all things" (Heb. 1:2). Meantime, we need to recognize the present truth of Calvin's statement: "The whole of Satan's kingdom is subject to the authority of Christ."[23] Again in his first sermon on Isaiah 53, Calvin exhorts us: "Let us not confine ourselves to His sufferings alone, but let us link the resurrection with the death and know that He, having been crucified, is nevertheless seated as Lieutenant of God his Father, to exercise sovereign dominion and to have all power in heaven and on earth."[24]

Calvin emphasizes the following features of Christ's kingly office:

• *The kingdom is spiritual, not material.*[25] Calvin clarifies this assertion by quoting the words of Jesus recorded in John's gospel: "My kingdom is not of this world" (18:36). Calvin writes, "For we see that everything which is earthly and of the world is temporary and soon fades away."[26] Calvin presses the truth of this home by adding, "We must therefore know that the happiness which is promised to us in Christ does not consist in external advantages—such as leading a joyful and tranquil life, abounding in wealth, being secure against all injury, and having an affluence of delights, such as the flesh is wont to long for—but properly belongs to the heavenly life."[27]

• *The kingdom of God is within you (Luke 17:21).* Calvin thinks it probable that Jesus is here responding to the Pharisees, who may have asked Him in derision to produce His insignia. Therefore, Calvin writes,

We may not doubt that we shall always be victorious against the devil, the world and everything that can do us harm. . . . But to prevent those who were already more than enough inclined to the earth from dwelling on its pomp, he bids them enter into their consciences, "the kingdom of God is righteousness and peace and joy in the Holy Ghost." These words briefly teach what the Kingdom of Christ bestows upon us. Not being earthly or carnal, and so subject to corruption, but spiritual, it raises us even to eternal life so that we can patiently live at present under toil, hunger, cold, contempt, disgrace, and other annoyances; contented with this, that our King will never abandon us, but will supply our necessities until our warfare is ended and we are called to triumph. . . . Since then he arms and equips us by his power, adorns us with splendor and magnificence, enriches us with wealth, we here find most abundant cause of glorying.[28]

The whole concept of the threefold office of Christ is applied by Calvin to human spiritual need. Blind by nature and ignorant of the truth, we need the revelation that came in Jesus Christ, for He is our Prophet and Teacher. Above all, He shows us where we find the truth about Himself and ourselves, about sin and salvation, about pardon from sin and peace with God, and it is all in Holy Scripture. J. F. Jansen says, "Calvin, like Luther, never forgot that the whole Bible is the manger in which Christ is found."[29]

But the human plight is not only that we are ignorant of God and of the truth. We are also sinful, guilty, and objects of God's wrath, without hope of saving ourselves. In this situation in which we have no access to God, Jesus Christ comes as our Mediator, taking us by a new and living way to the Father, offering up Himself as a perfect sacrifice and thereby atoning for our sin. The distinction Calvin makes is that the former priesthood could only typify atonement through animal sacrifices, but Christ effected atonement by the sacrifice of Himself.

Finally, the need of the sinner is not only the knowledge of the truth and reconciliation to God by the sacrificial death of His Son. It is also deliverance from the power of Satan and a transfer into the kingdom of God. We need the sovereign hand of the King of kings upon our lives to guide us, rule us, and daily subdue in us everything that grieves Him.

The sum of the whole matter, of course, is that Calvin is concerned throughout all his writing, preaching, praying, and living with what Abraham Kuyper called "a life system."[30] That system derives power from Christ in a life where He has total supremacy. It was for transformed lives that Calvin lived, preached, taught, prayed, and died—all that Christ might be exalted and glorified. "To Him who loves us and has freed us from our sins by his blood, and made us a kingdom, priests to his God and Father, to him be glory and dominion for ever and ever. Amen" (Rev. 1:5b–6).

I have always found that nothing sums up Calvin so admirably as the two stanzas of the hymn "Salutation to Jesus Christ," which is attributed to him:

I greet Thee, who my sure Redeemer art,
My only trust and Savior of my heart,
Who so much toil and woe and pain didst undergo,
For my poor, worthless sake;
And pray Thee, from our hearts, all idle griefs and smarts
And foolish cares to take.

Thou art the King of mercy and of grace,
Reigning omnipotent in every place:
So come, O King! and deign within our hearts to reign
And our whole being sway;
Shine in us by Thy light and lead us to the height
Of Thy pure, heavenly day.

NOTES

[1] John Calvin, *Institutes of the Christian Religion*, ed. John T. McNeill; trans. Ford Lewis Battles; Library of Christian Classics, XX–XXI (Philadelphia: Westminster John Knox, 1960), 2.15.3.

2 Stephen Edmondson, *Calvin's Christology* (Cambridge: Cambridge University Press, 2004), 169.

3 J. I. Packer, *The Collected Shorter Writings of J. I. Packer* (Carlisle, U.K.: Paternoster, 1999), 4:19.

4 Ibid., 4:20.

5 John Calvin, *The Commentaries of John Calvin*, 46 vols. (repr. Grand Rapids: Eerdmans, 1948–1950).

6 Sinclair B. Ferguson, essay in *The Practical Calvinist* (Ross-shire, U.K.: Christian Focus, 2002), 117.

7 Paul Wells, *Cross Words: The Biblical Doctrine of the Atonement* (Ross-shire, U.K.: Mentor, 2005), 168.

8 Ibid., 174.

9 Calvin, *Institutes of the Christian Religion*, trans. Henry Beveridge (London: James Clarke & Co., 1953), 2.12.2.

10 Ibid., 2.15.2.

11 Ibid.

12 John Calvin, *Commentary on Isaiah*, trans. William Pringle (Edinburgh: Calvin Translation Society, 1850; repr. Grand Rapids, Baker, 2003), 1:203.

13 Calvin, *Institutes of the Christian Religion* (Beveridge translation), 1.18.4.

14 Calvin, *Commentary on Isaiah*, 1:379.

15 Calvin, *Institutes of the Christian Religion* (Beveridge translation), 1.7.1.

16 Ibid., 2.15.6.

17 Calvin, *Institutes of the Christian Religion* (Beveridge translation), 2.17.4.

18 Ibid., 2.16.16.

19 Ibid., 2.15.6.

20 John Calvin, *Commentary on the Book of Psalms*, trans. James Anderson (Edinburgh: Calvin Translation Society, 1845; repr. Grand Rapids: Baker, 2003), 5:157.

21 Calvin, *Institutes of the Christian Religion* (Beveridge translation), 2.16.6.

22 R. C. Sproul, *The Heart of Reformed Theology* (London: Hodder & Stoughton, 1997), 98.

23 John Calvin, *Commentary on a Harmony of the Evangelists, Matthew, Mark, and Luke* (Edinburgh: Calvin Translation Society, 1845; repr. Grand Rapids: Baker, 2003), 1:430.

24 Quoted in John F. Jansen, *Calvin's Doctrine of the Work of Christ* (Cambridge: James Clarke & Co., 1956), 60.

25 Calvin, *Institutes of the Christian Religion* (Beveridge translation), 2.15.3.

26 Ibid.

27 Ibid., 2.15.4.

28 Ibid.

29 Jansen, *Calvin's Doctrine of the Work of Christ*, 64.

30 Abraham Kuyper, *Lectures on Calvinism* (Grand Rapids: Eerdmans, 1931), 9.

Chapter 10

THE TRANSFORMING WORK OF THE SPIRIT

THABITI ANYABWILE

Because of the rudeness and weakness that is in us, we must allow ourselves to be governed by God's Spirit, which is the chief key by which the gate of paradise is opened to us.[1]

—JOHN CALVIN

Our Reformation forebears understood clearly that the church constantly needed reforming according to the Word of God. Their rallying cry became "*Ecclesia reformata, semper reformanda*" ("the church reformed, always reforming"). Reformation was their goal *and* their strategy, all in accord with the plumb line of God's infallible Word.

In our day, however, the Reformers' rallying cry has faded into a distant and indistinguishable whisper. On the one hand, many exhibit zeal for reforming the church, but not according to the Word of God. They appear to prefer business techniques, psychology, and cultural trends as standards of reform over the Word of God. They are zealous, but not according to knowledge. Then there are those who seem to think the church is not in need of reform at all. Many are indifferent to the cancerous infections of worldliness and doctrinal drift. Where the

119

Reformers would have taken up arms, today some church leaders and Christians shrug in disinterest and carry on without recognizing the great eclipse of biblical truth that is taking place among us.

What the church needs today is a recovery of the vision and zeal of men like Calvin—a vision and zeal informed from first to last by the loftiness, centrality, authority, and glory of God's Word.

Calvin, insofar as he understood the Bible well, turns out to be a most excellent and edifying help to Christians today. The Bible is timeless, just as thoughtful works about the Bible sometimes take on that quality. Calvin's books are in that category. In our day, students desiring to understand the Bible can profit immensely from Calvin. And perhaps nowhere is that more evident than in Calvin's writings on God the Holy Spirit.

What we seem to be missing, which Calvin comprehended, is a firm commitment to the necessity of the Holy Spirit in the conversion of sinners, as well as a deep dependence upon the ongoing work of the Spirit in the Christian life and the church. Concerning these things, Calvin reminds us of our desperate need to rely on the third person of the Trinity.

THE HOLY SPIRIT IN CONVERSION AND UNION WITH CHRIST

Our reliance upon the Holy Spirit begins with our conversion, according to Calvin. Salvation lies well beyond the means of fallen man apart from the "secret workings" of God's Spirit. As a kind of preamble to the third book of the *Institutes*, Calvin opens by asking, "How do we receive those benefits which the Father bestowed on his only begotten Son—not for Christ's own private use, but that he might enrich poor and needy men?" Demonstrating the vital role the Spirit plays in conversion, Calvin answers that it is through "the secret energy of the Spirit, by which we come to enjoy Christ and all His benefits."[2]

In the *Institutes*, Calvin explains that saving faith is owing to the Spirit's divine work. In Calvin's theology, the Spirit acts as "the inner teacher by whose efforts the promise of salvation penetrates into our minds, a promise that would otherwise only strike the air or beat upon our ears."[3] Without the Holy Spirit, man's "blindness and perversity," and his "inclination to vanity," prevent him from "cleav[ing] fast" and leave him "always blind to the light of God's truth."[4] According to Calvin, "faith is a singular gift of God, both in that the mind of man is purged so as to be able to taste the truth of God and in that his heart is established therein. For the Spirit is not only the initiator of faith, but increases it by degrees, until by it he leads us to the Kingdom of Heaven."[5]

God the Holy Spirit turns a person's mind from the darkness and foolishness of the world to the light of the kingdom of God by the preaching of the gospel. Otherwise, "the Word of God is like the sun, shining upon all those to whom it is proclaimed, but with no effect among the blind . . . [because] all of us are blind by nature in this respect."[6]

Calvin seemed to rejoice in this truth, exalting and exulting in the work of the Spirit in producing and growing such faith. He almost sings as he writes, "Our eyes are worse than put out until He enlightens them by His Holy Spirit."[7] He adds, "Because of the rudeness and weakness that is in us, we must allow ourselves to be governed by God's Spirit, which is the chief key by which the gate of paradise is opened to us."[8]

The Spirit's work, according to Scripture and Calvin's exegesis, does not end with producing faith in the sinner. Calvin often detailed his view that the mere beginning of faith was insufficient for eternal salvation given the weak nature of man. He believed the Holy Spirit is necessary for salvation on two fronts:

Let us notice how volatile men are. He that is best disposed to follow God will soon fall, for we are so frail that the devil will overcome us every minute of time, if God does not hold us up with a strong hand. And for that reason it is said that God manifests his power in upholding us when He has elected us and given us to our

Lord Jesus Christ. For if He did not fight for us, alas, what would become of us? We should be absolutely confounded, and not by reason of one stroke only, but there would be an infinite number of falls, as I said before. As soon as we were in the way of salvation, we should at once be turned out of it by our own frailty, lightness and inconstancy, if we were not restrained and if God did not so work in us that we might, by His Holy Spirit, overcome all the assaults of the devil and the world. Thus God's Spirit does a twofold work in us with respect to faith. For He enlightens us to make us understand things which otherwise would be hidden from us, and to receive God's promises with all obedience. That is the first part of His work. The second is that the same Spirit is pleased to abide in us and to give us perseverance, that we do not draw back in the midst of our way.[9]

From first to last, the Christian owes his salvation to the enlightening, converting, and saving work of the Holy Spirit. Borrowing from the biblical imagery of Ephesians 1:13–14, Calvin pictured the Holy Spirit "engraved like a seal upon our hearts, with the result that it seals the cleansing and sacrifice of Christ." A few sentences later he writes, "the Holy Spirit is the bond by which Christ effectually unites us to himself."[10]

One is left to wonder whether this solid biblical truth is believed at all anymore. The Lord once granted me the privilege of leading a Bible study on the doctrine of the Holy Spirit. I began by asking, "How many of you have ever heard any substantial teaching about the Holy Spirit or have been involved in a church where this doctrine was explained?" In the room were adult Christians of many nationalities, denominational backgrounds, and ages. Some had walked with the Lord for forty or fifty years. Of the group of about forty people, maybe four or five raised their hands in the affirmative.

It is really no wonder, then, that evangelism and gospel preaching appear to be largely non-existent and ineffective in some quarters today. Instead, outreach and preaching seem to be designed around the persuasiveness of the preacher and emotional appeal rather than the sovereign and secret working of the Holy Spirit. We desperately need to recover a biblical view of conversion and the Holy Spirit's sovereign working in saving sinners so that we might free ourselves from the tyranny of methodological pragmatism and faddish trends.

THE HOLY SPIRIT AND CHRISTIAN LIVING

Calvin lived and ministered during a time of significant social, political, and religious upheaval and strife. Almost overnight, entire provinces switched their allegiances to either the Roman Catholic or Protestant causes. Struggles were intense and sometimes severe. Calvin himself evaded capture and certain death on occasion.

It is not surprising, then, that the Reformer thought of the Christian life principally in terms of warfare and struggle. His experience perhaps augmented the Bible's own use of warfare imagery to describe Christian living.

Chief among the Christian's enemies are the world, the flesh, and the Devil—the principal forces against which Christ's army is arrayed. Commenting on Galatians 5:14–18, Calvin writes:

> Until the day that we leave this world, there will always be spots and stains within us, and we will always be bent down with the burden of our sins and weaknesses. This is in order to humble us and to show that our life is to be a constant battle. Thus, though sin dwells within us, it must not have dominion, but the Spirit of God must conquer it. This can only happen if we flee to God with fervent zeal, and pray that he will remedy the evil that we cannot change. Also, that he would grant us more of the gifts of His Spirit so that we might overcome all that has weighed us down.[11]

Calvin clearly perceived that the Christian faces an ongoing battle with indwelling sin. He knew this conflict would remain with us, but he was no defeatist. He knew also that the Holy Spirit accompanies us, and that the Christian must live by the Spirit in order to conquer sin.

Christian sanctification was central to Calvin's thinking, and he understood that the Spirit's anointing of Christ as Prophet, Priest, and King in some way vouchsafed the Christian's sanctification. In other words, Calvin believed that our holiness is bound together with Christ's completed work by the Holy Spirit. Calvin put it this way: "Christ came endowed with the Holy Spirit in a special way: that is, to separate us from the world and to gather us unto the hope of the eternal inheritance. Hence he is called the 'Spirit of sanctification' because he not only quickens and nourishes us by a general power that is visible both in the human race and in the rest of the living creatures, but he is also the root and seed of heavenly life in us."[12]

The Holy Spirit, "the root and seed of heavenly life in us," sanctifies the Christian by "persistently boiling away and burning up our vicious and inordinate desires, [and thus] He enflames our hearts with the love of God and with zealous devotion."[13] According to Calvin, the Spirit "breathes divine life into us [so] that we are no longer actuated by ourselves, but are ruled by His action and prompting. Accordingly, whatever good things are in us are the fruits of His grace; and without Him our gifts are darkness of mind and perversity of heart."[14]

Calvin regarded this work of the Spirit as evidence of genuine regeneration. He insisted that "it is not enough for people to claim that the Spirit of God dwells in their hearts, for he is not idle; if he is there, his presence will reveal itself."[15] He also believed the Spirit's work was essential for growth. "It is only in [the anointing of the Holy Spirit] that we are invigorated," he writes. "Especially with regard to heavenly life, there is no drop of vigor in us save what the Holy Spirit instills. For the Spirit has chosen Christ as his seat, that from him might abundantly flow the heavenly riches of which we are in such need. The believers stand unconquered through the strength of their king, and his spiritual riches abound in them. Hence they are justly called Christians."[16]

In this warfare, the true Christian receives assurance of victory:

Christ enriches his people with all things necessary for the eternal salvation of souls and fortifies them with courage to stand unconquerable against all the assaults of spiritual enemies. From this we infer that He rules—inwardly and outwardly—more for our own sake than His. Hence we are furnished, as far as God knows to be expedient for us, with the gifts of the Spirit, which we lack by nature. By these fruits we may perceive that we are truly joined to God in perfect blessedness. Then, relying upon the power of the same Spirit, let us not doubt that we shall always be victorious over the devil, the world, and every kind of harmful thing.[17]

In his own life and ministry, Calvin relied on this truth:

God's Spirit is our pledge during the time that we wait to be taken out of this transitory life and to be set free from all miseries, especially from the bondage of sin, which is the heaviest burden of all. Until such time, then, as we are delivered from all those things, we must rest on this, that God's Spirit dwells in us.[18]

This is why Calvin so freely and fully rejoiced in the Holy Spirit. In one sense, he even summed up the Christian life as rejoicing in the Holy Spirit. He writes, "Christians . . . glory in the presence of the Holy Spirit, without which glorying Christianity itself does not stand!"[19]

Where is our glorying today? Do Christians today rejoice in the sanctifying work of the Holy Spirit and in their union with Christ by the Spirit? Do our lives demonstrate a consistent and conscious dependence upon the Spirit of God for victory and power in this life as we await the glorious return of the Savior Christ Jesus? If not, Calvin speaks especially to us today:

We should pray to God to renew us and to strengthen us by His Holy Spirit, and to increase His gifts in us more and more, so that in passing through this world, we may always aim at that mark, and

125

be here simply as pilgrims, in order that our Lord may confess us as His children, and keep for us the heritage which He has promised us and bought so dearly for us by the death and passion of our Lord Jesus Christ.[20]

THE HOLY SPIRIT AND THE CHURCH

Finally, we may learn a tremendous amount from Calvin when it comes to the necessity of the Holy Spirit in living out the Christian faith corporately, as the church.

Again, Calvin perceived the intertwining of Jesus' person and work with that of the Holy Spirit and the local church. According to Calvin:

> [Jesus] was anointed by the Spirit to be herald and witness of the Father's grace. We must note this: he received anointing, not only for himself that he might carry out the office of teaching, but for his whole body that the power of the Spirit might be present in the continuing preaching of the gospel.[21]

Calvin understood what some habitually forget—effective gospel preaching depends wholly on the power of the Spirit as Christ offers Himself in the gospel. If we neglect to proclaim the work of Christ or to beseech the work of the Spirit, all preaching is lifeless and impotent.

But Calvin reminds us also that the Spirit is necessary for producing the unity fitting for renewed life. In His atonement, Christ becomes "our peace," and purchases and makes for Himself "one new man" (Eph. 2:14–15). But the Spirit is the agent who applies this reality.

Commenting on Ephesians 2:16–19, Calvin writes, "We must all participate in one Spirit." That participation in the Spirit of God produces "such a union among us as might show that we are in very deed the body of our Lord Jesus Christ. It is not enough for us to be piled up together like a heap of stones, but we must be joined together with cordial affection."[22] Calvin unswervingly proclaimed that "when God's Spirit governs us, He reforms our affections in such a way that our souls are joined together."[23]

What a beautiful picture of life together in the local church. But this was no preacher's flourish for Calvin; he believed Scripture teaches that unity is a mark of the church of God. He writes:

> We must keep the unity of the Spirit in the bond of peace. For here he puts down the unity of the Spirit as a mark that is required in the church and flock of God, insomuch that if we are divided among ourselves, we are estranged from God. And with this, he shows us what we have seen briefly before, which is that if we are not at one among ourselves, God disclaims us and tells us we do not belong to Him. This unity therefore is something which ought to be valued nowadays seeing it is the way in respect of which we are acknowledged as God's children.[24]

If this unity was to be prized in Calvin's day, it is no less needed in our day. Unity in the truth and in God's Spirit is essential. It must be among the ends for which gospel preachers and all Christians labor, remembering that our love and unity commend to a perishing world the truth of the gospel of Jesus Christ (John 17:20–21).

The twenty-first-century church needs a number of things, including a deeper understanding of saving faith and conversion, a greater desire for sanctification and deliverance from worldliness, a resurgence of powerful gospel preaching, and a unwavering commitment to unity in the church. Five hundred years after his life and ministry, Calvin teaches us that essential to meeting all of these needs is daily reliance on God the Holy Spirit, "the chief key by which the gate of paradise is opened to us."[25]

NOTES

1   John Calvin, *Sermons on Ephesians* (1562; repr. Edinburgh: Banner of Truth Trust, 1998), 207.

2   John Calvin, *Institutes of the Christian Religion*, ed. John T. McNeill; trans. Ford Lewis Battles; Library of Christian Classics, XX–XXI (Philadelphia: Westminster John Knox, 1960), 3.1.1.

3   Ibid., 3.1.4.

4   Ibid., 3.2.33.

5   Ibid.

6   Ibid., 3.2.34.

7   John Calvin, *Sermons on Ephesians*, 92.

8   Ibid., 207.

9   Ibid., 73.

10 Calvin, *Institutes of the Christian Religion*, 3.1.1.

11 John Calvin, *Sermons on Galatians*, trans. Kathy Childress (1563; repr. Edinburgh: Banner of Truth Trust, 1997), 530.

12 Calvin, *Institutes of the Christian Religion*, 3.1.2.

13 Ibid., 3.1.3.

14 Ibid.

15 Calvin, *Sermons on Galatians*, 560.

16 Calvin, *Institutes of the Christian Religion*, 2.15.5.

17 Ibid., 2.15.4.

18 Calvin, *Sermons on Ephesians*, 78.

19 Calvin, *Institutes of the Christian Religion*, 3.2.39.

20 Calvin, *Sermons on Ephesians*, 287.

21 Calvin, *Institutes of the Christian Religion*, 2.15.2.

22 Calvin, *Sermons on Ephesians*, 326.

23 Ibid.

24 Ibid., 323.

25 Ibid., 207.

Chapter 11

MAN'S RADICAL CORRUPTION

JOHN MACARTHUR

The Scripture testifies often that man is a slave of sin. The Scripture means thereby that man's spirit is so alienated from the justice of God that man conceives, covets, and undertakes nothing that is not evil, perverse, iniquitous, and soiled.[1]

—JOHN CALVIN

False belief systems always seem to downplay human depravity. Some even deny it altogether, insisting that people are fundamentally good. This is a tendency of nearly all quasi-Christian heresies, humanistic philosophies, and secular worldviews. Apostles of those religions and philosophies seem to think describing human nature in upbeat and optimistic terms somehow makes their viewpoint nobler. That fact alone perfectly epitomizes the blind illogic that goes hand in hand with unbelief and false religion. After all, humanity's moral dilemma should be patently obvious to anyone who seriously considers the problem of evil. As G. K. Chesterton famously remarked, original sin is the one point of Christian theology that easily can be proved empirically.[2]

The fallenness of the human race is a profound, destructive, and universal predicament—inexplicable by any merely naturalistic rationale, but undeniably obvious. Wherever you find humanity, you see ample evidence that the entire race is held captive under sin's corrupting influence.

We see such proof, for example, in the dominant themes of popular entertainment. It is boldly exhibited across the face of civilization on large billboards, in neon lights, and in slick magazine ads. We see it delivered every day in vivid color and surround sound on the evening news, as well as in local, regional, and world headlines. Our closest personal relationships also offer constant reminders that no one is sin-free and the very best of people fall far short of God's righteous standard. Finally, each of us knows our own fallenness by experience, because we feel the weight of our guilt. (Even the determined sinner who utterly sears his own conscience is merely suppressing a truth he knows all too well.) We cannot do what we know we should, and we cannot will ourselves to be what we ought to be. Reminders of our own hopeless corruption plague us in one way or another practically every hour of every day. There's no escaping it (except by sheer, groundless denial): the human race is fatally infected with sin.

Yet the idea that sinners are totally in bondage to sin and therefore unable to come to God by their own free will has been one of the most controversial and constantly assaulted principles of biblical theology since the earliest days of the church. Surprisingly, some of the most tenacious opposition to the doctrine has come from within the church community. In fact, theologians and church leaders who despise or derogate the doctrine of human depravity have probably done as much to confuse and impede the advance of gospel truth as the most openly hostile adversaries of Christianity. And much controversy over the extent and nature of depravity continues even today.

KEY CHAPTERS IN THE CONFLICT OVER TOTAL DEPRAVITY

The quintessential episode in the whole debate, of course, was the Pelagian controversy. This conflict arose early in the fifth century when Pelagius and Celestius objected to Augustine's teaching that sinners are totally unable to obey God unless He intervenes by grace to free them from sin.[3]

Augustine was merely affirming the plain truth of Romans 8:7–8: "The mind that is set on the flesh is hostile to God, for it does not submit to God's law; indeed, it cannot. Those who are in the flesh cannot please God." But according to *Pelagianism*, anyone who simply chooses to obey God can do so. In contradiction to Romans 5:12–19, Pelagius steadfastly denied that human nature was in any way defiled or disabled by our first parents' sin. He insisted Adam alone fell when he ate the forbidden fruit, and neither guilt nor corruption was passed from Adam to his progeny because of his disobedience. Instead, the Pelagians said, every person possesses perfect freedom of the will just as Adam himself did at the beginning. So when we sin, it's purely by choice, not because our nature is depraved. They furthermore said sinners have the ability to change their hearts and free themselves from sin by the exercise of sheer willpower.

In effect, the Pelagians denied the need for divine grace and reduced salvation to a shallow notion of self-reformation. Of course, they utterly failed to make any compelling rational or biblical case for such a system, and their view was formally denounced as heresy by the Council of Ephesus in 431.

Yet no sooner was the original wave of Pelagian teaching turned aside than a new movement arose to explain away the seriousness of human depravity—with a more subtle doctrinal sleight of hand. While formally acknowledging that Adam's sin in some measure infected and disabled all his offspring, this view insisted that sinners nevertheless have just enough freedom of will left to make the first motion of faith toward God without the aid of divine grace. Today, we commonly refer to this view as *Semi-Pelagianism*, because it is something of a middle position between the views of Augustine and Pelagius. The name is a more recent coinage, dating back to the early Reformation, but the idea first arose not long after the Pelagian controversy began.

The gist of Semi-Pelagianism is that human depravity, while real, is not really *total*. Sinners are still good enough to be able to lay hold of saving grace on their own. Saving grace, therefore, is a response to human initiative rather than the efficient cause of our salvation.

The central principle underlying Semi-Pelagianism has been denounced by several church councils, starting with the Second Council of Orange in 529.[4] But numerous influential teachers through-out church history have proposed variations and modifications, trying to avoid being labeled Pelagian or Semi-Pelagian but still seeking a way to prop up the notion that human free will is in some way the hinge on which the salvation of sinners turns.

Arminianism takes precisely that approach. This view, of course, arose in reaction to Calvinism; it wasn't a significant factor until some fifty years after John Calvin's death. But in order to understand the various ways people have tried to avoid the implications of total deprav-ity, it might be helpful to summarize Arminianism before we examine Calvin's doctrine of total depravity in closer detail.

The Arminian position is based on a slight modification of the Semi-Pelagian principle. (In fact, many who call themselves Arminians today are actually Pelagians or Semi-Pelagians.) No true Arminian would deliberately deny that Adam's sin left his progeny depraved and in bondage to sin. But according to the Arminian scheme, a measure of "prevenient grace" has been universally granted to sinners, nullifying or mitigating the effects of the fall. It's not enough grace for salvation, but just enough to restore a small measure of volitional liberty to the sinner. Therefore, Arminians believe it is now possible for sinners who hear the gospel to make their own free-will choice about whether to receive it.

In other words, universal prevenient grace renders sin's bondage moot and restores free will to the sinner. So the Arminian scheme (just like Semi-Pelagianism) gives lip service to the doctrines of origi-nal sin and humanity's universal fallenness, but in practice it portrays the actual condition of fallen sinners as something less than *total* depravity.

CALVIN'S POSITION

Now let's go back in our thinking to a few generations before the time of Calvin. Pelagianizing influences in the medieval church had eclipsed the biblical stress on the sinner's depravity for some five hundred years.[5] But a century and a half before Calvin, a number of key writers, theologians, and early Reformers rediscovered and revived Augustine's position on the sinner's helplessness and the primacy of divine grace. It is not without significance that virtually all the early Reformers and their immediate predecessors were thoroughgoing Augustinians (including John Hus, John Wycliffe, William Tyndale, and Martin Luther). All of them emphasized the biblical and Augustinian principle of total depravity—and thus they stressed the sinner's total inability to repent and believe without the prior intervention of divine grace.

Calvin likewise affirmed that human depravity utterly destroys human free will and leaves sinners hopelessly in thrall to sin. He emphatically rejected every Pelagian and Semi-Pelagian attempt to tone down the seriousness of the human plight. He pointed out that the language Scripture employs to describe sin's effect on human nature leaves no room for thinking sinners have any capability to turn their own hearts to God. The Bible says sinners' hearts are "deceitful above all things, and desperately sick" (Jer. 17:9). Sinners themselves are "dead in . . . trespasses and sins" (Eph. 2:1, 5). They are blind to the truth of God (2 Cor. 4:4; cf. 3:14). They are no more able to do good than an Ethiopian can change his skin or a leopard can alter its spots (Jer. 13:23). And divine grace does not merely grant freedom of volition to the sinner; it resurrects him from spiritual death, draws him irresistibly to Christ, and grants him faith to believe (Eph. 2:4–10; Col. 2:13; John 6:44–45, 65).

It is impossible to overstate the importance of the doctrine of total depravity in Calvin's theology. It is the starting point and the logical linchpin for both anthropology and soteriology in the Calvinist system. It is a point to which Calvin invariably refers, no matter what other doctrine is under discussion. For example, his magnum opus, the *Institutes of the Christian Religion,* begins with an entire volume on the knowledge of God. But Calvin's very first point is that a true knowledge of oneself is inextricably related to a right understanding of God. So in the opening paragraph of that massive work, he makes a pointed reference to human depravity: "From the feeling of our own ignorance, vanity, poverty, infirmity, and—what is more—depravity and corruption, we recognize that the true light of wisdom, sound virtue, full abundance of every good, and purity of righteousness rest in God alone. To this extent we are prompted by our own ills to contemplate the good things of God."[6] Throughout that volume, Calvin returns again and again to the issue of total depravity, continually stressing the truth that sinners "never consider God at all unless compelled to; and they do not come nigh until they are dragged there despite their resistance."[7]

THE BONDAGE OF THE WILL

Scripture compares the sinner's plight to several irreversible conditions—death, total blindness, hopeless slavery, utter hardness of heart, permanent dullness of hearing, and incurable sickness. Of these, Calvin stressed the idea of slavery more than any other, placing the strongest accent on the bondage of the will. The volitional inability of sinners to love God, obey Him, or believe in Him was, in Calvin's view, the heart of the doctrine of depravity.

In his own brief summary of major doctrines designed for simple readers who couldn't fully digest the *Institutes,* Calvin dealt with depravity under the heading "Free Will." He wrote:

> The Scripture testifies often that man is a slave of sin. The Scripture means thereby that man's spirit is so alienated from the justice of God that man conceives, covets, and undertakes nothing that is not evil, perverse, iniquitous, and soiled. Because the heart, totally imbued with the poison of sin, can emit nothing but the fruits of sin. Yet one must not infer therefrom that man sins as constrained

by violent necessity. For, man sins with the consent of a very prompt and inclined will. But because man, by the corruption of his affections, very strongly keeps hating the whole righteousness of God and, on the other hand, is fervent in all kinds of evil, it is said that he has not the free power of choosing between good and evil—which is called free will.[8]

Calvin's most detailed discussion of the bondage of the will is found in book 2, chapter 2 of the *Institutes*. This chapter, together with chapter 3 (titled "Only Damnable Things Come Forth from Man's Corrupt Nature"), constitutes the very heart of Calvin's teaching on human depravity.

He starts the section on the human will (after a brief warning about the pitfalls of the subject) with a short survey of philosophers' opinions on the subject. He notes that philosophers generally describe the will as an arbiter between feeling and reason, and they usually admit the difficulty of governing the will by the mind rather than the emotions. Yet, Calvin observes, they inconsistently tend to treat the notion of free will as a certainty—as if "virtues and vices are in our power."[9]

Next, Calvin turns to church history and traces how Christianity's earliest writers dealt with the topic of our bondage to sin. Calvin, who was thoroughly familiar with the writings of the church fathers, observes that they tended to be unclear and naive on the question of free will. Though they knew and acknowledged Scripture's language about sin's utter dominion over sinners' hearts and minds, they often failed to appreciate the full import of how sin cripples the human will. In his words, "[They] recognized both that the soundness of reason in man is gravely wounded through sin, and that the will has been very much enslaved by evil desires. Despite this, many of them have come far too close to the philosophers."[10] Specifically, Calvin complained that too many writers in the early church severely understated the effects of sin on the sinner's power to choose between good and evil. Calvin notes, however, that the church fathers nevertheless consistently stressed the necessity of divine grace to assist fallen men to do good.

Calvin's survey is instructive, showing how the post-apostolic church's understanding of depravity "gradually fell from bad to worse, until it came to the point that man was commonly thought to be corrupted only in his sensual part and to have a perfectly unblemished reason and a will unimpaired."[11] Calvin also suggests that the term "free will" was too often bandied about without definition.

In this context, Calvin plainly states his appreciation for the clarity Augustine brought to this issue in the aftermath of the Pelagian controversy. Borrowing strongly from Augustine, Calvin shows how the human will is (in a very narrow sense) "free"—in that fallen sinners are under no external compulsion to sin. In other words, we cannot cite our enslavement to sin as an excuse for sin's guilt. On the other hand, because our choices are governed by our desires and our desires are corrupt, our wills are by no means "free" in any absolute sense. We are slaves of whom we obey (Rom. 6:16), and therefore in our fallen state we are stuck in a perfect bondage to sin from which we are helpless to extricate ourselves.

Calvin's position on the matter may be best summed up in a quotation he cites from Augustine:

[Why] do miserable men either dare to boast of free will before they have been freed, or of their powers, if they have already been freed? . . . If, therefore, they are slaves of sin, why do they boast of free will? For a man becomes the slave of him who has overcome him. Now, if they have been freed, why do they boast as if it had come about through their own effort? Or are they so free as not to wish to be the slaves of Him who says: "Without me, you can do nothing" [John 15:5]?[12]

Incidentally, both Augustine and Calvin are echoing a major theme of the New Testament: that when sinners become believers, they are released from sin's enslavement in order to become slaves of Christ (Rom. 6:17–18). A clear understanding of that truth is essential to understanding what it means to follow Christ.[13] And, in turn, the concept of being a slave to Christ can be fully understood only by someone who truly grasps what it means to be enslaved to sin. So the point Calvin is making about depravity and the bondage of the will is a vital truth.

HOW IS DEPRAVITY "TOTAL"?

The phrase "total depravity" (not an expression of Calvin's but a phrase descriptive of his view) has an unfortunate ambiguity about it. Many who are exposed to that terminology for the first time suppose it means Calvin taught that all sinners are as thoroughly bad as they possibly can be.

But Calvin expressly disclaimed that view. He acknowledged that "in every age there have been persons who, guided by nature, have striven toward virtue throughout life."[14] Calvin suggested that such people (even though there are "lapses . . . in their moral conduct"[15]) are of commendable character, from a human point of view. "They have by the very zeal of their honesty given proof that there was some purity in their nature."[16] He went even further: "These examples, accordingly, *seem* to warn us against adjudging man's nature wholly corrupted, because some men have by its prompting not only excelled in remarkable deeds, but conducted themselves most honorably throughout life."[17]

Nevertheless, Calvin went on to say, such thinking actually points the wrong direction. Instead, "it ought to occur to us that amid this corruption of nature there is some place for God's grace; not such grace as to cleanse it, but to restrain it inwardly."[18]

Calvin was describing here what later theologians called "common grace"—the divine restraining influence that mitigates the effects of our sin and enables even fallen creatures to display—never perfectly, but always in a weak and severely blemished way—the image of God that is still part of our human nature, marred though it was by the fall.

In other words, depravity is "total" in the sense that it infects every part of our being—not the body only; not the feelings alone; but flesh, spirit, mind, emotions, desires, motives, and will together. We're not always as bad as we can be, but that is solely because of God's restraining grace. We ourselves are thoroughly depraved, because in one way or another sin taints everything we think, do, and desire. Thus, we never fear God the way we should, we never love Him as much as we ought, and we never obey Him with a totally pure heart. That, for Calvin, is what depravity means.

Calvin's thorough treatment of human depravity is one of his most important legacies. Next to his work on the doctrine of justification by faith, it may be the most vital aspect of his doctrinal system. He brought clarity to a crucial principle that had practically fallen into obscurity over the centuries since Augustine's conflict with Pelagius: *to magnify human free will or minimize the extent of human depravity is to downplay the need for divine grace, and that undermines every aspect of gospel truth.*

Once a person truly grasps the truth of human depravity, the more difficult and controversial principles of Calvinist soteriology fall into place. Unconditional election, the primacy and efficacy of saving grace, the need for substitutionary atonement, and the perseverance of those whom God graciously redeems are all necessary consequences of this principle.

While this brief chapter cannot be any more than an introduction and short summary of Calvin's work on the doctrine of depravity, we can see in his handling of this issue all the best aspects of the great Reformer's ministry and approach to Bible doctrine. Here is Calvin at his very finest—thoroughly knowledgeable about church history, human philosophy, and the best aspects of Christian tradition, but steadfastly and unconditionally determined to submit his mind and his teaching to the truth of Scripture. His uncanny ability to grapple with hard issues candidly, explain his view simply, and support the truth biblically is never seen more powerfully or put to better use than in his landmark treatment of total depravity.

NOTES

---

[1] John Calvin, *Instruction in Faith (1537)*, trans. Paul T. Fuhrmann (London: Lutterworth, 1949), 22.

[2] G. K. Chesterton, *Orthodoxy* (Garden City, N.J.: Doubleday, 1959), 15.

[3] Pelagius' famous complaint was a response to a short section in book 10 of Augustine's *Confessions* (ch. 29, para. 40), in which Augustine expresses his deep gratitude for divine grace and acknowledges that he can obey God only if God Himself graciously enables and empowers him. Then Augustine prays, "Give what You command, and command what You will." This was an explicit acknowledgement that the will of a sinner is in no sense "free." Augustine later recorded that Pelagius was livid and became instantly argumentative when that paragraph was read to him.

[4] The Council of Orange unfortunately muddied matters by suggesting that "the grace of baptism" automatically frees people from the bondage of sin. But the council nonetheless recognized that the fall utterly destroyed both Adam's and his offspring's liberty of will, and that only God's grace can free sinners from that condition. Orange's Canon 13 says: "The freedom of will that was destroyed in the first man can be restored only by [grace], for what is lost can be returned only by the one who was able to give it. Hence the Truth itself declares: 'So if the Son makes you free, you will be free indeed' (John 8:36)."

The Council of Trent in the mid-1500s took precisely the position condemned by Orange and declared it the magisterial Roman Catholic view. Canon 5 of Trent's sixth session (on justification) says this: "If any one saith, that, since Adam's sin, the free will of man is lost and extinguished . . . let him be anathema." In effect, Trent affirmed a variety of semi-Pelagianism and made it binding Catholic dogma.

[5] John McNeill writes, "After Gottschalk of Orbais, who was condemned for heresy in 849, the first eminent representative of unqualified Augustinianism was the scholarly theologian and ecclesiastic, Thomas Bradwardine, called Doctor Profundus, who died immediately after his consecration as archbishop of Canterbury in 1349." John Calvin, *Institutes of the Christian Religion*, ed. John T. McNeill; trans. Ford Lewis Battles; Library of Christian Classics, XX–XXI (Philadelphia: Westminster John Knox, 1960), 1:lvii.

[6] Ibid., 1.1.1.

[7] Ibid., 1.4.4.

[8] Calvin, *Instruction in Faith (1537)*, 22.

[9] Calvin, *Institutes of the Christian Religion*, 2.2.3.

[10] Ibid., 2.2.4.

[11] Ibid.

[12] Ibid., 2.2.8.

[13] There is insufficient space to develop the theme of our slavery to Christ here, but I have dealt with it in some detail in chapter 1, "What Does Jesus Mean When He Says, 'Follow

Me?'" in the anniversary edition of my book *The Gospel According to Jesus* (Grand Rapids: Zondervan, 2008).

[14] Calvin, *Institutes of the Christian Religion*, 2.3.3.

[15] Ibid.

[16] Ibid.

[17] Ibid., emphasis added.

[18] Ibid.

Chapter 12

ELECTION AND REPROBATION

RICHARD D. PHILLIPS

We have it from the words of the apostle that the salvation of believers has been founded upon the decision of divine election alone, and that this favor is not earned by works but comes from free calling. [1]

—JOHN CALVIN

John Calvin is probably known today more for his teaching of predestination than for anything else. However, in popular culture, his doctrine usually is represented as a dark and gloomy fatalism. As a lifelong Boston Red Sox baseball fan, I have read countless sports columns decrying the "Calvinistic pessimism" of the Red Sox fan base (if anything, it was Calvinistic *optimism* that kept Sox fans going in the long decades between championships). In the Christian subculture, Calvinists are looked on as those with a highbrow theological bent, exemplified above all in their adherence to the reason-shattering doctrine of election.

It is a shame that Calvin's reputation is so narrowly linked with the doctrine of predestination, also known as election. Calvin's contributions far surpassed the horizons of any one doctrine, and even of doctrine as a whole, as I hope this book has demonstrated. And yet, to those who know and appreciate Calvin's thought, his identification with election is not to his shame but his glory. Whenever I am asked, "Do you, a Calvinist, really believe in predestination?" I always answer in two ways. First, I say, "Being a Calvinist means a lot more than believing in election." But then I hasten to add, "But I most certainly do believe the wonderful doctrine of predestination, and I praise the Lord for the legacy of John Calvin in promoting this most God-glorifying and soul-elevating truth."

CALVIN'S DOCTRINE OF ELECTION

In this short study of Calvin's doctrine of election, the place to begin is with his own words. First, with respect to those who are saved, i.e., the elect, Calvin taught that the ultimate cause of their salvation is the sovereign choice (election) and predestination of God. Likewise, when it comes to those who are not saved and finally are condemned, the ultimate cause is also God's sovereign predestination. This is true because God's sovereign decree is the ultimate cause of all things. Calvin writes: "We call predestination God's eternal decree, by which he compacted with himself what he willed to become of each man. . . . Eternal life is foreordained for some, eternal damnation for others. Therefore, as any man has been created to one or the other of these ends, we speak of him as predestined to life or to death."[2]

Moreover, Calvin asserts that the reason behind God's predestination of individuals rests in God and not in the creature. In other words, the elect are chosen by God apart from any positive consideration in themselves. This is why Calvin's doctrine is known as *unconditional election*. The same goes for reprobation: the reprobate, or the non-elect, are passed over by God's grace for reasons ultimately found only in God's decree. Calvin explains, "We assert that, with respect to the elect, this plan was founded upon his freely given mercy, without regard to human worth; but by his just and irreprehensible but incomprehensible judgment he has barred the door of life to those whom he has given over to damnation."[3]

This does not mean that the reprobate will be judged without reference to their transgressions, for their condemnation will be perfectly just. Rather, having first ordained that all mankind should fall into sin (Rom. 11:32), and through sin into judgment, God also decreed that certain persons would be chosen for salvation through faith in Jesus Christ. All destinies, Calvin asserts, flow from God's eternal and sovereign decree, the governing principle being God's own perfect will. Calvin cites the apostle Paul's statement that election is "according to the purpose of his will" (Eph. 1:5) and "his purpose" (Eph. 1:9). Calvin comments: "For to say that 'God purposed in himself' means the same thing as to say that he considered nothing outside himself with which to be concerned in making his decree. Therefore [Paul] adds at once that the whole intent of our election is that we should be to the praise of divine grace (cf. Eph. 1:6)."[4]

Recognizing the difficulty many have with this doctrine, Calvin often urged prudence in the study of predestination. Careless and unbiblical speculation should be strictly avoided. To this end, Calvin issues a warning that many of both his followers and his detractors would have done better to heed: "If anyone with carefree assurance breaks into this place, he will not succeed in satisfying his curiosity and he will enter a labyrinth from which he can find no exit."[5]

A BIBLICAL DOCTRINE

Because of his concern for the faithful and prudent handling of doctrine, Calvin's approach to predestination was carefully and rigorously biblical. One will occasionally hear Calvin charged with rationalism in his doctrine of election, but nothing could be further from the truth. The sole reason that Calvin insisted on teaching a doctrine so likely to give offense was his commitment to the plain teaching of Holy Scripture. He writes in this context, "the Word of the Lord is the sole way that can lead us in our search for all that is lawful to hold concerning him, and is the sole light to illumine our vision of all that we should see of him."[6] Moreover, in constructing the contours of his doctrine of predestination, Calvin was scrupulously determined to follow the Scriptures wherever they went, but no further: "Let this, therefore, first of all be before our eyes: to seek any other knowledge of predestination than what the Word of God discloses is not less insane than if one should purpose to walk in a pathless waste (cf. Job 12:24), or to see in darkness. And let us not be ashamed to be ignorant of something in this matter, wherein there is a certain learned ignorance."[7]

This commitment to Scripture addresses the question of the necessity of teaching predestination. In our day, sermon series on the book of Romans often cease after chapter 8. And how many studies of Ephesians have omitted chapter 1 for fear of the "controversy" of teaching predestination? Calvin's response was instructive of his whole approach to doctrine, namely, that Christians have a duty to know and believe all that God has seen fit to teach us in the Scriptures. Therefore the teachers of the church have no right to withhold anything taught in the Bible.

Calvin was sympathetic to the motive behind the hesitation to teach predestination, writing, "Their moderation in this matter is rightly to be praised, because they feel that these mysteries ought to be discussed with great soberness." Nonetheless, he countered, "because they descend to too low a level, they make little progress with the human understanding, which does not allow itself to be easily restrained."[8] People are bound to wonder about God's foreordination and will, Calvin insists, so they should be instructed soundly from the Scriptures rather than be left open to vain speculation. Moreover, he argues, it is irreverent for any creature to disdain matters thought necessary for us by the Holy Spirit:

For Scripture is the school of the Holy Spirit, in which, as nothing is omitted that is both necessary and useful to know, so nothing is taught but what is expedient to know. Therefore we must guard against depriving believers of anything disclosed about predestination in Scripture, lest we seem either wickedly to defraud them of the blessing of their God or to accuse and scoff at the Holy Spirit for having published what it is in any way profitable to suppress.[9]

It is not surprising, then, that Calvin defended his doctrine of predestination by direct appeal to the Scriptures and the necessary implications thereof.

On what basis does Calvin teach predestination? First, he points to Israel's national election in the Old Testament. He appeals to Deuteronomy 7:6b–8a, which asserts that Israel was chosen only because of God's electing love: "The LORD your God has chosen you to be a people for his treasured possession, out of all the peoples who are on the face of the earth. It was not because you were more in number than any other people that the LORD set his love on you and chose you . . . but it is because the LORD loves you." Among many other texts, Calvin also cites Psalm 47:4a, "He chose our heritage for us," and Psalm 33:12, "Blessed is the nation whose God is the LORD, the people whom he has chosen as his heritage."

Calvin recognizes that there is a difference between God's election of Israel as a nation and the predestination of individuals for salvation. Therefore, he points to "a second, more limited degree of election, or one in which God's more special grace was evident, that is, when from the same race of Abraham God rejected some but showed that he kept others among his sons by cherishing them in the church."[10] That is, the Bible plainly shows that God discriminates between individuals by sovereign election and predestination. Calvin's primary examples are Ishmael/Isaac and Esau/Jacob. He admits that Ishmael and Esau, whom God rejected, deserved to be condemned by God, "for the condition had been laid down that they should faithfully keep God's covenant, which they faithlessly violated."[11] But the same easily could be said of Isaac and Jacob. When the Bible explains this matter, it attributes God's distinction solely to the sovereign predestination of God. God says through Malachi: "Is not Esau Jacob's brother? . . . Yet I have loved Jacob but Esau I have hated" (Mal. 1:2b–3a). This is, of course, the text cited by the apostle Paul to state the doctrine of predestination:

> When Rebecca had conceived children by one man, our forefather Isaac, though they were not yet born and had done nothing either good or bad—in order that God's purpose of election might continue, not because of works but because of his call—she was told, "The older will serve the younger." As it is written, "Jacob I loved, but Esau I hated." (Rom. 9:10–13)

Calvin therefore comments: "We have it from the words of the apostle that the salvation of believers has been founded upon the decision of divine election alone, and that this favor is not earned by works but comes from free calling. . . . Jacob, therefore, is chosen and distinguished from the rejected Esau by God's predestination, while not differing from him in merits."[12] When pressed for a clear explanation, Calvin observes, Paul makes this very point: "For [God] says to Moses, 'I will have mercy on whom I have mercy, and I will have compassion on whom I have compassion'" (Rom. 9:15). This, says Calvin, "is simply the Lord's clear declaration that he finds in men themselves no reason to bless them but takes it from his mercy alone."[13]

Those who find Calvin's doctrine of predestination hard to swallow will see his doctrine of reprobation as even more difficult. Yet here, too, Calvin's doctrine arises strictly from the Scriptures. In this regard, Calvin makes the unavoidable observation that saving election and sovereign reprobation are mutually required: "Election itself could not stand except as set over against reprobation."[14] When it comes to predestination, it is truly double or nothing: unless God predestines both salvation and damnation, He predestines neither. Yet, as noted above,

Calvin's argument is not based merely on reason. He argues from the Scriptures, especially Paul's handling of this matter in Romans 9.

Following Paul, Calvin points out that Scripture ascribes Pharaoh's hardening of heart specifically to God's sovereign action: "For the Scripture says to Pharaoh, 'For this very purpose I have raised you up, that I might show my power in you, and that my name might be proclaimed in all the earth'" (Rom. 9:17). Calvin notes that "Paul does not . . . labor anxiously to make false excuses in God's defense; he only warns that it is unlawful for the clay to quarrel with its potter."[15] This quote is a reference to the analogy Paul employs to defend his teaching: "Will what is molded say to its molder, 'Why have you made me like this?'" (Rom. 9:20b). Calvin further notes that some would seek to soften predestination by observing that all the reprobate are condemned justly, so that God merely permits their damnation. Calvin responds by citing Augustine: "Where might is joined to long-suffering, God does not permit but governs by his power."[16] Calvin further urges that since Paul insists that God "prepared" the reprobate "for destruction" (Rom. 9:22), "it is utterly inconsistent to transfer the preparation for destruction to anything but God's secret plan."[17] Thus, Calvin demonstrates from Scripture that both salvation and reprobation result from the sovereign and eternal decree of God.

ANSWERS TO OBJECTIONS

In responding to objections to predestination, Calvin displays his typical vast reading and extensive experience, dealing with a great many challenges and arguments. For brevity's sake, I will consider only those most frequently heard today.

First among these is the assertion that election is based on God's foreknowledge. This approach seeks to counter Calvin's doctrine of election by asserting that God foresees which people will believe His Word in the future, then predestines them for salvation on that basis. Likewise, God foreknows those who will not believe, and thus elects them for condemnation. Calvin explains, "These persons consider that God distinguishes among men according as he foresees what the merits of each will be."[18]

In reply, Calvin first notes that the true issue involves the origin of salvation. Under the foreknowledge view, God's grace finds its origin in the worthiness of the recipient; since God can give grace only in response to foreseen merit, it is not His freely to give. But the Bible presents a different picture: as Calvin states, "God has always been free to bestow his grace on whom he wills."[19]

Calvin then unfolds the teaching of Scripture, which insists that salvation originates not in the worthiness of the recipient but in the free grace of God. He notes that the Bible's teaching that God chose His people before the creation of the world (Eph. 1:4) clearly means merit plays no part in their election. We are chosen "in Christ"—since we have nothing in ourselves to commend us to God's grace, God views us by our union with Christ. This shows that the elect possess no merit of their own for God to foresee. In fact, Calvin says, Ephesians 1:4 declares that "all virtue appearing in man is the result of election."[20]

Here, then, is the question: is our faith the *cause* or the *result* of our election? If we are elected because of foreseen faith, then we can make no sense of Paul's teaching: "He chose us in [Christ] before the foundation of the world, that we should be holy and blameless before him" (Eph. 1:4). As Calvin explains, the foreknowledge objection inverts the order of Paul's reasoning: "If he chose us that we should be holy, he did not choose us because he foresaw that we would be so."[21] This is abundantly confirmed in Paul's subsequent teaching, when he states that our election is "according to the purpose of his will" (Eph. 1:5) and "according to his purpose" (Eph. 1:9). Paul uses similar language in 2 Timothy 1:9, writing that God "saved us and called us to a holy calling, not because of our works but because of his own purpose and grace." Preaching on this text, Calvin asserts: "He saith not that God hath chosen us because we have heard the gospel, but on the other hand, he attributes the faith that is given us to the highest cause; to wit, because God hath fore-ordained that He would save us."[22] Therefore, instead of teaching that salvation originates in what God foresees in us, Calvin insists, "all benefits that God bestows for the spiritual life, as Paul teaches, flow from this one source: namely, that God has chosen whom he has willed, and before their birth has laid up for them individually the grace that he willed to grant them."[23]

Another common objection is the charge that predestination is unjust. People complain that if the reprobate are predestined to sin and condemnation, then it is not fair for God to hold them accountable for their actions. Calvin counters by arguing the impudence of any charge of injustice toward God, for the simple reason that God is Himself the only standard of justice. "For God's will," he writes, "is so much the highest rule of righteousness that whatever he wills, by the very fact that he wills it, must be considered righteous." To use some standard of justice to judge God is "seeking something greater and higher than God's will, which cannot be found."[24]

Moreover, the condemnation of the reprobate is, in fact, just. But were they not predestined to this? Calvin's rejoinder is eloquent, pointing out how alien to Scripture is this line of argument: "Let all the sons of Adam come forward; let them quarrel and argue with their Creator that they were by his eternal providence bound over before their begetting to everlasting calamity. What clamor can they raise against this defense when God, on the contrary, will call them to their account before him."[25]

Calvin observes that Paul plainly ascribes reprobation to God's predestining decree, saying that God the Potter has made some vessels "for dishonorable use" and "prepared" them "for destruction" (Rom. 9:21–22). Yet the Scriptures never allow sinful man to use this truth as an excuse to escape from just condemnation. "Is [God] not, then, unjust who so cruelly deludes his creatures?"[26] Calvin asks rhetorically. His answer is none other than Paul's own: "Who are you, O man, to answer back to God?" (Rom. 9:20a). As Calvin puts it, "The apostle did not look for loopholes of escape as if he were embarrassed in his argument but showed that the reason of divine righteousness is higher than man's standard can measure, or than man's slender wit can comprehend."[27]

Moreover, when we consider the salvation of the elect, justice is simply the wrong category. Justice offers only condemnation, since "all have sinned and fall short of the glory of God" (Rom. 3:23). It is not as if God looked down on a neutral humanity, deciding to make some believe and others reject him. Rather, he looked on a humanity already guilty in sin and unbelief. Calvin writes, "If all are drawn from a corrupt mass, no wonder they are subject to condemnation!"[28] This is why election is "in Christ"—it is joined with God's intention to send His Son to die for the sins of the elect. God passes by some sinful rebels, allowing them to continue in their chosen, hell-bound course to the praise of His justice. Others He saves to the glory of His mercy, for as Paul says in Romans 9:16, "It depends not on human will or exertion, but on God, who has mercy." Those who object to this, Calvin states, "so act toward [God] as if either mercy were to be forbidden to him or as if when he wills to show mercy he is compelled to renounce his judgment completely."[29]

Lastly, some object that predestination renders the Bible's admonitions meaningless. Calvin considered this a "malicious" and "shameless" misrepresentation of the Bible's doctrine.[30] He first appeals to the example of Paul: "What a plain and outspoken preacher of free election Paul was has previously been seen. Was he therefore cold in admonition and exhortation? Let these good zealots compare their earnestness with his: theirs will be found ice compared with his intense fervor."[31] The same might be said of Christ:

> Christ commands us to believe in him. Yet when he says, "No one can come to me unless it has been granted him by my Father" (Jn. 6:65), his statement is neither false nor contrary to his command. Let preaching, then, take its course that it may lead men to faith, and hold them fast in perseverance with continuing profit. And yet let not the knowledge of predestination be hindered, in order that

those who obey may not be proud as of something of their own but may glory in the Lord.[32]

But might not believing that all depends on God's predestination lead us to slothfulness and promote sin? Calvin admits, "there are many swine that pollute the doctrine of predestination with their foul blasphemies, and by this pretext evade all admonitions and reproofs."[33] But a proper consideration of election will show that we are chosen to be holy (cf. Eph. 1:4). Therefore, "if election has as its goal holiness of life, it ought rather to arouse and goad us eagerly to set our mind upon it than to serve as a pretext for doing nothing. What a great difference there is between these two things: to cease well-doing because election is sufficient for salvation, and to devote ourselves to the pursuit of good as the appointed goal of election!"[34]

ADVANTAGES OF PREDESTINATION

It is sometimes assumed that predestination must promote pride in its adherents. But according to Calvin, one of the chief virtues of the doctrine is its humbling effect on the hearts of believers. In the Old Testament, Israel was informed of its election primarily for this purpose: "in order more effectively to crush all pride, he reproaches them as deserving no such thing, since they were a stubborn and stiff-necked people (Ex. 32:9; cf. Dt. 9:6)."[35] The true root of godly humility is gratitude for free and unmerited grace, Calvin insists, "For neither will anything else suffice to make us humble as we ought to be nor shall we otherwise sincerely feel how much we are obliged to God."[36]

The doctrine of predestination is so humbling because it does not ascribe salvation to any merit in the Christian, but fully embraces the Bible's teaching of our total depravity. It says that unless salvation is wholly of God, none could be saved, so great is mankind's sin and enmity to the things of God. As Calvin preached in a sermon on 1 Timothy 2:3–5: "Thus we see how profitable this doctrine of election is to us: it serveth to humble us, knowing that our salvation hangeth not upon our deserts, neither upon the virtue which God might have found in us: but upon the election that was made before we were born, before we could do either good or evil."[37]

Calvin also saw the doctrine of predestination as possessing great pastoral value, especially in rightly grounding our assurance of salvation. But first he warned against a vain and dangerous attempt to base our assurance on direct knowledge of God's decree. One must not attempt, he writes, "to break into the inner recesses of divine wisdom . . . in order to find out what decision has been made concerning himself at God's judgment seat."[38] No mere creature has direct access to God's eternal counsel, so to seek assurance through knowledge of election is to be dashed against the rocks like a shipwrecked mariner.

So how does the doctrine of election contribute to assurance? Calvin preached: "How do we know that God has elected us before the creation of the world? By believing in Jesus Christ. . . . Whosoever then believes is thereby assured that God has worked in him, and faith is, as it were, the duplicate copy that God gives us of the original of our adoption. God has his eternal counsel, and he always reserves to himself the chief and original record of which he gives us a copy by faith."[39] Election is always "in Christ" (Eph. 1:4), so the distinguishing mark of the elect is their union with Christ in faith. "Therefore," Calvin explains, "if we desire to know whether God cares for our salvation, let us inquire whether he has entrusted us to Christ, whom he has established as the sole Savior of all his people."[40]

On this basis, true believers can and should look to the future without anxiety, knowing that their faith in Christ testifies to their eternal election. But this does not encourage presumptuous abuse of our privileges, since apart from discipleship to Christ our grounds for confidence vanish. Most importantly, Christians look for perseverance in faith not to themselves but to the promise of Christ: "This is the will of him who sent me, that I should lose nothing of all that he has given me, but raise it up on the last day" (John 6:39). Likewise, we rely for our perseverance in faith on the determination of God's sovereign will, since, Paul writes, "He who began a good work in you will bring it to completion at the day of Jesus Christ" (Phil. 1:6).

How many Christians stumble on in weakness, burdened with doubts that would be erased if only they knew their salvation rested not in themselves but in God? The doctrine of election tells us that it was God who sought us and not we who sought Him; that God called us to Himself in time because He chose us in eternity. No longer seeking confidence in a decision we have made or in our feeble resolves for the future, we put our confidence in God, as Paul insists: "God's firm foundation stands, bearing this seal: 'The Lord knows those who are his'" (2 Tim. 2:19a). Notice Calvin's pastoral sensitivity as he preaches on this theme:

> We are as birds upon the boughs, and set forth as a prey to Satan. What assurance then could we have of tomorrow, and of all our life; yea, and after death, were it not that God, who hath called us, will end His work as He hath begun it. How hath He gathered us together in the faith of His gospel? Is it grounded upon us? Nay, entirely to the contrary; it proceedeth from His free election. Therefore; we may be so much the more freed from doubt.[41]

A GOD-GLORIFYING DOCTRINE

It is evident that Calvin considered the doctrine of predestination to be of great value in humbling Christians, while giving them a firm ground for assurance of salvation. But anyone who reads Calvin on this topic will realize quickly that he sees the chief virtue of predestination lying elsewhere. This doctrine's main benefit is in ascribing all the praise and glory of salvation where it belongs: to God alone. Calvin cites his beloved Augustine in asserting the chief reason why predestination must be preached: "that he who has ears to hear of God's grace may glory, not in himself but in God."[42] This is precisely the note with which the apostle Paul concluded his long section in Romans dealing with

153

God's sovereign decree: "For from him and through him and to him are all things. To him be glory forever. Amen" (Rom. 11:36).

God purposed salvation; He planned it; He chose us and now in Christ He has saved us. All our spiritual blessings and an eternity in glory are because of His wonderful sovereign grace. As noted Calvinist preacher James Montgomery Boice put it in a hymn:

Since grace is the source of the life that is mine—
and faith is a gift from on high—
I'll boast in my Savior, all merit decline,
and glorify God 'til I die.[43]

Calvin asserts, "The goodness of God shall never be thoroughly known until this election be laid before us; and we are taught that we are called at this time, because it pleased God to extend His mercy to us before we were born." Therefore, he urges, in words as appropriate for the twenty-first century as for his own sixteenth century, "This doctrine must be explained more at large."[44]

NOTES

[1] John Calvin, *Institutes of the Christian Religion*, ed. John T. McNeill; trans. Ford Lewis Battles; Library of Christian Classics, XX–XXI (Philadelphia: Westminster John Knox, 1960), 3.21.3.

[2] Ibid., 3.21.5.

[3] Ibid., 3.21.7.

[4] Ibid., 3.22.3.

[5] Ibid., 3.21.1.

[6] Ibid., 3.21.2.

[7] Ibid.

[8] Ibid., 3.21.3.

[9] Ibid.

[10] Ibid., 3.21.6.

[11] Ibid.

[12] Ibid., 3.22.5–6.

[13] Ibid., 3.22.6.

[14] Ibid., 3.23.1.

[15] Ibid.

[16] Ibid.

[17] Ibid.

[18] Ibid., 3.22.1.

[19] Ibid.

[20] Ibid., 3.22.2.

[21] Ibid., 3.22.3.

[22] John Calvin, *The Mystery of Godliness and Other Sermons* (1830; repr. Morgan, Pa.: Soli Deo Gloria, 1999), 46.

[23] Calvin, *Institutes of the Christian Religion*, 3.22.2.

[24] Ibid., 3.23.2.

[25] Ibid., 3.23.3.

[26] Ibid., 3.23.4.

[27] Ibid.

[28] Ibid., 3.23.3.

[29] Ibid., 3.23.11.

[30] Ibid., 3.23.13.

[31] Ibid.

[32] Ibid.

[33] Ibid., 3.23.12.

[34] Ibid.

[35] Ibid., 3.21.5.

[36] Ibid., 3.21.1.

[37] Calvin, *The Mystery of Godliness*, 103.

[38] Calvin, *Institutes of the Christian Religion*, 3.24.4.

[39] John Calvin, *Sermons on the Epistle to the Ephesians* (1577; repr. Edinburgh: Banner of Truth Trust, 1973), 47.

[40] Calvin, *Institutes of the Christian Religion*, 3.24.6.

[41] Calvin, *The Mystery of Godliness*, 103–104.

[42] Calvin, *Institutes of the Christian Religion*, 3.23.13.

[43] James Montgomery Boice, *Hymns for a Modern Reformation* (Philadelphia: Tenth Presbyterian Church, 2000), 25.

[44] Calvin, *The Mystery of Godliness*, 34–35.

Chapter 13

REDEMPTION DEFINED

THOMAS K. ASCOL

In all the creatures, indeed, both high and low, the glory of God shines, but nowhere has it shone more brightly than in the cross, in which there has been an astonishing change of things, the condemnation of all men has been manifested, sin has been blotted out, salvation has been restored to men; and, in short, the whole world has been renewed, and every thing restored to good order.[1]

—JOHN CALVIN

The crucifixion of Jesus Christ is the hinge on which all biblical revelation turns. Together with the resurrection of Christ, it is the apex of redemptive history. Everything prior to it anticipated it and was calculated by God to set it up and bring it to pass in the right way at the right time. Everything after the death of Jesus derives its meaning and significance from it.

Despite its centrality, the cross remains a "stumbling block" and a "folly" to many who hear of it, but that is because they do not understand its necessity or nature. By contrast, as the apostle Paul teaches, for those who are called, Christ crucified is "the power of God and the wisdom of God" (1 Cor. 1:23–24).

John Calvin deeply appreciated the centrality of the work of Christ. "Our salvation," he stated, "consists in the doctrine of the cross."[2]

His insights help us appreciate why Jesus had to die and what He accomplished.

THE NECESSITY OF ATONEMENT

What makes atonement for sin necessary? Calvin was careful to establish every aspect of salvation on the decree of God so that we might recognize that all that comes to us is by divine mercy and grace. Thus, he rejected the idea that the incarnation and atoning work of Christ were driven by any kind of "absolute necessity."[3] In a sermon on the death of Christ, he declares, "God was well able to rescue us from the unfathomable depths of death in another fashion, but he willed to display the treasures of his infinite goodness when he spared not his only Son."[4]

Given God's gracious determination to save sinners, Calvin established the foundation of our need for atonement in his *Institutes of the Christian Religion* long before he formally addressed the redeeming work of Christ. In fact, the reason atonement is necessary is found in the famous opening line of that work: "Nearly all the wisdom that we possess, that is to say, true and sound wisdom, consists of two parts: the knowledge of God and of ourselves."[5] A superficial knowledge of God and a superficial view of human nature prevent a person from regarding the cross as the saving wisdom of God.

Where God's self-revelation is muted and the biblical testimony about human sin and depravity is rejected, the atoning work of Jesus loses its *raison d'etre*. H. Richard Niebuhr's apt criticism of liberalism shows the close connection; he writes that, in the liberal view, "A God without wrath brought men without sin into a kingdom without judgment through the ministrations of a Christ without a cross."[6]

We can grasp the necessity of the atonement only when we see that the creatures' sin has provoked the wrath of the holy Creator. These two biblical ideas, human depravity and divine wrath, are fundamental to understanding both the necessity and nature of the atonement that was accomplished by the suffering and death of Jesus on the cross.

It would be hard to find an evangelical description of the atonement that does not highlight the love of God in providing it. That emphasis is certainly justified in light of New Testament teaching (John 3:16; Rom. 5:8; 1 John 4:10). However, the glorious reality of God's love in sending His Son to atone for sin must never be construed in a way that negates any of His other attributes, particularly when the work of Jesus on the cross is being considered.

One aspect of God's nature that often is ignored when contemplating the atoning work of Christ is His wrath. Some have difficulty with the concept altogether, believing it to be in conflict with God's love. Divine wrath, however, clearly is taught in both the Old and New Testaments. More than twenty different Hebrew words are used nearly six hundred times in the Old Testament to describe God's wrath.[7] Any inability to reconcile God's love and wrath stems from unbiblical notions of morality. As Leon Morris notes: "It is a necessary part of moral character to abhor evil as well as to love good. God is actively and strongly opposed to all forms of evil; and the biblical writers express this opposition, in part at least, by speaking of the wrath of God."[8]

Divine wrath should not be reduced to the mere natural retribution that occurs in a moral world as if it were some kind of impersonal effect that automatically follows certain causes.[9] Rather, God's wrath is personally and purposefully directed against human sin. Scripture describes God as "angry with the wicked every day" (Ps. 7:11, KJV), as threatening to pour out His wrath and "spend" His anger against people for their "abominations" (Ezek. 7:8), as "burning with his anger" and having "lips . . . full of fury" (Isa. 30:27), and as planning a day of wrath when His righteous judgment will be revealed (Rom. 2:5).

There is nothing capricious about God's wrath. It is simply "his response to sin."[10] This means that there is a predictable consistency about what provokes God to anger. One need not wonder what will arouse divine wrath. When His law is violated, His response to the violator is wrath. Granted, God's wrath is not usually expressed immediately, as it was in the cases of Nadab and Abihu (Lev. 10:1–3), Uzzah (1 Chron.

13:5–11), and Ananias and Sapphira (Acts 5:1–11). Those dramatic displays are illustrative of God's response to sin but, fortunately, are not indicative of how His response is always or even usually executed. It is precisely because God does not always respond immediately in this way to sin that many are skeptical about the whole idea of divine wrath. However, as Paul warns in Romans 2:1–11, those who practice unrighteousness are "storing up wrath for [themselves] on the day of wrath when God's righteous judgment will be revealed."

Calvin explains that even though God does not immediately punish every instance of sin, He "cannot bear injury or wrong" and "will yet be the defender of his own glory." At the right time, God will carry out his judgment against sin. Calvin writes,

> God is not to be rashly judged of on account of his delay, when he does not immediately execute his judgments; for he waits for the seasonable opportunity. But, in the meantime there is no reason for us to think that he forgets his office when he suspends punishment, or for a season spares the ungodly. When, therefore, God does not hasten so very quickly, there is no ground for us to think that he is indifferent, because he delays his wrath, or retains it, as we have already said; for it is the same thing to retain wrath, as to be the Lord of wrath, and to possess it.[11]

God's response toward all sinners is anger and opposition. His wrath is provoked and stored up against all sin.

The distinction that Roman Catholicism makes between venial and mortal sins is baseless. While Protestants rightly reject that kind of distinction theologically, it often subtly informs much of their thinking about sin and judgment. Many are under the false impression that God's wrath in general, or hell in particular, is reserved for those guilty of "major sins," such as Adolf Hitler or Saddam Hussein. Lesser sinners are tempted to hope that their case is significantly different. This is why even the title of Jonathan Edwards' famous sermon, "Sinners in the

Hands of an Angry God," so often evokes scorn. It is assumed that while it might be conceivable that some sinners would be in that horrible position, surely it is not true of all.

To this Calvin answers, "Every sin is a deadly sin!"[12] In saying this, he was merely echoing the prophet Ezekiel, who teaches, "the soul who sins shall die" (18:4, 20), and the apostle Paul, who writes in Romans 6:23, "The wages of sin is death." Calvin exhorts Christians to acknowledge this fundamental, vital point of biblical teaching: "Let the children of God hold that all sin is mortal. For it is rebellion against the will of God, which of necessity provokes God's wrath, and it is a violation of the law, upon which God's judgment is pronounced without exception."[13]

This is true even for those whom God chose before the foundation of the world to receive salvation (Eph. 1:4). Though they are the objects of eternal, divine love, they are nevertheless liable to God's anger because of their sin. Paul reminds the Ephesians of this fact when he writes that Christians were "by nature children of wrath, like the rest of mankind" (2:3). This means that, before their conversion, the elect are both deeply loved by God and at enmity with Him. Calvin explains the matter quite starkly by quoting Augustine after invoking Romans 5:8:

> Therefore, [God] loved us even when we practiced enmity toward him and committed wickedness. Thus in a marvelous and divine way he loved us even when he hated us. For he hated us for what we were that he had not made; yet because our wickedness had not entirely consumed his handiwork, he knew how, at the same time, to hate in each one of us what we had made, and to love what he had made.[14]

This apparent contradiction, or "duality," within God's attitude toward sinners is seen elsewhere in Scripture, most graphically in the book of Hosea. In chapter 11, God speaks passionately both about the wrath Israel justly deserves from Him and the love He has for her, which will not allow Him to "give [her] up" or "hand [her] over" (vv.

8–9). John Stott notes, "We must never think of this duality within God's being as irreconcilable." While we may "find it difficult to hold in our minds simultaneously the images of God as the Judge who must punish evil-doers and the Lover who must find a way to forgive them," nevertheless "he is both, at the same time."[15]

It is because of this duality that atonement had to be secured in the way that it was, by the death of Jesus Christ. For divine love to be fulfilled in the salvation of sinners, someone had to pay for their sins. The holy love of God can be neither compromised nor thwarted. It must be satisfied by the atoning death of one who represents those who are beloved. This is precisely what took place in the crucifixion of Jesus.

THE NATURE OF THE ATONEMENT

The New Testament speaks of the atoning work of Jesus in objective and definite terms. His death on the cross actually accomplished something definitive. When we consider its accomplishment, a clearer understanding of the nature of the atonement emerges.

Three New Testament words are particularly important in explaining what actually took place on the cross—*redemption, propitiation,* and *reconciliation.*

• *Redemption.* Calvin recognized the whole course of Jesus' life as complicit in the work of redemption. He writes, "From the time when he took on the form of a servant, he began to pay the price of liberation in order to redeem us."[16] This was in keeping with Paul's consideration of the whole life of Christ—including his death—as "one man's obedience" by which "the many will be made righteous" (Rom. 5:19). Nevertheless, Scripture does speak more precisely in defining salvation by ascribing redemption as "peculiar and proper to Christ's death."[17]

In the first century, the word *redemption* (Greek, *lutron*) did not have the religious connotation that it does today. It was primarily used to describe deliverance that came through payment.[18] This applied to prisoners of war who were ransomed from captivity, as well as to slaves who were granted freedom through the payment of a set fee. This same idea is found in the Old Testament in the laws governing the redemption of firstborn sons and male animals (Ex. 13:12–13; Num. 3:40–49). Their freedom could be secured through the payment of a price.

In the New Testament, the concept of redemption is found primarily in Paul's writings. He associates it closely with the death of Christ, in whom, he writes, "we have redemption through his blood, the forgiveness of our trespasses" (Eph. 1:7; Col. 1:14; cf. Gal. 3:13). Jesus' work on the cross ("his blood") is the means by which our redemption is accomplished.

This accords perfectly with Jesus' teaching that He came to "give his life as a ransom for many" (Mark 10:45). The freedom that is gained by payment is redemption. The actual payment itself is the ransom, and Jesus says the giving of His life (on the cross) is the payment that results in the deliverance of many.

So the death of Jesus was redemptive. It secured the deliverance of sinners by providing the payment necessary for their deliverance. As Calvin puts it, Christ "made himself a ransom" and thereby provided redemption.[19]

• *Propitiation.* There are only four passages in the New Testament where the word *propitiation* is used in particular connection with the atoning work of Jesus on the cross (Rom. 3:25; Heb. 2:17; 1 John 2:2; 4:10). However, the concept of propitiation is pervasive.[20] It is a personal idea (someone must be propitiated) that means more than the impersonal notion of expiation, which means to take away or remove something (as in sin and guilt). To propitiate someone is to "appease or pacify his anger."[21]

Propitiation, then, necessarily presupposes anger that needs to be appeased. When the death of Christ is described in propitiatory terms, it is the holy wrath of God against sin that is in view. Jesus propitiates God by substituting Himself in the place of sinners and enduring divine wrath that justly should be unleashed on them. Calvin explains how this took place on the cross:

He placed himself in our room, and thus became a sinner, and subject to the curse, not in himself indeed, but in us, yet in such a manner, that it became necessary for him to occupy our place. He could not cease to be the object of his Father's love, and yet he endured his wrath. For how could he reconcile the Father to us, if he had incurred his hatred and displeasure? . . . Again, how would he have freed us from the wrath of God, if he had not transferred it from us to himself? Thus, "he was wounded for our transgressions," (Isaiah 53:5) and had to deal with God as an angry judge. This is the foolishness of the cross, (1 Corinthians 1:18) and the admiration of angels, (1 Peter 1:12) which not only exceeds, but swallows up, all the wisdom of the world.[22]

This understanding of the atonement is repulsive to many modern sensibilities. Steve Chalke has scandalously charged that the propitiatory, substitutionary death of Jesus was "cosmic child abuse."[23] Apart from draining the meaning from biblical texts that speak of the cross as redemption and propitiation, Chalke's accusation betrays a superficial appreciation of the sinfulness of human sin and the wrath of God against it. Sin has made us the objects of divine wrath. Calvin writes, "Christ was the price of our 'chastisement,' that is, of the chastisement which was due to us. Thus, the wrath of God, which had been justly kindled against us, was appeased."[24]

  • *Reconciliation.* Because the cross is a work of redemption and propitiation, it accomplishes reconciliation between God and sinners. Because of sin, the original friendship between God and man that was established at Creation was exchanged for enmity. God thus regards sinners as His enemies. For reconciliation to occur, the cause for the enmity must be removed—sin must be taken away.

Christ accomplished exactly this in His death. Paul writes that it was "while we were enemies we were reconciled to God by the death of His Son" (Rom. 5:10). What Jesus did on the cross removed the cause of the breach in the relationship between God and sinners. His death expiated our sins.

Calvin's comments on the announcement of John the Baptist upon seeing Jesus for the first time (John 1:29) underscore this truth. Calvin writes:

> The principal office of Christ is briefly but clearly stated; that he *takes away the sins of the world* by the sacrifice of his death, and reconciles men to God. There are other favors, indeed, which Christ bestows upon us, but this is the chief favor, and the rest depend on it; that, by appeasing the wrath of God, he makes us to be reckoned holy and righteous. For from this source flow all the streams of blessings, that, by not imputing our sins, he receives us into favor. Accordingly, John, in order to conduct us to Christ, commences with the gratuitous forgiveness of sins which we obtain through him.[25]

In the old covenant, expiation of sins was portrayed by means of animal sacrifices. All of the ceremony surrounding the sacrificial offerings was designed to point to the work of Christ on the cross. Calvin elaborates:

> The sacrifice was offered in such a manner as to expiate sin by enduring its punishment and curse. This was expressed by the priests by means of the laying on of hands, as if they threw on the sacrifice the sins of the whole nation. (Exodus 29:15) And if a private individual offered a sacrifice, he also laid his hand upon it, as if he threw upon it his own sin. Our sins were thrown upon Christ in such a manner that he alone bore the curse. . . . [This describes] the benefit of Christ's death, that by his sacrifice sins were expiated, and God was reconciled towards men.[26]

Without the right starting point, it is impossible to come to a right conclusion about what Jesus accomplished by His death on the cross.

God's holy love that issues forth in wrath against all that is unrighteous (both sin and sinners), along with mankind's universal and all-pervasive sinfulness, assure us that there can be no salvation without atonement. God must be appeased, sin must be removed, and peace must be reestablished in the relationship between the two. Jesus secured all of this through His sacrificial death. Those who, by faith, entrust themselves to Him receive all of these benefits of His work on the cross.

It is in the cross that we discover the depth of God's wrath against us and His love for us. Because of our sin, He is hostile toward us. Because of His grace, He loves us. His wrath we deserve. His love comes to us freely. By delivering up His Son on the cross, God satisfies them both. This led Calvin to call the cross of Christ "a magnificent theatre" for the glory of God:

[In it], the inestimable goodness of God is displayed before the whole world. In all the creatures, indeed, both high and low, the glory of God shines, but nowhere has it shone more brightly than in the cross, in which there has been an astonishing change of things, the condemnation of all men has been manifested, sin has been blotted out, salvation has been restored to men; and, in short, the whole world has been renewed, and every thing restored to good order.[27]

NOTES

[1] John Calvin, *Commentary on the Gospel According to John*, trans. William Pringle (London: Calvin Translation Society, 1847; repr. Grand Rapids: Baker, 1981), 2:73.

[2] John Calvin, *Commentary on a Harmony of the Evangelists, Matthew, Mark, and Luke* (Edinburgh: Calvin Translation Society, 1845; repr. Grand Rapids: Baker, 1981), 3:274–75.

[3] John Calvin, *Institutes of the Christian Religion*, ed. John T. McNeill, trans. Ford Lewis Battles; Library of Christian Classics, XX–XXI (Philadelphia: Westminster John Knox, 1960), 2.12.1.

[4] Cited in Timothy George, *Theology of the Reformers* (Nashville: Broadman, 1988), 221.

[5] Calvin, *Institutes of the Christian Religion*, 1.1.1.

[6] H. Richard Niebuhr, *The Kingdom of God in America* (New York: Harper and Row, 1959), 193.

[7] Leon Morris, *The Atonement, its Meaning and Significance* (Downers Grove, Ill.: InterVarsity Press, 1983), 153, 156.

[8] Leon Morris, "Wrath of God," in *New Dictionary of Theology*, ed. Sinclair B. Ferguson and David F. Wright (Downers Grove, Ill.: InterVarsity Press, 1988), 732.

[9] In the twentieth century, C. H. Dodd was the most prominent spokesman against this view, arguing that the wrath of God should be regarded as impersonal. For extensive rebuttal of this view, see Leon Morris, *The Apostolic Preaching of the Cross*, 3rd ed. (Grand Rapids: Eerdmans, 1965), 145–213. See also Roger Nicole, "C. H. Dodd and the Doctrine of Propitiation," in *Standing Forth* (Ross-shire, U.K.: Christian Focus: 2002), 343–385.

[10] John Frame, *The Doctrine of God* (Phillipsburg, N.J.: P&R, 2002), 464.

[11] John Calvin, *Commentaries on the Twelve Minor Prophets*, trans. John Owen (Edinburgh: Calvin Translation Society, 1845; repr. Grand Rapids: Baker, 1981), 2:421.

[12] Calvin, *Institutes of the Christian Religion*, 2.8.59. In his commentary on Hab. 1:13 (*Commentaries on the Twelve Minor Prophets*, 4:45), Calvin paraphrases the prophet's complaint to God by saying, "It is not consistent with thy nature to pass by the vices of men, for every iniquity is hateful to thee."

[13] Ibid.

[14] Ibid., 2.14.4.

[15] John Stott, *The Cross of Christ* (Downers Grove, Ill.: InterVarsity, 1986), 131. Stott treats this subject very helpfully on pages 129–132.

[16] Calvin, *Institutes of the Christian Religion*, 2.16.5.

[17] Ibid.

[18] Morris has an excellent study of the *lutron* word group in both its biblical and extra-biblical usages in *The Apostolic Preaching of the Cross*, 11–64.

[19] John Calvin, *Commentary on the Epistles of Paul the Apostle to the Corinthians* , trans. John Pringle (London: Calvin Translation Society, 1848; repr. Grand Rapids: Baker, 1981), 1:94. See also Robert Peterson, *Calvin and the Atonement* (Ross-shire, U.K.: Christian Focus, 1999), 91–99.

[20] Morris, *The Apostolic Preaching of the Cross*, 144.

[21] Stott, *The Cross of Christ*, 169. Stott has a helpful summary of the debate over the meaning of the *i°la¿skomai* word group on pages 169–173.

[22] Calvin, *Commentaries on the Epistles of Paul to the Galatians and Ephesians*, trans. William Pringle (London: Calvin Translation Society, 1854; repr. Grand Rapids: Baker, 1981), 92.

[23] Steve Chalke and Alan Mann, *The Lost Message of Jesus* (Grand Rapids: Zondervan, 2003), 182–183.

[24] John Calvin, *Commentary on the Prophet Isaiah*, trans. William Pringle (London: Calvin Translation Society, 1850; repr. Grand Rapids: Baker, 1981), 4:116.

25 John Calvin, *Commentary on the Gospel According to John*, 1:63.

26 John Calvin, *Commentary on the Prophet Isaiah*, 4:124–125. Calvin further explains his point: "Hence it follows that nowhere but in Christ is found expiation and satisfaction for sin. In order to understand this better, we must first know that we are guilty before God, so that we may be accursed and detestable in his presence. Now, if we wish to return to a state of favor with him, sin must be taken away. This cannot be accomplished by sacrifices contrived according to the fancy of men. Consequently, we must come to the death of Christ; for in no other way can satisfaction be given to God. In short, Isaiah teaches that sins cannot be pardoned in any other way than by betaking ourselves to the death of Christ. If any person think that this language is harsh and disrespectful to Christ, let him descend into himself, and, after a close examination, let him ponder how dreadful is the judgment of God, which could not be pacified but by this price; and thus the inestimable grace which shines forth in making Christ accursed will easily remove every ground of offense" (Ibid., 4:125).

27 Calvin, *Commentary on the Gospel According to John*, 2:73.

Chapter 14

TRANSFORMING GRACE

KEITH A. MATHISON

*It is entirely the work of grace and a benefit conferred by it that
our heart is changed from a stony one to one of flesh, that our will
is made new, and that we, created anew in heart and mind, at
length will what we ought to will.* [1]

—John Calvin

In 1610, the followers of the Dutch pastor and professor Jacob
Arminius drafted a protest called "the Remonstrance."[2] The document contained five negative statements that rejected specific
Calvinistic doctrines, followed by five articles stating Arminian doctrines.[3] Among the Calvinistic teachings with which the Remonstrance
took issue was the doctrine of irresistible grace.

In the fourth negative statement, the Arminians rejected the following: "That the Holy Spirit works in the elect by irresistible grace, so
that they *must* be converted and be saved; while the grace necessary and
sufficient for conversion, faith, and salvation is withheld from the rest,
although they are externally called and invited by the revealed will of
God."[4] The statement of the Arminian doctrine was then presented in
the fourth article on *Resistible Grace*: "Grace is the beginning, continuation, and end of our spiritual life, so that man can neither think nor
do any good or resist sin without prevening, co-operating, and assisting

grace. But as for the manner of co-operation, this grace is not irresistible, for many resist the Holy Ghost (Acts vii)."[5]

The publication of the Remonstrance led to a lengthy debate between Calvinists and Arminians in the Netherlands. Eventually, in order to resolve the debate, the Dutch Estates General called an ecclesiastical assembly, the Synod of Dort, which met from November 1618 until May 1619. In addition to the approximately seventy Dutch delegates present, there were twenty-six delegates from eight foreign nations, including England, Switzerland, and parts of Germany. The synod set forth its conclusions in the Canons of Dort. This document contains "the decision of the Synod of Dort on the five main points of doctrine in dispute in the Netherlands."[6] Each main point in the canons contains a positive exposition of the Calvinist doctrine, followed by a rejection of the corresponding Arminian error.

The synod's defense of the doctrine of irresistible grace is found in Main Point III/IV of the canons. After setting forth the effects of the fall upon human nature and the inability of the light of nature or of the law to convert fallen man, the synod declares that what neither nature nor the law can do, God "accomplishes by the power of the Holy Spirit" (Art. 6). In eternity, God chose His own, and within time He effectively calls them and grants them faith (Art. 10). The Holy Spirit supernaturally regenerates God's chosen ones in an incomprehensible manner (Arts. 11–13). This regenerating work is irresistible: "all those in whose hearts God works in this marvelous way are certainly, unfailingly, and effectively reborn and do actually believe" (Art. 12).

The Westminster Confession of Faith, which was completed in 1646, sets forth the same doctrine of irresistible (or effectual) grace that was defended at Dort. Its statement of the doctrine is found in Chapter 10, "Of Effectual Calling":

> I. All those whom God hath predestinated unto life, and those only, he is pleased, in his appointed and accepted time, effectually to call, by his Word and Spirit, out of that state of sin and death

in which they are by nature, to grace and salvation by Jesus Christ: enlightening their minds, spiritually and savingly, to understand the things of God, taking away their heart of stone, and giving unto them an heart of flesh; renewing their wills, and by his almighty power determining them to that which is good; and effectually drawing them to Jesus Christ; yet so as they come most freely, being made willing by his grace.

II. This effectual call is of God's free and special grace alone, not from any thing at all foreseen in man, who is altogether passive therein, until, being quickened and renewed by the Holy Spirit, he is thereby enabled to answer this call, and to embrace the grace offered and conveyed in it.

III. Elect infants, dying in infancy, are regenerated and saved by Christ through the Spirit, who worketh when, and where, and how he pleaseth. So also are all other elect persons who are incapable of being outwardly called by the ministry of the Word.

IV. Others, not elected, although they may be called by the ministry of the Word, and may have some common operations of the Spirit, yet they never truly come to Christ, and therefore can not be saved: much less can men, not professing the Christian religion, be saved in any other way whatsoever, be they never so diligent to frame their lives according to the light of nature, and the law of that religion they do profess; and to assert and maintain that they may is without warrant of the Word of God.

This doctrine is found as well in the Westminster Larger Catechism, Question 67.[7]

We see, then, that by the seventeenth century, the doctrine of irresistible grace was considered to be an established point of Reformed orthodoxy. Here the Reformed churches were following the lead of John Calvin, who had simply set forth the teaching of Scripture.

As we have seen, the doctrine of irresistible grace involves several doctrinal issues, including effectual calling and regeneration. Calvin addressed these themes in his biblical commentaries, his *Institutes of the Christian Religion*, and in several treatises, including one specifically addressed to the topics.[8] Calvin found the doctrine of effectual grace in several texts of Scripture. One of the clearest of these references is John 6. Commenting on verse 44, Calvin explains how God draws sinners to Himself.

> The statement amounts to this, that we ought not to wonder if many refuse to embrace the Gospel; because no man will ever of himself be able to come to Christ, but God must first approach him by his Spirit; and hence it follows that all are not *drawn*, but that God bestows this grace on those whom he has elected. True, indeed, as to the kind of *drawing*, it is not violent, so as to compel men by external force; but still it is a powerful impulse of the Holy Spirit, which makes men willing who formerly were unwilling and reluctant.[9]

Jesus had said, "No one can come to me unless the Father who sent me draws him" (John 6:44a). As Calvin explains, this verse clearly expresses the truth that God is sovereign in man's salvation. Man does not initiate the process, for he cannot come to Christ unless God acts *first*. This is the case because man is dead in sin, and a dead man can do nothing for himself.

Calvin's most extended systematic treatment of the doctrine of irresistible grace is found in his 1559 edition of the *Institutes*.[10] Here Calvin explains that God must begin the good work of salvation in us because our wills are evil and set against Him. Man's will cannot turn to the good in its own power, but must be changed by God. As Calvin explains, this divine change is efficacious: "He does not move the will in such a manner as has been taught and believed for many ages—that it is afterward in our choice either to obey or resist the motion—but by disposing it efficaciously."[11]

Because salvation is God's work, from beginning to end, perseverance ultimately depends on Him. It is a free gift of God, not a reward based on man's merit.

In 1542, the Dutch Roman Catholic theologian Albert Pighius wrote a work titled *Ten Books on Human Free Choice and Divine Grace*. Pighius was critiquing Calvin's teaching on the subject of free will and predestination as found in the 1539 edition of the *Institutes*. In 1543, Calvin wrote a response to Pighius titled *The Bondage and Liberation of the Will*. This book contains Calvin's most extended treatment of the relationship between God's grace and man's will. In it, Calvin sums up his argument against Pighius in the following statement:

> But all that we say amounts to this. First, that what a person is or has or is capable of is entirely empty and useless for the spiritual righteousness which God requires, unless one is directed to the good by the grace of God. Secondly, that the human will is of itself evil and therefore needs transformation and renewal so that it may begin to be good, but that grace itself is not merely a tool which can help someone if he is pleased to stretch out his hand to [take] it. That is, [God] does not merely offer it, leaving [to man] the choice between receiving it and rejecting it, but he steers the mind to choose what is right, he moves the will also effectively to obedience, he arouses and advances the endeavor until the actual completion of the work is attained.[12]

Contrary to Pighius, Calvin affirms that grace is efficacious:

> [In the *Institutes*] I say, then, that grace is not offered to us in such a way that afterwards we have the option either to submit or to resist. I say that it is not given merely to aid our weakness by its support as though anything depended on us apart from it. But I demonstrate that it is entirely the work of grace and a benefit conferred by it that our heart is changed from a stony one to one of flesh, that our will is made new, and that we, created anew in heart and mind, at

length will what we ought to will. For Paul bears witness that God does not bring about in us [merely] that we are able to will what is good, but also that we should will it right up to the completion of the act. How big a difference there is between performance and will! Likewise, I determine that our will is effectively formed so that it necessarily follows the leading of the Holy Spirit, and not that it is sufficiently encouraged to be able to do so if it wills.[13]

As we see, Calvin clearly taught that in order for man to be saved, the Holy Spirit had to work efficaciously and irresistibly to bring him from a state of spiritual death to spiritual life.

In his teaching on the subject of saving grace, Calvin merely followed the doctrine set forth in the Scriptures. The doctrine of efficacious grace is necessary because of the state of fallen man. Man is born dead in sin (cf. Rom. 5:12; Eph. 2:1; Col. 2:13), with his mind and heart corrupted (Gen. 6:5; Jer. 17:9; Rom. 8:7–8; 1 Cor. 2:14). He is a slave to sin (Rom. 6:20; Titus 3:3) and therefore unable to repent and come to God (Jer. 13:23; Matt. 7:18; John 6:44, 65). Because of this, man must be born again (John 3:5–7). Those whom God elected and for whom Christ died are brought to life by the Holy Spirit (John 1:12–13; 3:3–8; 5:21; Eph. 2:1, 5; Titus 3:5). God gives them faith and repentance (Acts 5:31; 11:18; 13:48; Eph. 2:8–9; Phil. 1:29; 2 Tim. 2:25–26), and they are justified.

A SUMMARY OF THE BIBLICAL DOCTRINE

The work of the Holy Spirit in the salvation of sinners involves effectual calling and regeneration. Effectual calling must be distinguished from the external call that is made to all who hear the gospel (cf. Matt. 28:19). The external call involves the presentation of the gospel to all human beings. The effectual internal call is connected to and mediated by the external call, but it is not the same thing, and it is not given to all who hear the external call. The internal call is given only to the elect,[14] and it is always effectual. In other words, the one so called will be saved (cf. Rom. 8:30).

Regeneration is the act of the Holy Spirit by which he brings a man from the state of spiritual death to spiritual life. It is, in effect, spiritual "resurrection." In the act of regeneration, the Holy Spirit changes the disposition of the soul and renews the will. The new life given in regeneration immediately manifests itself in faith and repentance. Regeneration is, therefore, not the result of faith, as Arminians and others assert. Rather, faith is the result of regeneration. The state of the sinner is analogous to the state of Lazarus in the tomb (John 11:1–44). Like the unbeliever, Lazarus was dead, unable to do anything to change his condition. Jesus commands this corpse to come out of the tomb (in one brief statement, He destroys the claim of those who say that if God commands something we must have the natural ability to do it).

The command Jesus gives to Lazarus is analogous to the external call made to all unbelievers. Like Ezekiel preaching to the valley of dry bones (37:1–14), the external call is made to the spiritually dead. Those who proclaim the gospel preach in a graveyard. Lazarus cannot obey Christ's command until he is given new life, and this is something only God can do. When Lazarus is given new life, he immediately responds and exits the tomb. In the same way, the spiritually dead sinner cannot respond to the gospel until he is given new life through the regenerating work of the Holy Spirit. Once he is regenerated, however, he immediately responds, placing his faith in Jesus. He is then justified by God.

A GLORIOUS DOCTRINE

Irresistible, or efficacious, grace is not a dry and dusty old doctrine that was invented by curmudgeonly Calvinists. It is, in fact, a glorious biblical doctrine, for without the efficacious work of the Holy Spirit, we would all be without hope in this world and the next. When we come to a full understanding of how serious our situation is as fallen human beings, our perspective on these doctrines changes dramatically. If we view fallen man as merely disabled or sick, we will never understand the full riches of God's grace. When we see ourselves as God sees us, however, the truth of the matter is sobering. When we realize that we were spiritually stillborn, rebels against the Almighty and Most Holy God, the Creator of heaven and earth, wicked to our core, we will not have an overinflated sense of our own goodness and abilities. We will not delude ourselves into thinking that God chose us because of some innate goodness within us. We will not flatter ourselves in thinking that we are saved because we made the first move to come to God.

On the contrary, we will fall down on our knees and thank God every day for His amazing grace. We will thank God that He came to *our* tomb, when *we* were dead and helpless in sin, and cried out to *us*, "Come forth!" We will thank Him for giving us new life, for turning our wills from evil, for granting us faith and repentance, for bringing us out of the tomb and loosing us from the burial cloths in which we were bound. If we walked out of the tomb, it was not because of any power in us. It was not because we made a decision for Christ. Rather, it was solely because of the irresistible grace of God, the sovereign and mysterious work of the Holy Spirit, who gave us new life. When we finally learn this, we will, with Calvin and our Reformed forefathers, ascribe all glory to God alone for our salvation.

NOTES

[1] John Calvin, *The Bondage and Liberation of the Will: A Defence of the Orthodox Doctrine of Human Choice Against Pighius*, ed. A. N. S. Lane, trans. G. I. Davies; Texts and Studies in Reformation and Post-Reformation Thought (Grand Rapids: Baker, 1996), 174.

[2] Thereafter the Arminian party was often known as the Remonstrants.

[3] For the full text of the Remonstrance, see Philip Schaff, *A History of the Creeds of Christendom* (London: Hodder and Stoughton, 1877), 517–519.

[4] Ibid., 517.

[5] Ibid., 518.

6   *Ecumenical Creeds and Reformed Confessions* (Grand Rapids: CRC Publications, 1988), 123.

7   Q. 67. What is effectual calling? A. Effectual calling is the work of God's almighty power and grace, whereby (out of his free and special love to his elect, and from nothing in them moving him thereunto) he doth, in his accepted time, invite and draw them to Jesus Christ, by his word and Spirit; savingly enlightening their minds, renewing and powerfully determining their wills, so as they (although in themselves dead in sin) are hereby made willing and able freely to answer his call, and to accept and embrace the grace offered and conveyed therein.

8   See the discussion of Calvin's response to Pighius below.

9   John Calvin, *Commentary on the Gospel According to John*, trans. William Pringle (London: Calvin Translation Society, 1847; repr. Grand Rapids: Baker, 2003), 1:257.

10 John Calvin, *Institutes of the Christian Religion*, ed. John T. McNeill; trans. Ford Lewis Battles; Library of Christian Classics, XX–XXI (Philadelphia: Westminster John Knox, 1960), 2.3.6–11.

11 Ibid., 2.3.10.

12 Calvin, *The Bondage and Liberation of the Will: A Defence of the Orthodox Doctrine of Human Choice Against Pighius*, 114.

13 Ibid., 174

14 Cf. Louis Berkhof, *Systematic Theology*, 4th ed. (Grand Rapids: Eerdmans, 1941), 469.

Chapter 15

A CERTAIN
INHERITANCE

JAY E. ADAMS

Paul calls the Spirit, whom [believers] receive, both "Spirit of adoption" and the "seal" and "guarantee of the inheritance to come." For he surely establishes and seals in their hearts by his testimony the assurance of the adoption to come. [1]

—JOHN CALVIN

Throughout his writings, John Calvin sounded the note of certainty, and that certainty had a powerful influence on the Reformation. He was especially concerned that believers should know the certainty of their salvation. The Roman Catholic Church's ceremonialism and system of merit had utterly obscured the biblical truth that people can know in this life that they will spend eternity in the presence of God. As a result, many believed that those once saved could be lost again. Calvin wanted to remove the fear that salvation can be lost. Rather, he wanted believers to know that their salvation is assured in Christ, resulting in confidence and love in place of fear.

The scriptural doctrine of the perseverance of the saints, which Calvin strongly championed, was the key to maintaining certainty of salvation. I am delighted to reexamine the biblical evidence for the cheerful and soul-warming teaching of the perseverance of the saints, especially at the present time, when in some "evangelical" circles all of the doctrines established at the Reformation are considered up for grabs.

NOTHING CAN GO WRONG WITH OUR INHERITANCE

The clearest statement of the doctrine of perseverance is found in 1 Peter 1:3–5:

> Blessed be the God and Father of our Lord Jesus Christ! According to his great mercy, he has caused us to be born again to a living hope through the resurrection of Jesus Christ from the dead, to an inheritance that is imperishable, undefiled, and unfading, kept in heaven for you, who by God's power are being guarded through faith for a salvation ready to be revealed in the last time.

Peter makes it clear that the heavenly inheritance of the saints is secure. There is nothing that can destroy or even mar it, because it is "imperishable, undefiled, and unfading." Earthly things, as Jesus pointed out, have the very opposite characteristics: "moth and rust destroy" them (Matt. 6:19). But the heavenly inheritance is of such a nature that it cannot be so affected. Being a spiritual inheritance, in God's spiritual realm, it is entirely out of the reach of such things.

Calvin writes: "In this way we are assured of the inheritance of the Heavenly Kingdom; for the only Son of God, to whom it wholly belongs, has adopted us as his brothers. 'For if brothers, then also fellow heirs with him' [Rom. 8:17]."[2] So there is no doubt about the integrity of the inheritance—the salvation that Jesus purchased for His own.

Moreover, this inheritance, as Peter says, is "kept in heaven." It is a trust that God has committed into His own hands for safekeeping. If the almighty preserving power of God is being exerted to protect it, then we can be absolutely certain that nothing can go wrong with our future inheritance.

NOTHING CAN GO WRONG WITH THE HEIR

But those who believe that people once saved may lose their salvation often point to the vulnerability of the believer himself. The believer, they think, is the weak link in the chain. "Of course," they say, "no one can snatch him from God's hand, but he can wander and fall from grace on his own." But Peter will have nothing to do with this notion. He knows of no weak link; his words make it perfectly clear that God has covered all the bases. He assures his readers that just as nothing can go wrong with the inheritance, so nothing can go wrong with the heir. He, too, is "guarded by God's power," and there is no power greater than God's—least of all the power of a believer to tear himself loose from God's safekeeping.

Moreover, as some might fail to notice, Peter makes it absolutely plain that the guarding takes place "through faith." That can mean nothing else than that the faith that saves (a gift from God, according to Eph. 2:8–9) is so nurtured and cared for by the Spirit of God that no genuine believer ever apostatizes. The phrase "through faith" is telling for the argument, since it is a supposed loss of faith that is the thrust of the attack by those who believe in the possibility of losing salvation. It is here that they believe the weak link is to be found. But Peter parries their thrust by saying that it is precisely through—by means of—faith that God preserves His people. God's safekeeping "power" works through the faith of the believer. In other words, it is precisely because the power of God is manifested in preserving the Christian's faith that he can be assured of never losing his salvation.

In describing Christ's work as the Mediator of our salvation, Calvin explains how we are heirs according to God's pledge:

[The Mediator's] task was to restore us to God's grace as to make of the children of men, children of God; of the heirs of Gehenna, heirs of the Heavenly Kingdom. Who could have done this had not the self-same Son of God become the Son of man, and had not so taken what was ours as to impart what was his to us, and to make what was his by nature ours by grace? Therefore, relying on this pledge, we trust that we are sons of God.[3]

The perseverance of believers in the faith is also clearly taught in John 17, a powerful passage that is often misinterpreted. Here we are privileged to listen in on what has been called the High Priestly Prayer of Christ. In it, He speaks of believers becoming "one" so that "the world may believe that you have sent me" (v. 21). This prayer has been consistently understood by liberals (and, sadly, of late by conservatives, as well) as teaching that organic union (or, at least, corporate expressions of unity) among Christians will lead the world to believe in Christ. If that were true, then Jesus' prayer has never been answered in the affirmative. Indeed, it could only be declared an utter failure. From the beginning, there have been strife and division among Christians, as the New Testament itself and church history so plainly testify. But, of course, we must maintain that Christ's prayer for unity has not failed. How, then, do we explain the failure of churches to unite? The fact is that He prayed for nothing of the sort.

For what then did Jesus pray? Surely He asked the Father that His followers might become one, didn't He? Yes, He did. But the unity for which He prayed was not a horizontal unity among men; rather, He prayed for a vertical unity with Himself, as He is one with the Father. Many have failed to understand this truth. The entire prayer is a petition that genuine believers may not be "lost" as Judas was (v. 12). Since Christ was about to leave His own, He prayed that God would continue to "guard" them, just as He previously had "kept" them under His watchful care (v. 12). And He prayed not only for the apostles, but also for those who would come to believe under their preaching (v. 20). The kind of guarding that Jesus had in mind is explained in verse 21: "that they may all be one, just as you, Father, are in me, and I in you, that they also may be in us, so that the world may believe that you have sent me."

AN INSEPARABLE UNITY

The unity involved in these words is a unity with the Father and the Son, a unity that is as inseparable as that which these members of the Trinity enjoy. And in answer to His Son's prayer, the Father continues to bring disciples into such union with Jesus and Himself, so that they are "guarded" from anything that might destroy them (vv. 12, 20–21). The world believed when, in the face of great persecution, true Christians refused to abandon their faith. The world could not fail to see that there was something different about them. Many came over to the faith when they saw that neither flame nor rack nor wild beasts could separate them from their love for God and His love for them (Rom. 8:35–39). They recognized that something beyond mere human grit filled the hearts of the martyrs who endured to the end. That something was the Father's answer to Jesus' prayer.

Nothing could be simpler. God doesn't make a promise, then change His mind. He never hands us something with one hand, only to take it back with the other. He would never give eternal life to a person and then later kill him spiritually. Eternal life is just that—life that lasts eternally in God's presence. God is true to His word. The certainty that Calvin taught was nothing new; it was first taught by Jesus, and then by Peter and Paul.

Add one more proof from Romans—the chain of certainty found in Romans 8:30: "And those whom he predestined he also called, and those whom he called he also justified, and those whom he justified he also glorified." There is no weak link in the chain. It moves inexorably from predestination to glorification. The several declarations given by Paul are tied together in such a way that they are not subject to interruptions or alterations. Calvin writes:

> "Those whom he appointed beforehand, he also called; those whom he called, he also justified" [Rom. 8:30] that he might sometime glorify them. Although in choosing his own the Lord already

has adopted them as his children, we see that they do not come into possession of so great a good except when they are called; conversely, that when they are called, they already enjoy some share of their election. For this reason, Paul calls the Spirit, whom they receive, both "Spirit of adoption" [Rom. 8:15] and the "seal" and "guarantee of the inheritance to come" [Eph. 1:13–14; cf. II Cor. 1:22; 5:5]. For he surely establishes and seals in their hearts by his testimony the assurance of the adoption to come.[4]

WHAT ABOUT APOSTASY?

When, for instance, preachers from the heretical denomination called the Churches of Christ[5] speak of "the possibility of apostasy," they mean that those who are truly saved may leave the faith, lose their salvation, and turn against the Lord Jesus Christ. Plainly, the Bible speaks about apostasy, but that is not what it means by the word. A very important verse that makes the truth about apostasy clear is 1 John 2:19: "They went out from us, but they were not of us; for if they had been of us, they would have continued with us. But they went out, that it might become plain that they all are not of us."

In this verse, John is addressing the fact that certain gnostic teachers who had been in the fold had left and had begun teaching their heresy. Previously, they had seemed to be true Christians, because they gave no outward indication of their heretical belief. But their false views of the nature of Christ solidified and came to the fore, and they found that they could no longer fellowship with genuine Christians. So they apostatized and denied that Christ died for our sins.[6]

In this verse, two important facts emerge. First, those who apostatized were never true believers. John says that by leaving they made it clear that this was so ("they were not of us"). While they had been a part of the visible church, they had never belonged to the invisible church. Their profession of faith was false. This problem of a false profession of faith in Jesus Christ, which we so often encounter in our churches today, was a problem in apostolic times and in the sixteenth century as well. In fact, Calvin describes it as a "daily" occurrence:

> Yet it daily happens that those who seemed to be Christ's, fall away from him again, and hasten to destruction. Indeed, in that same passage, where he declares that none of those whom the Father had given to him perished, he nevertheless excepts the son of perdition [John 17:12]. True indeed, but it is also equally plain that such persons never cleaved to Christ with the heartfelt trust in which certainty of election has, I say, been established for us.[7]

Those who teach that believers may apostatize from the church disregard John's plain explanation of the facts. We must not do so. Instead, we must maintain that those who denounce the faith never had true faith in the first place. They may have been among believers, but they were not of them. Otherwise, as John says, they would not have failed to persevere with them.

Second, note the corollary: John affirms that "if they had been of us, they would have continued with us." True believers remain in the faith and in the church. They endure to the end. It is certainly possible for a believer to defect for a time, but, like Peter or John Mark—who both had temporary lapses—in the end they repent and return.

THE AUTHOR OF HEBREWS AGREES

The letter to the Hebrews addresses this problem in strong language in two places (Heb. 6:4–9; 10:26–29). Throughout the book, the writer shows a concern that his readers might "drift" from the truth in the face of persecution (Heb. 2:1; 12:3). This concern about those who might "fall away" leads him to warn of the fearful eventualities that will come to those who do. As a result, the book is replete with both warnings and encouragements.

While he knew that true believers would not repudiate their Savior, the writer recognized the possibility that some among his readers might not be genuine Christians after all. Therefore, he shows that people may become a part of the visible body of Christ, participating in all of God's wonderful benefits that are provided for the life of the church, but eventually turn their backs on everything they have experienced. There is no way to renew such people to a genuine profession of faith, he says, because there is only one true message—the very one they have rejected. So he describes how great a dishonor to Christ it is for one to hear and taste the gospel only to reject it, and how terrible are the consequences.

But as he describes the situation in terms of an example, he seems to conclude that his readers' faith is genuine—at least the faith of most of those to whom he is writing. The example is that of the rain watering the ground. The very same rain (teaching, Christian fellowship, etc.) falls on two patches of ground. One produces fruit, while the other produces thorns and thistles. The first result refers to those who believe and persevere; the latter refers to those who do not.

Then, applying that example to his readers, he declares: "In your case, beloved, we feel sure of better things—things that belong to salvation." Here the writer says that those who have salvation do not fall away. They do not apostatize.

GOD IS A GOOD FATHER

To teach that a saved person may be lost is to impugn the fatherhood of God. It is to say that He so poorly raises His children that many become delinquents who "drop out" or must be disowned by Him. But the Bible teaches otherwise. Hebrews says that the Lord "disciplines" each of His children in order to bring them into line when they go the wrong way; if they receive no discipline, the book teaches, they are illegitimate (Heb. 12:5–11). Such discipline, we are assured, "yields the peaceful fruit of righteousness to those who have been trained by it" (v. 11). God disciplines all of His legitimate children, and His discipline gets positive results.[8] God does not allow rebellious children to wander away from the family or become so incorrigible that He must put them out. Those members who leave, or who are permanently put out of the church, as we have seen, are false professors. Calvin writes:

> In order that we may quickly summarize the whole matter, let this stand as the first of two distinctions: wherever punishment is for vengeance, there the curse and wrath of God manifest themselves, and these he always withholds from believers. On the other hand, chastisement is a blessing of God and also bears witness to his love, as Scripture teaches [Job 5:17; Prov. 3:11–12; Heb. 12:5–6].[9]

This is by no means a merely academic discussion. To believe that one can be saved and lost leads to several serious consequences. For instance, a young man who had been taught this unbiblical doctrine once told me that he had finally "given up." Since, as he had discovered, he could not "keep himself saved," but supposedly kept falling in and out of salvation, he had concluded that he might as well live it up for whatever pleasures he could enjoy here and now in this life. After all, he would never reach heaven. According to all indications, he was not using this description and explanation of his experience as an excuse.

PERSEVERANCE IS THE KEY

If you have been taught the "once saved, always saved" doctrine, you may think that there is no difference between that teaching and the doctrine of the perseverance of the saints. But while it is certainly true that those who are once saved will always be saved, the concept of the perseverance of the saints encompasses a vitally important truth that is rarely emphasized by people who teach the "once saved, always saved" view. That missing emphasis is the fact that a person is saved *through* perseverance, not apart from it. The "once saved, always saved" view may lead those who hold it into quietistic thinking. That is to say, they may think that they have little or no part to play in maintaining their salvation, but that God does it all for them. While a person is not saved by works (as Romanists believe) and does not remain saved because of works (as the Churches of Christ believe), God saves only those who persevere in the faith.

In a section of the *Institutes of the Christian Religion* titled "Perseverance is exclusively God's work; it is neither a reward nor a complement of our individual act," Calvin writes:

> Perseverance would, without any doubt, be accounted God's free gift if a most wicked error did not prevail that it is distributed according to men's merit, in so far as each man shows himself receptive to the first grace. But since this error arose from the fact that men thought it in their power to spurn or to accept the proffered grace of God, when the latter opinion is swept away the former idea also falls of itself. However, there is here a twofold error. For besides teaching that our gratefulness for the first grace and our lawful use of it are rewarded by subsequent gifts, they add also that grace does not work in us by itself, but is only a co-worker with us.[10]

Perseverance is the result of the work of the Spirit in believers' hearts. Nevertheless, it is a work that enables them to keep on believing, as Peter says. God does not believe for them. Rather, they are "guarded" through faith.

In John 15, we read about the sanctification that is necessary for a believer to be saved.[11] A so-called "abiding" condition, which some Higher Life adherents take to mean a special sort of holiness, is not taught in the passage. That idea distorts the apostle's teaching. The Greek word *meno*, which the King James Version translates as "abide," means "remain, continue, stay." It does not refer to some special state of "resting" in Christ that only super saints achieve. Rather, this abiding is equivalent to persevering in the faith. And it is true not of a select few, such as the apostles only, but of all Christians. Indeed, persevering in one's faith in Christ is necessary not only for bearing "much fruit," as the passage teaches, but also for salvation.

Unless one remains in the vine, "he is thrown away like a branch and withers," eventually to be burned up (v. 6). Jesus, therefore, commands, "Abide [or remain] in my love" (v. 9b). The apostles had to persevere in their faith or be cast aside like a branch broken off the vine, and the same is true for all believers. Christ, the Vine, requires every professed Christian to remain in Him by genuine faith or eventually be thrown into the fire.

So perseverance is the result of true faith, nourished and maintained by the Spirit. But the believer himself must continue to exercise it. He may never sit back and say, "I'm saved, I may do as I please, since I can never be lost." To think that way indicates either that he has received very faulty teaching or that he is not a believer. No one who is truly converted can think that way for very long, if at all. True Spirit-given and Spirit-nourished faith leads to biblical thinking. A professed Christian must persevere—remain, continue, stay—in the Vine.

Jesus spoke not only of believers remaining in Him, but also of His "words" remaining in believers (v. 7). Moreover, in verse 14 He said, "You are my friends if you do what I command you." After justification, by means of divinely guarded faith, one remains in salvation by the work of the Spirit, who, through that faith, enables him to continue obeying Jesus' words and commandments. That is perseverance.

This precious doctrine of the perseverance of the saints, coming down to us from the Reformation, must be preserved at all costs. We may neither abandon it nor compromise with those who would do so. The certainty of salvation, which Calvin so dearly wished his congregation to know and which he bequeathed to subsequent generations, must not be lost.

NOTES

1. John Calvin, *Institutes of the Christian Religion*, ed. John T. McNeill; trans. Ford Lewis Battles; Library of Christian Classics, XX–XXI (Philadelphia: Westminster John Knox, 1960), 3.24.1.
2. Ibid., 2.12.2.
3. Ibid.
4. Ibid., 3.24.1.
5. This is an Arminian group, founded by Thomas and Alexander Campbell, that claims to be the only true church. Campbellites refuse to capitalize the word *church* and claim not to be a denomination.
6. The verb *apostatize* means "to stand off from."
7. Calvin, *Institutes of the Christian Religion*, 3.24.7.
8. Cf. Rev. 3:19.
9. Calvin, *Institutes of the Christian Religion*, 3.4.32.
10. Ibid., 2.3.11.
11. I.e., the sanctification that is always present, giving evidence of the fact that one is saved.

Chapter 16

THE BELIEVER'S UNION WITH CHRIST

PHILIP GRAHAM RYKEN

Christ, having been made ours, makes us sharers with him in the gifts with which he has been endowed. We do not, therefore, contemplate him outside ourselves from afar in order that his righteousness may be imputed to us but because we put on Christ and are engrafted into his body—in short, because he deigns to make us one with him. [1]

—JOHN CALVIN

When people think of Calvinism as a theology, they usually think first of John Calvin's belief in the sovereignty of God, or more specifically of his doctrine of predestination. Yet there is another doctrine that distinguishes his thought and helps to organize his theology of salvation, namely, the doctrine of union with Christ. Even the angels, Calvin said, "wonder at the riches that God has displayed in uniting us with the body of his Son."[2]

Put in simple terms, the doctrine of union with Christ teaches that the Holy Spirit joins believers to Jesus by faith, and that by virtue of this spiritual bond we receive both Christ Himself and all His benefits. Calvin believed this doctrine to be of the highest importance, one of the great mysteries of the gospel. Broadly speaking, the first half of his famous *Institutes of the Christian Religion* explains what God has done *for us* as Creator (Book I) and Redeemer (Book II), while the second half explains what God has done *in us*, both individually (Book III) and corporately (Book IV). Calvin's theology thus turns on the spiritual reality of being in Christ.

IN CHRIST

Union with Christ is one of the central theological principles of the Christian faith. Its pervasive presence in the New Testament typically is indicated by the word *in*, a simple preposition with profound implications.

Believers often are said to be in Christ: "If anyone is in Christ, he is a new creation" (2 Cor. 5:17). Sometimes this phrase passes by so rapidly that we may hardly notice, as in Paul's opening address to "the saints in Christ Jesus who are at Philippi" (Phil. 1:1). But even such passing expressions are grounded in the deep spiritual truth of our faith-union with Jesus Christ. The reason we are called "saints in Christ" is because our true and ultimate identity is found in Him: "you are all one in Christ Jesus" (Gal. 3:28).

On other occasions, the Bible teaches the reciprocal principle that Jesus Christ is in the believer: "It is no longer I who live, but Christ who lives in me" (Gal. 2:20). Similarly, Paul wrote of the gospel mystery that has been "hidden for ages and generations but now revealed to his saints" (Col. 1:26). What is this glorious mystery? "Christ in you, the hope of glory" (Col. 1:27).

Christ is in us and we are in Christ. The two sides of this mutual relationship sometimes appear together in Scripture. For example, in teaching His disciples about the vine and the branches—a metaphor for union with Christ—Jesus said, "Abide in me, and I in you" (John 15:4). Similarly, the apostle John described union with Christ as a double habitation by the Holy Spirit: "We know that we abide in him and he in us, because he has given us of his Spirit" (1 John 4:13).

By virtue of this mutual relationship of spiritual indwelling—our union with Christ—we receive all the saving blessings of God. In being united to Christ, we receive not only Christ Himself, but also His benefits. What is His becomes ours, for God "has blessed us in Christ with every spiritual blessing" (Eph. 1:3). Thus we see, said Calvin, that "our whole salvation and all its parts are comprehended in Christ."[3] Indeed, union with Christ is the heart of the gospel, for when the apostle Paul "defines the Gospel, and the use of it, he says that we are called to be partakers of our Lord Jesus Christ, and to be made one with Him, and to dwell in Him, and He in us; and that we be joined together in an inseparable bond."[4]

When Calvin considered how "we receive those benefits which the Father bestowed on his only-begotten Son," his answer was that we receive them by our union with Christ.[5] Christ must "present Himself to us and invite us into such a relationship that truly we are united to Him, that He dwells in us in such a way that everything that belongs to Him is ours."[6] Thus Calvin made union with Christ one of the controlling principles of his soteriology, or doctrine of salvation.

Apart from union with Christ, it is impossible to receive any of the saving blessings of God. Not even the cross and the empty tomb can save us unless we are joined to Jesus Christ. Calvin was emphatic:

> We must understand that as long as Christ remains outside of us, and we are separated from him, all that he has suffered and done for the salvation of the human race remains useless and of no value for us. Therefore, to share with us what he has received from the Father, he had to become ours and to dwell within us. . . . We also, in turn, are said to be "engrafted into him" [Rom. 11:17], and to "put on Christ" [Gal. 3:27]; for, as I have said, all that he possesses is nothing to us until we grow into one body with him.[7]

Simply put, if we are not in Christ, we have no part in His death on the cross to atone for sins and no share in His resurrection from the dead. We are not justified, adopted, sanctified, or glorified without being united to Christ. "I do not see," wrote Calvin, "how anyone can trust that he has redemption and righteousness in the cross of Christ, and life in his death, unless he relies chiefly upon a true participation in Christ himself. For those benefits would not come to us unless Christ first made himself ours."[8] Union with Christ, therefore, is nothing less than a matter of spiritual life and death.

THE DOUBLE BOND

The New Testament uses a variety of images to describe our incorporation into Christ. Jesus used the organic metaphor of a vine with its branches (John 15:1–8), but there are other metaphors as well: the marital union of a bride and groom (Eph. 5:31–32), the familial union of members in a household (Eph. 2:19–22), the architectural union of stones in a building (1 Peter 2:5), and the anatomical union of parts in a body (1 Cor. 12:12–27).

Each of these images highlights a different aspect of union with Christ. The image of the vine and the branches shows that this union is life-giving. The metaphor of marriage shows how intimate it is. The household analogy shows that union with Christ is corporate as well as individual, and so forth.

Regardless which image is used, the union in view is always spiritual. That is to say, union with Christ is the work of God the Holy Spirit. For Calvin, "the Holy Spirit is the bond by which Christ effectually unites us to himself."[9] This is because the "Spirit alone causes us to possess Christ completely and have him dwelling in us."[10] This means that the doctrine of union with Christ is not narrowly Christ-centered but encompasses the wide-spanning work of the entire Trinity.

The role of the Spirit in uniting us to Christ is made necessary by the ascension. If Christ has been raised to the right hand of God and we are still on earth, how can we be united to Him? The answer is that Christ "diffuses his life in us by the secret efficacy of the Spirit."[11] We are able to abide in Christ, and He in us, because "he has given us of his Spirit" (1 John 4:13; cf. Rom. 8:9).

The work of the Holy Spirit in connecting us to Christ makes it clear that in being united to Christ we do not actually *become* Christ. Our union with Christ is spiritual, not physical. To say that we are "one with the Son of God" is not to say that He "conveys his substance to us," but that "by the power of his Spirit, he imparts to us his life and all the blessings which he has received from the Father."[12]

We should not think, however, that the role of the Spirit as the bond of union somehow distances us from Jesus Christ. On the contrary, the Holy Spirit brings us into the closest possible union and communion with the Son of God. Christ "so labors by the virtue of his Holy Spirit that we are united with him more closely than are the limbs with the body."[13]

Jesus Christ unites us to Himself by the Holy Spirit; this is how union with Christ is viewed from the perspective of God's initiative. Yet viewed from our perspective, there is a second bond of union with Christ: we are joined to Him by faith.

This, too, is the teaching of Scripture, for the New Testament constantly describes faith as something we put "in Christ." "Believe in the Lord Jesus," Paul told the Philippian jailer, "and you will be saved" (Acts 16:31). This is not merely a verbal expression, but a profound theological truth: Christ dwells in our hearts by faith (Eph. 3:17). Or as Calvin put it, faith "does not reconcile us to God at all unless it joins us to Christ; . . . [Saving faith is the instrument that] engrafts us in the body of Christ."[14] Thus, our union with Christ is secured by the double bond of faith and the Holy Spirit.

It should be kept clearly in mind, however, that even faith itself is a gift of the Holy Spirit. The grace that saves us through faith is not our own doing; it is the gift of God (Eph. 2:8). Indeed, Calvin described faith as the Holy Spirit's "principal work" in the life of a believer.[15] The Spirit's divine agency means that the sovereignty of God's grace is as evident in Calvin's doctrine of union with Christ as it is anywhere else in his theology. God takes the gracious initiative to join us to Christ by the Holy Spirit, giving us the very faith that establishes a double bond with our Savior.

THE DOUBLE BENEFIT

Of all the blessings that come from being united to Christ, Calvin emphasized two that are distinct yet inseparable: "By partaking of him, we principally receive a double grace: namely, that being reconciled to God through Christ's blamelessness, we may have in heaven instead of a Judge a gracious Father; and secondly, that sanctified by Christ's spirit we may cultivate blamelessness and purity of life."[16] To put this in theological terms, by virtue of our union with Christ we receive the double benefit of justification and sanctification.

To be justified is to be declared righteous—not on the basis of our own righteousness, but on the basis of the righteousness of Jesus Christ, received by faith alone. This was the central doctrine of the Protestant Reformation, and for Calvin, "the main hinge on which religion turns."[17]

As important as it is in its own right, Calvin's doctrine of justification finds its proper context in his doctrine of union with Christ. The blessing of justifying righteousness becomes ours when we are united to Christ by faith. According to Calvin, we are "deprived of this utterly incomparable good until Christ is made ours" and it is only by the "indwelling of Christ in our hearts" that His righteousness is declared to be our own.[18] He then adds:

> Christ, having been made ours, makes us sharers with him in the gifts with which he has been endowed. We do not, therefore, contemplate him outside ourselves from afar in order that his righteousness may be imputed to us but because we put on Christ and are engrafted into his body—in short, because he deigns to make us one with him. For this reason, we glory that we have fellowship of righteousness with him.[19]

Justification is not the only benefit that belongs to us by union with Christ, however, for we are sanctified in Christ as well as justified in Him. To say this another way, we are not simply *declared* righteous in Christ, but also *made* righteous in Him. The second grace of our union with Christ is sanctification by the Spirit.

The double benefit of justification and sanctification provides an immediate answer to the Roman Catholic objection that Calvin and the other Reformers wrongly divided these doctrines, or removed good works from their proper place in the Christian life. On the contrary, Calvin's doctrine of union with Christ unifies his theology of salvation. Viewing both justification and sanctification from the perspective of union with Christ shows how intimately these saving benefits are related.

Calvin was convinced that the several benefits of salvation, though distinct, could never be divided. To receive Christ by faith is to receive the whole Christ, not just part of Him. Thus, in coming to Christ we receive both justification and sanctification. To separate these benefits, Calvin said, would virtually tear Christ in two. But of course "Christ cannot be torn into parts, so these two which we perceive in him together and conjointly are inseparable—namely, righteousness and sanctification."[20]

A key text for Calvin's doctrine of salvation was 1 Corinthians 1:30, where Christ is described as "our righteousness and sanctification." "If you would properly understand how inseparable faith and works are," Calvin wrote, "look to Christ, who, as the Apostle teaches, has been given to us for justification and for sanctification."[21]

First Corinthians 1:30 clearly distinguishes the two benefits of union with Christ, so that we comprehend God's full work of salvation in declaring us and making us righteous. Yet justification and sanctification are also joined together as inseparable benefits we receive simultaneously in Christ:

Although we may distinguish them, Christ contains both of them inseparably in himself. Do you wish, then, to attain righteousness in Christ? You must first possess Christ; but you cannot possess him without being made partaker in his sanctification, because he cannot be divided into pieces (1 Cor. 1:13). Since, therefore, it is solely by expending himself that the Lord gives us these benefits to enjoy, he bestows both of them at the same time, the one never without the other.[22]

If it is true that justification and sanctification are inseparable, then good works are a necessary part of the Christian life. Although they have no part to play in justification, which is by faith alone, good works are indispensable to sanctification. Yet sanctification, no less than justification, is by union with Christ. "Thus it is clear," Calvin writes, "how true it is that we are justified not without works yet not through works, since in our sharing in Christ, which justifies us, sanctification is just as much included as righteousness."[23]

UNION AND COMMUNION WITH CHRIST

In addition to serving as a fundamental principle of theology, union with Christ is an abiding source of true joy and lasting hope in the Christian life. To be united to Christ is to have a loving relationship with Him of growing intimacy. Thus, our union with Christ is the basis for our communion with Christ—our living fellowship with our risen Lord.

In uniting us to himself, Christ shares His life with us—the life of God in the believer's soul: "Christ is not outside us but dwells within us. Not only does he cleave to us by an indivisible bond of fellowship, but with a wonderful communion, day by day, he grows more and more into one body with us, until he becomes completely one with us."[24]

The joy of union and communion with Christ is strengthened by participation in baptism and the Lord's Supper, which bear sacramental witness to our participation in Christ. Baptism is the visible sign and seal of initiation into Christ, of incorporation into His body, of "implanting in Christ."[25] Similarly, the Lord's Supper is the visible sign and seal of continuation in Christ, of communion with Him by the presence of the Holy Spirit. It is "a help whereby we may be engrafted into Christ's body, or, engrafted, may grow more and more together with him until he perfectly joins us with him in the heavenly life."[26]

As we share Christ's table together, feeding spiritually on the bread of His body and the cup of His blood, we participate in Christ Himself, with all His benefits. The very purpose of the sacrament is to give us a tangible experience of the spiritual mystery of our union with Christ. "When we come to this holy table," Calvin told his congregation in Geneva, "we must know that our Lord Jesus Christ presents Himself to confirm us in the unity which we have already received by the faith of the Gospel, that we may be grafted into His body in such a manner that He will dwell in us and we in Him."[27]

What is true in the sacraments is true for the whole Christian life: Christ is not separated from us, but shares Himself with us. By the double bond of faith and the Holy Spirit, we are united to Christ, and thus we gain the double benefit of His justifying and sanctifying righteousness. Yet as Calvin wisely recognized, it is not simply salvation that we need, but the Savior. This is the beauty and joy of union with Christ, in which Christ "makes us, ingrafted into his body, participants not only in all his benefits but also in himself."[28]

NOTES

[1] John Calvin, *Institutes of the Christian Religion*, ed. John T. McNeill; trans. Ford Lewis Battles; Library of Christian Classics, XX–XXI (Philadelphia: Westminster John Knox, 1960), 3.11.10.

[2] Quoted in Francois Wendel, *Calvin: The Origins and Development of His Religious Thought*, trans. Philip Mairet (London: Collins, 1963), 238.

[3] John Calvin, *Institutes of the Christian Religion*, 2.16.19.

[4] John Calvin, quoted in Ronald S. Wallace, *Calvin's Doctrine of the Word and Sacrament* (Edinburgh: Oliver and Boyd, 1953), 143.

[5] Calvin, *Institutes of the Christian Religion*, 3.1.1.

6 John Calvin, quoted in Ronald S. Wallace, *Calvin's Doctrine of the Christian Life* (Edinburgh: Oliver and Boyd, 1959), 17.

7 Calvin, *Institutes of the Christian Religion*, 3.1.1.

8 Ibid., 4.17.11.

9 Ibid., 3.1.1.

10 Ibid., 4.17.12; cf. 4.17.33.

11 Calvin, quoted in Wendel, *Calvin: The Origins and Development of His Religious Thought*, 239.

12 John Calvin, *Commentary on the Gospel According to John*, trans. William Pringle (London: Calvin Translation Society, 1848; repr. Grand Rapids: Baker, 2003), 2:184.

13 Calvin, quoted in Wendel, *Calvin: The Origins and Development of His Religious Thought*, 235.

14 Calvin, *Institutes of the Christian Religion*, 3.2.30.

15 Ibid., 3.1.4.

16 Ibid., 3.11.1.

17 Ibid.

18 Ibid., 3.11.10.

19 Ibid.

20 Ibid., 3.11.6.

21 John Calvin, *Responsio*, in *Ioannis Calvini opera selecta*, ed. P. Barth, W. Niesel, and Dora Scheuner (Munich: Chr. Kaiser, 1926–1952), 1:470.

22 Calvin, *Institutes of the Christian Religion*. 3.16.1.

23 Ibid.

24 Ibid., 3.2.24.

25 Calvin, quoted in Wallace, *Calvin's Doctrine of the Word and Sacrament*, 149.

26 Calvin, *Institutes of the Christian Religion*, 4.17.33.

27 Calvin, quoted in Wallace, *Calvin's Doctrine of the Word and Sacrament*, 144.

28 Calvin, *Institutes of the Christian Religion*, 3.2.24.

Chapter 17

THE PRINCIPAL ARTICLE
OF SALVATION

MICHAEL HORTON

*We explain justification simply as the acceptance with which
God receives us into his favor as righteous men. And we say that
it consists in the remission of sins and the imputation of Christ's
righteousness.*[1]

—JOHN CALVIN

Ever since the nineteenth century, historical theologians have
often sought to locate a central dogma from which all other
teachings can be deduced. For Rome, it was ecclesiology (the
doctrine of the church); for Lutherans, justification; for Anabaptists,
discipleship. For the Reformed, predestination was regarded as the
central principle.

While we can rejoice that this reductionistic method and its conclusion have been completely discarded among specialists, it is still
often maintained by friend and foe alike that anyone who believes in
the sovereignty of God or in predestination is a Calvinist. However,
John Calvin's soteriology (doctrine of salvation) is too rich and inte-
grated to be reduced to a central dogma.[2] For him, every doctrine is a

facet of a glimmering jewel that attests to God's fatherly mercy toward sinners; one doctrine leads us to another doctrine, displaying to our growing astonishment the condescension of the Father, the Son, and the Holy Spirit.

Nevertheless, Christ was clearly central in Calvin's thinking, and by his own testimony he regarded justification as "the primary article of the Christian religion,"[3] "the main hinge on which religion turns,"[4] and "the principal article of the whole doctrine of salvation and the foundation of all religion."[5] It is impossible to drive a wedge between Martin Luther and Calvin on the doctrine of justification. In fact, wherever there are divergences even in emphasis between Ulrich Zwingli and Luther, Calvin explicitly sides with the latter and is especially attentive to Philip Melanchthon's refinements.[6]

Although references to justification appear throughout Calvin's *Institutes of the Christian Religion*, this survey follows the logic of Calvin's unfolding argument in chapters 11–19 of Book 3, along with some citations from his commentary on Romans. The argument from the *Institutes* may be summarized as follows:

1. To save us from judgment, the Son became flesh and merited our salvation (2.15–17).

2. Thus, the righteousness by which we are saved is alien to us (3.11.2).

3. Yet Christ must not only be given for us; He must be given to us (3.1.1).

4. We are recipients not only of Christ's gifts but of Christ Himself with His gifts (3.1.1; 3.1.4; 3.2.24; 4.17.11).

5. Faith unites us to Christ (3.1.1), but it is the Holy Spirit who gives faith, and it is Christ who always remains the sole ground of salvation rather than faith itself. In other words, faith is nothing in itself; it receives *Christ* and with Him all treasures (3.11.7; 3.18.8). After all, "if faith in itself justified one by its own virtue, then, seeing that it is always weak and imperfect, it would be only partly effectual and give us only a part of salvation."[7]

JUSTIFICATION AND CHRIST

Against the backdrop of the medieval definition of justification as a process of moral transformation that begins with baptism, increases through cooperation, and (it is hoped) yields a final justification, Luther launched his famous protest that Calvin later joined with his immense intellectual and pastoral energies. Returning to the New Testament understanding of justification as a purely legal (forensic) declaration, Calvin argued that God's justifying righteousness was not an infused quality within the believer, but a gift of an alien righteousness. This righteousness "consists in the remission of sins, and in this: that the righteousness of Jesus Christ is imputed to us."[8]

Therefore, justification is not a process of transformation from a condition of sinfulness to a state of justice. Believers are *simultaneously* justified and sinful.[9] Sin's dominion has been toppled, but it still indwells believers.[10] Consequently, whatever works believers perform will always fall short of that righteousness that God's law requires.

This orientation stood in sharp contrast both with Rome and the radical sects. Rome taught that Christ's sacrifice remitted the guilt but not the punishment of sins.[11] Meanwhile, Calvin relates, "Certain Anabaptists of our day conjure some sort of frenzied excess instead of spiritual regeneration," thinking that they can attain perfection in this life.[12] In either case, justification was understood as a process of inner transformation rather than as God's free acquittal of sinners for the sake of Christ and His imputation of Christ's righteousness to their account. Of course, there is a diversity of moral character evident to us as human beings, but Calvin reminds us (repeating Luther's contrast) that righteousness before humanity (*coram hominibus*) is not the same as righteousness before God (*coram Deo*).[13]

"Therefore," Calvin responds, "we explain justification simply as the acceptance with which God receives us into his favor as righteous. And we say that it consists in the remission of sins and the imputation of Christ's righteousness."[14]

Calvin appeals to Augustine and Bernard, among others, for his conclusion that we find all of our justifying righteousness in Christ and none in ourselves.[15] The law of God arraigns us before God's judgment, leaving us with no hope. It cannot give the righteousness that it commands because of our own turpitude. Calvin writes: "Removing, then, mention of law, and laying aside all consideration of works, we should, when justification is being discussed, embrace God's mercy alone, turn our attention from ourselves, and look only to Christ. . . . If consciences wish to attain any certainty in this matter, they ought to give no place to the law."[16]

Calvin repeatedly speaks of Christ having merited our salvation. Furthermore, he attributes this not only to Christ's atoning sacrifice (which would have yielded only forgiveness) but to His lifelong obedience (meriting a positive status by fulfilling the law in our place). In fact, this is one of Calvin's criticisms of the heterodox Lutheran Andreas Osiander, whom I discuss below. Our Savior not only had to be fully human and sinless in order to be the appropriate sacrifice for sin; in that humanity, He had to fulfill all righteousness. Thus, justification is not only forgiveness (i.e., not imputing our sins to us), but the positive imputation of Christ's merits.

As François Wendel observes, "Calvin goes on to point out that it is by the obedience of Christ that we are justified, but that he could not have manifested that obedience except in his quality as a servant; that is, according to his human nature." In His obedience, Christ offered His merits, and in handing His body over to death, He offered Himself as a sacrifice for sin. All of this He could do only as a human servant.[17] Thus, Rome's charge that the Reformation doctrine of justification constituted a legal fiction was unfounded: Christ discharged the office of covenant head, claiming by right (condign merit) that status of perfect justice that He shares with His body, the church.

Calvin believed that the whole epistle to the Romans can be summarized as saying "that man's only righteousness is through the mercy of God in Christ, which being offered by the Gospel is apprehended by faith."[18] There will be rewards, but "it is an absurd inference, to deduce merit from reward."[19] Calvin was aware of the exegesis of Romans 2:13 ("For it is not the hearers of the law . . . but the doers of the law who will be justified") that defended a justification (at least, final justification) by works. "They who pervert this passage for the purpose of building up justification by works, deserve most fully to be laughed at even by children," he wrote in response. He added that since it was obvious from Paul's argument that the purpose was to show that the Jews were in fact under the law's curse along with the Gentiles for failing to do what the law requires, "another righteousness must be sought."[20] Not only the ceremonies but the entire law—including the moral law—is included when Paul opposes the law to faith as the way of justification.[21] Calvin writes, "For if there be any righteousness by the law or by works, it must be in men themselves; but by faith they derive from another what is wanting in themselves; and hence the righteousness of faith is rightly called imputative."[22]

Also echoing Luther—and, more importantly, Paul—is Calvin's insistence that the logic of works-righteousness (what Luther called a "theology of glory") is opposed to the logic of righteousness through faith alone. Intuitively, we know that good people go to heaven and bad people go to hell; that God cannot declare someone righteous who is at that moment inherently unrighteous. We have to examine the actual state of affairs and judge people by what we see. However, the gospel is counterintuitive. Here, God's promise must override our moral sensibilities, which judge by appearances. With Abraham, faith clings to a promise, against all human "possibilities":

> All things around us are in opposition to the promises of God: He promises immortality; we are surrounded with mortality and corruption: He declares that he counts us as just; we are covered with our sins: He testifies that he is propitious and kind to us; outward judgments threaten his wrath. What then is to be done? We must with closed eyes pass by ourselves and all things connected

with us, that nothing may hinder or prevent us from believing that God is true.[23]

When Paul speaks of Christ being crucified for our sins and raised for our justification in Romans 4:25, Calvin observes, "For if justification means renovation, then that he died for our sins must be taken in the same sense, as signifying that he acquired for us grace to mortify the flesh, which no one admits. . . . He therefore still speaks of imputative justification."[24] The careless unbeliever, like "the Pharisee," cannot know this peace with God through justification.[25] There are no "preparations" of our own that can give us "access" to God.[26]

From this we can conclude that, for Calvin, justification was an exclusively forensic declaration of God, imputing Christ's righteousness to sinners through faith alone. The righteousness that justifies is never inherent within the believer—even by grace, through the work of the Spirit, indeed even by union with Christ. It is always the righteousness of another, imputed rather than imparted, that renders the ungodly just before a holy God.

JUSTIFICATION AND FAITH

Book 2 of the *Institutes* concentrates on "The Knowledge of God the Redeemer," elucidating all that God in Christ has accomplished for us *extra nos*—outside ourselves. Christ's perfect person and work cannot be extended, completed, augmented, or improved. Our righteousness before God is alien: extrinsic, not inherent; perfect, not progressive. Yet, Calvin writes:

> As long as Christ remains outside of us, and we are separated from him, all that he has suffered and done for the salvation of the human race remains useless and of no value for us. Therefore, to share with us what he has received from the Father, he had to become ours and dwell within us. For this reason, he is called "our

Head" (Eph. 4:15), and "the first-born among many brethren" (Rom. 8:29).[27]

Apart from any virtues or actions that might improve our inherent moral condition, Calvin writes, "faith adorns us with the righteousness of another, which it seeks as a gift from God."[28] He adds:

Faith then is not a naked knowledge either of God or of his truth; nor is it a simple persuasion that God is, that his word is the truth; but a sure knowledge of God's mercy, which is received from the gospel, and brings peace of conscience with regard to God, and rest to the mind. The sum of the matter then is this,—that if salvation depends on the keeping of the law, the soul can entertain no confidence respecting it, yea, that all the promises offered to us by God will become void: we must thus become wretched and lost, if we are sent back to works to find out the cause or the certainty of salvation . . . for as the law generates nothing but vengeance, it cannot bring grace.[29]

At the place where Rome spoke of infused habits of virtue, Calvin spoke of faith as a grasping or clinging to Christ and the gift of the Holy Spirit, who creates this faith through the gospel.

At the same time, Calvin was concerned to keep faith from being perceived as the one work we can perform in order to merit our justification. In itself, faith is nothing; its efficacy lies in its object, the person to whom it clings. Faith itself is imperfect, "for the mind is never so illuminated, but that many relics of ignorance remain; the heart is never so strengthened, but that much doubting cleaves to it."[30] Even faith is partial and weak, so if we were justified by faith itself, our case would be as hopeless as if we had to merit it by our works.[31]

According to Calvin, faith *is* assurance. One does not look to Christ for justification and to oneself for assurance of being justified. Therefore, the popular thesis of the sociologist Max Weber—namely, that Calvinism engendered an activist spirit in the world by linking assurance of election to one's works—is untenable, at least in relation to Calvin (and his heirs, who equated faith and assurance in their confessions). As Wilhelm Niesel reminds us: "The much discussed activism of Calvin is rooted in the fact that we belong to Christ and thus can go our way free from care and confess our membership in Christ; but it does not arise from any zealous desire to prove one's Christian faith by good works."[32]

Not only at the moment of our justification but throughout the Christian life, our works remain under the curse of God's law if they are measured by the standard of God's law. But Calvin is quick to add:

> But if, freed from this severe requirement of the law, or rather from the entire rigor of the law, [believers] hear themselves called with fatherly gentleness by God, they will cheerfully and with great eagerness answer, and follow his leading. To sum up: Those bound by the yoke of the law are like servants assigned certain tasks for each day by their masters. . . . But sons, who are more generously and candidly treated by their fathers, do not hesitate to offer them incomplete and half-done and even defective works, trusting that their obedience and readiness will be approved by our most merciful Father, however small, rude, and imperfect these may be. . . . But how can this be done amidst all this dread, where one doubts whether God is offended or honored by our works?[33]

Once works are no longer presented to God for justification, they can be accepted despite their imperfections by a merciful Father for the sake of Christ.

JUSTIFICATION AND UNION

Drawing, like Luther, on the wide range of biblical analogies for this union, Calvin complemented his judicial emphasis with respect to justification by the organic imagery of union and ingrafting in relation to inner renewal and communion with Christ, including His holiness. Thus, commenting on John 17, Calvin explains, "having been ingrafted into the body of Christ, we are made partakers of the Divine adoption, and heirs of heaven."[34] Elsewhere he writes, "This is the design of the gospel, that Christ may become ours, and that we may be ingrafted into his body."[35] We are not first united to Christ and then justified on the basis of His indwelling righteousness, but justified through faith by the imputation of Christ's alien righteousness. Nevertheless, one cannot grasp Christ without receiving all of His benefits. All of those who are justified are united to Christ and become fruit-bearing branches.

Calvin's emphasis on the person and work of the Holy Spirit, familiar to us especially in his formulation of the way in which Christ is communicated to us in the Lord's Supper, is already apparent in his treatment of the mystical union. The Spirit's mediation of Christ's person and work, not an immediate participation in the divine essence, is a critical aspect of his account. We are "one with the Son of God; not because he conveys his substance to us, but because, by the power of the Spirit, he imparts to us his life and all the blessings which he has received from the Father."[36] It is the Spirit who unites us here and now to Christ's work then and there, so that His righteousness really becomes ours—though it is always *His* righteousness rather than an inherent quality of ours.

Calvin's understanding of union with Christ, then, is the same as the federal theology that followed in his wake, with Christ replacing Adam as our federal, or covenantal, head. It is not an abstract participation in being, "as if it had been implanted in them by nature," but a personal union with the mediator of the covenant: "But Christ dwells principally on this, that the vital sap—that is, all life and strength—proceeds from himself alone."[37] Given the Trinitarian emphasis of Calvin's doctrine of union, including a high view of the Spirit's role in uniting us to Christ, it is not surprising that his treatment suggests a more dynamic understanding. Whereas justification is a once-and-for-all verdict, rendered at the moment one embraces Christ through the gospel, and the union itself is definitive, we grow more and more into Christ and His body.

On the legal basis of the imputation of Christ's righteousness, believers can be united to Christ, confident that everything that belongs properly to Him is given freely to us. In this marvelous exchange, all our debts become His and all His riches become ours. And in our union with Christ, we actually receive these benefits to which His imputed righteousness entitles us. Not even in our sanctification, therefore, can we lodge confidence in our inherent holiness. Calvin writes, "If you contemplate yourself, that is sure damnation."[38] He adds:

> Although we may distinguish them [justification and sanctification], Christ contains both of them inseparably in himself. Do you wish, then, to attain righteousness in Christ? You must first possess Christ; but you cannot possess him without being made partaker in his sanctification, because he cannot be divided into pieces [1 Cor. 1:13]. Since, therefore, it is solely by expending himself that the Lord gives us these benefits to enjoy, he bestows both of them at the same time, the one never without the other. Thus it is clear how true it is that we are justified not without works yet not through works, since in our sharing in Christ, which justifies us, sanctification is just as much included as righteousness.[39]

When discussing justification, Calvin cautions emphatically that "the question is not how we may become righteous but how, being unrighteous and unworthy, we may be reckoned righteous. If consciences wish to attain any certainty in this matter, they ought to give no place to the law."[40] Calvin recognizes here that justification need not be *confused* with sanctification by means of an all-encompassing ontology of union in order to recognize the *inseparability* of both legal (forensic) and organic (effective) aspects of that union.[41] Possess Christ and you will have both the perfect righteousness of justification and the beginning of sanctification in this life.

Regardless of whether union temporally preceded justification, Calvin is clear that the latter is the basis for the former: "Most people consider fellowship with Christ [*Christi esse participem*], and believing in Christ, to be the same thing; but the fellowship which we have with Christ [*participation quam habemus cum Christo*] is the consequence of faith [*fidei effectus*]."[42] Union with Christ does not provide a basis for God to discern in us a righteousness imparted; rather, on the basis of justification we are made partakers of Christ's vivifying life. The same act of faith that constantly looks to Christ alone for justification looks to Christ alone for sanctification and glorification.

Thus, there are not two sources of the Christian life: one that is forensic and found in Christ alone, and another that is moral and found within us. Forensic justification through faith alone is the fountain of union with Christ in all of its renewing aspects. We are justified through faith, not through union with Christ. As Wendel observes, for Calvin it is through faith that the justified are united to Christ and all of His benefits, becoming members of His own body, "although union with Christ cannot be regarded as the cause of the imputation of righteousness. Imputation and union with Christ are, rather, two inseparable aspects of one and the same divine grace: the one is not possible without the other."[43]

Therefore, Calvin speaks of a "double grace" in fellowship with Christ:

> Christ was given to us by God's generosity, to be grasped and possessed by us in faith. By partaking of him, we principally receive a double grace: namely, that being reconciled to God through Christ's blamelessness, we may have in heaven instead of a Judge a gracious Father; and secondly, that sanctified by Christ's spirit we may cultivate blamelessness and purity of life.[44]

This double grace entails a "twofold acceptance": Our persons are justified apart from works by the imputation of Christ's righteousness received through faith, so that our works can be justified or accepted by the Father not as meritorious but as the fruit of justification and union with His Son.[45]

In this way, Calvin subverts the charge (long repeated by countless Roman Catholic and Protestant critics) that justification leaves no place for good works in the Christian life. On the contrary, it frees us for the first time to obey God and serve our neighbor without fear of punishment for our shortcomings. Justification in no way depends on an impartation of Christ's righteousness through union, yet it is inseparable from it. Calvin writes: "This alone is of importance: having admitted that faith and good works must cleave together, we still lodge justification in faith, not in works. We have a ready explanation for doing this, provided we turn to Christ to whom our faith is directed and from whom it receives its full strength."[46] The believer does not keep one eye on Christ for justification and the other eye on himself for his own works, but looks to Christ for both. "You cannot grasp this [justification] without at the same time grasping sanctification also,"[47] Calvin affirms. Although they play no role in God's acceptance of us, even believers' imperfect works are welcomed by the Father because their corruption "is buried in Christ's purity, and is not charged to our account."[48] Only when we give no place to our works in justification are our works themselves "justified." This distinction between our persons and our works being justified is assumed in the different ways that the word *justification* is used by Paul and James.[49]

Calvin hardly substituted union with Christ for justification; rather, he appealed to Christ's external or alien righteousness imputed as the sole ground of justification and union with Christ as the source of our new life. Of course, union with Christ can be considered the ground of both justification and sanctification in an important sense: as the "marvelous exchange" in which Christ becomes our sin-bearer and we become the righteousness of God in Him. Nevertheless, imputative justification must always be distinguished as the forensic ground of God's acceptance. To whatever extent Calvin may have refined the notion of a "double righteousness," he was elaborating a conclusion that Luther arrived at early on, in his "Sermon on the Double Righteousness" (1519).[50]

DISPUTATION OVER JUSTIFICATION

As is often the case in church history, erroneous views provide an occasion for greater refinement and clarity, and the Lutheran Reformer Andreas Osiander is a case in point. Although his views were roundly condemned by his fellow Lutherans, it was perhaps Calvin who drew the sharpest attention to them and, in refuting them, helped to define critical aspects of the Reformation consensus on justification. So concerned was Calvin over Osiander's views that he added eight sections of refutation to the 1559 edition of the *Institutes* (3.11.5–12).

Osiander, Calvin wrote, "has introduced some strange monster of 'essential' righteousness."[51] In Calvin's view, it made little difference to say that one was justified by cooperation with an infused righteousness or by the "essential righteousness" of Christ indwelling the believer, since in either case the ground of justification would be an internal act of making the person righteous, rather than the imputation of an alien righteousness. Calvin admits that Osiander did not intend "to abolish freely given righteousness, he has still enveloped it in such a fog as to darken pious minds and deprive them of a lively experience of Christ's grace."[52] Besides indulging in "speculation" and "feeble curiosity," Osiander is guilty, Calvin says, of "something bordering on Manichaeism, in his desire to transfuse the essence of God into men," with the additional speculation "that Adam was formed to the image of God because Christ had already been destined as the prototype of human nature before the Fall."[53]

Since Osiander's confusion on justification and union is similar to a variety of recent proposals from various (mainly Protestant) quarters, and the debate helped Calvin to refine the doctrine that was embraced by Lutheran as well as Reformed interpreters, it is worth highlighting the main points. First, according to Calvin, Osiander's view confuses Christ's essential righteousness with our own. Osiander, Calvin says, does not understand justification as the imputation of "that righteousness which has been acquired for us by Christ's obedience and sacrificial death, but pretends that we are substantially righteous in God by the infusion both of his essence and of his quality." Second, "he throws in a mixture of substances by which God—transfusing himself into us, as it were—makes us part of himself." This not only introduces a Creator-creature confusion, it fails to recognize that "it comes about through the power of the Holy Spirit that we grow together with Christ, and he becomes our Head and we his members." The upshot is that justification is confused with regeneration and the believer is confused with the divine essence.

We can affirm a communion with Christ's person, Calvin counters, without surrendering the doctrine of forensic justification.[54] In Osiander's treatment, "to be justified is not only to be reconciled to God through free pardon but also to be made righteous, and righteousness is not a free imputation but the holiness and uprightness that the essence of God, dwelling in us, inspires."[55]

Justification and rebirth, Calvin writes, must be joined but never confused.[56] He also criticizes Osiander's view that "faith is Christ," rather than, as Calvin believes, an empty vessel that receives Christ.[57] Faith is the instrument through which we receive Christ, not to be confused with Christ (the material cause) Himself.[58]

Calvin also says that by conflating the new birth with justification, faith with Christ, and the believer with God, Osiander separated the two natures of Christ—an interesting twist on the running christological debates between these two traditions. Calvin notes that Osiander's view not only leads to a Nestorian Christology but to a doctrine of atonement that eliminates the saving humanity of Christ as Mediator.[59] Not even Christ was justified by His essential righteousness as divine, but by His obedience as a servant under the law.[60]

Consequently, there can be no saving deity of Christ apart from the covenantal obedience that He rendered in His humanity as the second Adam. Calvin writes: "For if we ask how we have been justified, Paul answers, 'By Christ's obedience' (Rom. 5:19). But did he obey in any other way than when he took upon himself the form of a servant (Phil. 2:7)? From this we conclude that in his flesh, righteousness has been manifested to us."[61] So once again we see that, far from representing antitheses to be negotiated, covenant and participation are integrally related themes.

Calvin observes that "mystical union" is "accorded by us the highest degree of importance, so that Christ, having been made ours, makes us sharers with him in the gifts with which he has been endowed." While our righteousness is indeed external to us—an alien righteousness that belongs properly to Christ rather than to us—Christ Himself does not remain alien, but joins Himself to us and us to Him. "We do not, therefore, contemplate him outside ourselves from afar in order that his righteousness may be imputed to us but because we put on Christ and are engrafted into his body—in short, because he deigns to make us one with him."[62] He adds:

> Osiander laughs at those who teach that "to be justified" is a legal term; because we must actually be righteous. Also, he despises nothing more than that we are justified by free imputation. Well then, if God does not justify us by acquittal and pardon, what does Paul's statement mean: "God was in Christ, reconciling the world to himself, not imputing men's trespasses against them" (2 Cor 5:19)? "For our sake he made him to be sin who had done no sin so that we might be the righteousness of God in him" (v. 21)?[63]

Calvin compares a number of New Testament texts to ordinary legal usage and then concludes, "Osiander objects that it would be insulting to God and contrary to his nature that he should justify those who actually remain wicked." To this Calvin replies with the familiar *simul iustus et peccator* (at the same time just and sinful), reminding Osiander that "they are always liable to the judgment of death before his tribunal" according to their own righteousness.[64]

The key, he says, is to distinguish justification and inward renewal without divorcing them. Sanctification is always partial in this life. "But [God] does not justify in part but liberally, so that they may appear in heaven as if endowed with the purity of Christ. No portion of righteousness sets our consciences at peace until it has been determined that we are pleasing to God, because we are entirely righteous before Him."[65] According to Calvin, Osiander, no less than Rome, denies this comfort to believers.[66] Only because justification is constituted by an imputed rather than an inherent righteousness are believers able "not to tremble at the judgment they deserve, and while they rightly condemn themselves, they should be accounted righteous outside themselves."[67] So we discern complementary emphases in Calvin's account: the righteousness of Christ that justifies us is "outside of us," although, by virtue of the mystical union, Christ Himself—including His righteousness—cannot remain outside us.

All supernatural gifts are found in Christ alone by the Spirit alone, though working through means. That we are in Christ *and* that Christ is in us are both because of the mediation of the Spirit. However, Calvin notes, "faith is the principal work of the Holy Spirit."[68] After all, it is faith that receives justification and is also active in love, yielding the fruit of good works. Since we are united to Christ through faith, this faith is the source not only of justification but also of sanctification and glorification.

Ever since Osiander and widely revived today, there have been attempts even in Protestant theologies to make sanctification the basis for justification rather than vice versa. However, they always end up omitting the crucial distinction between Christ *for* us and Christ *in* us. According to classic Reformed treatments of this connection, Christ alone is the basis for justification and union, but the act of justification is logically prior to union.[69] Nevertheless, once justification has provided the legal ground, all of the gifts of God's grace are freely given in union with Christ.

"HEAVENLY TREASURES"

If Luther was the "apostle" of the Reformation, as Calvin said, there can be little doubt that Calvin was a "Timothy" who refined the doctrine of justification that we find in our confessions. It is not simply one doctrine among many, much less a subtle point of theology that has little relevance for practical life and experience. Echoing Luther's "marvelous exchange," Calvin's comment offers a fitting conclusion:

> For in Christ he offers all happiness in place of our misery, all wealth in place of our neediness; in him he opens to us the heavenly treasures that our whole faith may contemplate his beloved Son, our whole expectation depend upon him, and our whole hope cleave to and rest in him. This, indeed, is that secret and hidden philosophy which cannot be wrested from syllogisms. But they whose eyes God has opened surely learn it by heart, that in his light they may see light [Ps. 36:9].[70]

NOTES

[1] John Calvin, *Institutes of the Christian Religion*, ed. John T. McNeill; trans. Ford Lewis Battles; Library of Christian Classics, XX–XXI (Philadelphia: Westminster John Knox, 1960), 3.11.2.

[2] For decisive criticism of the central dogma thesis, see especially Richard Muller, *The Unaccommodated Calvin* (New York: Oxford University Press, 2001), 3–17.

[3] Calvin, *Institutes of the Christian Religion*, 3.2.1.

[4] Ibid., 3.11.1.

[5] John Calvin, sermon on Luke 1:5–10, in *Corpus Reformatorum*, ed. Karl Gottlieb Bretschneider, et al. (Halle: Schwetske, 1863–1900), 46.23.

[6] See, for example, Muller, *The Unaccommodated Calvin*, 126–127.

[7] Calvin, *Institutes of the Christian Religion*, 3.11.7.

[8] Ibid., 3.11.2.

[9] Ibid., 3.3.10.

[10] Ibid., 3.3.11.

[11] Ibid., 3.4.30.

[12] Ibid., 3.3.14.

[13] Ibid., 3.12.2.

[14] Ibid., 3.11.2.

[15] Ibid., 3.12.3.

[16] Ibid., 3.19.2.

[17] François Wendel, *Calvin: Origins and Development of His Religious Thought*, trans. Philip Mairet (Durham: The Labyrinth Press, 1987), 260. I elaborate Calvin's argument on this point in *Lord and Servant: A Covenant Christology* (Louisville, Ky., and London: Westminster John Knox, 2006).

[18] John Calvin, *Commentaries on the Epistle of Paul the Apostle to the Romans*, trans. and ed. John Owen (repr. Grand Rapids: Baker, 1996), xxix–xxx.

[19] Ibid., 90.

[20] Ibid., 95–96.

[21] Ibid., 151.

[22] Ibid., 155.

[23] Ibid., 180.

[24] Ibid., 186.

[25] Ibid., 187.

[26] Ibid., 188.

[27] Calvin, *Institutes of the Christian Religion*, 3.1.1.

[28] Calvin, *Commentaries on the Epistle of Paul the Apostle to the Romans*, 159.

[29] Ibid., 171.

[30] Ibid., 179.

[31] Calvin, *Institutes of the Christian Religion*, 3.11.7. Doubtless, this emphasis was required not only for polemics against Rome, but also for opposing the perfectionistic teachings of the Anabaptists and even, as Wendel (*Calvin: Origins and Development of His Religious Thought*, 263) observes, Zwingli's tendency to treat faith as perfect. Calvin also may have already begun to detect among Protestants a tendency to regard faith as the basis rather than the instrument of justification (sometimes encouraged by the use of the phrase "justification *by* faith" as shorthand for "justification by Christ *through* faith").

[32] Wilhelm Niesel, *The Theology of John Calvin*, trans. Harold Knight (Philadelphia: Westminster, 1956), 99.

[33] Calvin, *Institutes of the Christian Religion*, 3.19.5.

[34] John Calvin, *Commentary on the Gospel According to John*, trans. William Pringle (repr. Grand Rapids: Baker, 1996), 2:166, commenting on John 17:3.

[35] John Calvin, *Commentary on the Epistles of Paul the Apostle to the Corinthians*, trans. John Pringle (repr. Grand Rapids: Baker, 2003), 1:60.

[36] Calvin, *Commentary on the Gospel According to John*, 2:184.

37 Ibid., 2:107, commenting on John 15:1.

38 Calvin, *Institutes of the Christian Religion*, 2.2.24.

39 Ibid., 3.16.1.

40 Ibid., 3.19.2.

41 On this point, see especially Philip Walker Butin, *Revelation, Redemption, and Response: Calvin's Trinitarian Understanding of the Divine-Human Relationship* (Oxford: Oxford University Press, 1995), and the excellent work by J. Todd Billings, *Calvin, Participation, and the Gift: The Activity of Believers in Union with Christ*, in Changing Paradigms in Historical and Systematic Theology (Oxford: Oxford University Press, 2007).

42 John Calvin, *Commentaries on the Epistles of Paul to the Galatians and Ephesians*, trans. William Pringle (repr. Grand Rapids: Baker 2003), 262.

43 Wendel, *Calvin: Origins and Development of His Religious Thought*, 258.

44 Calvin, *Institutes of the Christian Religion*, 3.11.1.

45 Ibid., 3.17.4–5.

46 Ibid., 3.16.1.

47 Ibid.

48 Ibid., 3.17.10.

49 Ibid., 3.17.11.

50 Wendel, *Calvin: Origins and Development of His Religious Thought*, 261.

51 Calvin, *Institutes of the Christian Religion*, 3.11.5, in refutation of Andreas Osiander's *Disputation on Justification* (1550). Osiander was a Lutheran theologian whose views were finally rejected in the Book of Concord. Similarities with the view of justification advanced especially by the New Finnish Perspective on Luther have been noted.

52 Ibid.

53 Ibid.

54 Ibid.

55 Ibid., 3.11.6.

56 Ibid.

57 Ibid., 3.11.7. The reference to Osiander is from his *Confession of the Only Mediator and of Justification by Faith* (1551). Faith is itself of no inherent worth, Calvin adds in this section; it only receives, yet "can justify us by bringing Christ, just as a pot crammed with money makes a man rich."

58 Ibid.

59 Ibid.

60 Ibid., 3.11.12.

61 Ibid.

62 Ibid., 3.11.10.

63 Ibid., 3.11.11.

64 Ibid.

65 Ibid.

[66] Ibid.

[67] Ibid.

[68] Ibid., 3.1.4.

[69] Louis Berkhof, *Systematic Theology*, 452. The mystical union in the sense in which we are now speaking of it is not the judicial ground, on the basis of which we become partakers of the riches that are in Christ. It is sometimes said that the merits of Christ cannot be imputed to us as long as we are not in Christ, since it is only on the basis of our oneness with Him that such an imputation could be reasonable. But this view fails to distinguish between our legal unity with Christ and our spiritual oneness with Him, and is a falsification of the fundamental element in the doctrine of redemption, namely, the doctrine of justification. Justification is always a declaration of God, not on the basis of an existing condition, but on that of a gracious imputation—a declaration which is not in harmony with the existing condition of the sinner. The judicial ground for all the special grace that we receive lies in the fact that the righteousness of Christ is freely imputed to us.

[70] Calvin, *Institutes of the Christian Religion*, 3.20.1.

Chapter 18

THE TRUE CHRISTIAN LIFE

JERRY BRIDGES

No one has rightly denied himself unless he has wholly resigned himself to the Lord and is willing to leave every detail to His good pleasure. If we put ourselves in such a frame of mind, then, whatever may happen to us, we shall never feel miserable or accuse God falsely because of our lot. [1]

—JOHN CALVIN

Because of his classic work, the *Institutes of the Christian Religion,* John Calvin is best known as a theologian, and he could rightly be called the father of Reformed theology. However, Calvin was primarily a pastor, and, as such, he was concerned with the outworking of theology in the everyday life of the believer. That is why in the *Institutes,* his development of the true Christian life follows immediately after his work on regeneration.

According to Calvin: "The object of regeneration . . . is to manifest in the life of believers a harmony and agreement between God's righteousness and their obedience and thus to confirm the adoption that they have received as sons."[2] How is this harmony between God's righteousness and our obedience to be pursued? Calvin leads us directly to

Scripture, for it is in obedience to Scripture that God's image is restored in us. Scripture first of all instructs us in the law to love righteousness, because by nature we are not inclined to do so. Second, Scripture provides us a guiding principle, namely, God's words to us: "You shall be holy, for I am holy" (1 Peter 1:16).

HOLINESS OF LIFE

Holiness consists in conformity to Christ. Calvin writes, "Because the Father has reconciled us to Himself in Christ, therefore He commands us to be conformed to Christ as to our pattern."[3] Indeed, he continues, "Unless we ardently and prayerfully devote ourselves to Christ's righteousness we do not only faithlessly revolt from our Creator, but we also abjure Him as our Savior."[4]

This is strong language. The word *ardently* conveys the idea of eager zealousness, or as we might say today, "going all out" or "giving 100 percent." The word *abjure* means "to renounce strongly," as in Peter's third denial of the Lord when "he began to invoke a curse on himself and to swear, 'I do not know the man'" (Matt. 26:74).

Calvin leaves no room for a middle ground. Either we ardently pursue the example of Christ or else we strongly renounce Him by our conduct and lifestyle. How different this standard is from the attitude of so many of today's Christians, who are quite casual or halfhearted in their pursuit of Christlikeness. But from Calvin's matter-of-fact writing style, it is clear that he regards a zealous pursuit of holiness as the *normal* Christian life.

Such an ardent pursuit of Christlikeness requires a strong motivation. To find it, Calvin appeals to the blessings of God:

• God has revealed Himself as a Father; therefore, we should behave as His children.

• Christ has purified us through His blood; therefore, we should not become defiled by fresh pollution.

- Christ has united us to His body as His members; therefore, we should not disgrace Him by any blemish.
- Christ has ascended to heaven; therefore, we should leave our carnal desires behind and lift our hearts upward to Him.
- The Holy Spirit has dedicated us as temples of God; therefore, we should exert ourselves not to profane His sanctuary, but to display His glory.
- Both our soul and body are destined to inherit an incorruptible and never-fading crown; therefore, we should keep them pure and undefiled.

For Calvin, there is no such thing as the so-called "carnal Christian." Rather, he writes, "The apostle denies that anyone actually knows Christ who has not learned to put off the old man, corrupt with deceitful lusts, and to put on Christ."[5] And again, "[The gospel] will be unprofitable if it does not change our heart, pervade our manners, and transform us into new creatures."[6] He continues: "Perfection must be the final mark at which we aim, and the goal for which we strive. It is not lawful for you to make a compromise with God, to try to fulfill part of your duties and to omit others at your own pleasure."[7]

At the same time, Calvin guards against setting too high a standard for other believers. He writes, "We should not insist on absolute perfection of the gospel in our fellow Christians, however much we may strive for it ourselves."[8] To use a contemporary expression, we should be tough on ourselves and tender with others. Unfortunately, the opposite is too often true. We expect a lot from others while excusing ourselves.

While urgently pressing the importance of our diligent pursuit of holiness, Calvin is realistic about our meager attainments. He acknowledges that the vast majority of Christians make only slight progress. But this is not to excuse us. Rather, he writes, "Let us not cease to do the utmost; that we may incessantly go forward in the way of the Lord; and let us not despair because of the smallness of our accomplishment."[9]

SELF-DENIAL

Given his stress on the importance of holiness, we might expect Calvin to proceed with some specific examples of how to pursue holiness in our lives, perhaps using the principle of "put off/put on" as Paul does in Ephesians 4:22–5:5. Instead, he first takes us to the root of the matter by directing our attention to Paul's words in Romans 12:1–2:

> I appeal to you therefore, brothers, by the mercies of God, to present your bodies as a living sacrifice, holy and acceptable to God, which is your spiritual worship. Do not be conformed to this world, but be transformed by the renewal of your mind, that by testing you may discern what is the will of God, what is good and acceptable and perfect.

He then writes, "It is a very important consideration that we are consecrated and dedicated to God; it means that we may think, speak, meditate, or do anything only with a view to His glory."[10] In pursuing the implications of this truth, he seems to unconsciously draw on Paul's words in 1 Corinthians: "You are not your own, for you were bought with a price" (6:19b–20a). He writes:

> If we are not our own, but the Lord's, it is plain what error we must flee, and to what purpose all our deeds must be directed. We are not our own, therefore neither our reason nor our will should guide us in our thoughts and actions. We are not our own, therefore we should not seek what is expedient to the flesh. We are not our own, therefore let us forget ourselves and our own interests as far as possible. But we are God's own; to him, therefore, let us live and die. We are God's own; therefore let his wisdom and will dominate all our actions. We are God's own; therefore let every part of our existence be directed toward him as our only legitimate goal.[11]

According to Calvin, self-denial also includes a life regulated by Paul's words in Titus 2:11–14:

> For the grace of God has appeared, bringing salvation for all people, training us to renounce ungodliness and worldly passions, and to live self-controlled, upright, and godly lives in the present age, waiting for our blessed hope, the appearing of the glory of our great God and Savior Jesus Christ, who gave himself for us to redeem us from all lawlessness and to purify for himself a people for his own possession who are zealous for good works.

Ungodliness means everything that hinders the sincere fear of God. And *worldly passion* means anything that panders to our sinful desires.

Turning to the positive traits of the new life in Titus 2:12, Calvin understands *self-control* to include "chastity, and temperance, as well as the pure and frugal use of temporal blessings and patience under poverty."[12] *Uprightness*, or righteousness, includes all the duties of justice and fairness in our dealings with others, and *godliness* "separates us from the pollutions of the world, and by true holiness unites us to God."[13]

According to Calvin, we should not crave wealth, honor, or power, but we should rest assured that everything depends on divine blessing alone. He writes, "A true Christian will not ascribe any prosperity to his own diligence, industry, or good fortune, but he will acknowledge that God is the author of it."[14]

While self-denial refers primarily to our relationship with God, it also applies to our relationships with other people. Paul's thought in Philippians 2:3—"in humility count others more significant than yourselves"—is Calvin's take-off point. This is an aspect of holiness that many of us seldom if ever think about. In vivid language, he exposes our lack of humility toward others. He writes:

> The vices of which we are full we carefully hide from others, and we flatter ourselves with the notion that they are small and trivial;

we sometimes even embrace them as virtues. . . . [But] if others have any vices, we are not content to criticize them sharply and severely, but we exaggerate them hatefully.[15]

Holiness of life even impacts how we view our talents and the talents of others. We must remember that whatever talents we have are free gifts from God. On the other hand, when we notice gifts of God in others, we are to value and esteem both the gifts and their possessors. And despite the faults of others, we are never to insult the person, but we are to show love and respect to everyone.

Calvin then raises the bar of self-denial even higher. Not only must we think of others as better than ourselves, we must actually seek their advantage. This, he says, is extremely difficult unless we set aside all selfish considerations and almost forget ourselves. He writes, "Let us rather seek the profit of others, and even voluntarily give up our rights for the sake of others."[16]

In fact, we should seek the good of everyone, friend and foe. "The Lord commands us to do good unto all men without exception, though the majority are very undeserving when judged according to their own merits."[17] The basis for this attitude is that all people are created in the image of God, to whom we owe all possible honor and love. This is especially true of other believers, because they have been made alive in Christ by the work of the Holy Spirit. But even if a person's actions are despicable and worthless, he still bears the image of God and is thus worthy of our respect and assistance as he needs it.

In a summary statement on self-denial, Calvin writes:

No one has rightly denied himself unless he has wholly resigned himself to the Lord and is willing to leave every detail to His good pleasure. If we put ourselves in such a frame of mind, then, whatever may happen to us, we shall never feel miserable or accuse God falsely because of our lot.[18]

PATIENCE IN CROSS-BEARING

As challenging as self-denial is, Calvin says, "it is fitting for the faithful Christian to rise to still a higher level where Christ calls every disciple to 'take up his cross.'"[19] Whereas self-denial is something we do or an attitude we maintain, cross-bearing for Calvin is to accept the hard, difficult, and painful circumstances of life from the hand of God as the means by which we might be conformed to the image of Christ (Rom. 8:29).

Calvin gives us five advantages of cross-bearing:

1. *The cross makes us humble.* We are too prone to have confidence in our own strength and our ability to endure hardship. Therefore, God afflicts us with calamity, and we soon sink under it. And so, being humbled, we learn to call upon His strength to endure.

2. *The cross makes us hopeful.* We experience the truth of God's promise that He will help us in our trials. This experience of God's faithfulness bolsters our assurance that God will keep His promises to us in the future, Calvin writes.

3. *The cross teaches obedience.* Through cross-bearing, we are taught to follow God's desire and not our own. If everything proceeded according to our wishes, we would not understand what it means to follow God.

4. *The cross makes for discipline.* Calvin says that God uses the cross we must bear to restrain and subdue our natural fleshly arrogance. This helps prevent us from becoming prideful if we acquire wealth, honor, or health.

5. *The cross brings repentance.* Calvin writes: "In every affliction we ought immediately to review our past life. When we do so, we shall certainly find that we deserved such chastisement."[20] Furthermore, we should acknowledge God's mercy and kindness even in our trials, for He sends afflictions as part of His design to deliver us from condemnation.

HOPEFULNESS FOR THE NEXT WORLD

Calvin's instructions on cross-bearing lead logically to his instructions on hopefulness for the next world. God knows we tend to love this world too much; we ought to learn the vanity of this world and raise our eyes to heaven to see the reward that awaits us. But Calvin recognized that our hearts will never seriously wish for and meditate on the future life unless we have first determined to forsake the vanities of this present life. He writes, "There is no golden mean between these two extremes; either this earthly life must become low in our estimation, or it will have our inordinate love."[21]

In a remarkable shifting of direction, however, Calvin warns us against despising this present life. He writes: "Nevertheless, our constant efforts to lower our estimate of the present world should not lead us to hate life or be ungrateful to God. For this life, though it is full of countless miseries, deserves to be reckoned among the divine blessings which should not be despised."[22] Here we see the careful balance that Calvin strikes between being overly engrossed in the things of this life on one hand, and despising them and failing to give thanks for them on the other.

THE RIGHT USE OF THE PRESENT LIFE

How, then, can we strike the right balance between an unhealthy occupation with the things of this life and an equally improper despising of the things of this life? We are to avoid unnecessary extremes. Calvin writes: "For if we must live, we must also use the necessary instruments for life. We cannot even avoid those matters which serve our pleasures rather than our needs. But that we may use them with a pure conscience, we should observe moderation, whether we mean the one or the other."[23] We should keep in mind "that the use of gifts of God cannot be wrong, if they are directed to the same purpose for which the Creator Himself has created and destined them."[24] But Calvin also suggests, "we must with equal zeal fight the lusts of the flesh, for if they are not firmly restrained, they will transgress every bound."[25]

Calvin wrote these words in the sixteenth century. Compared with our present day, with our modern conveniences and medical care, the lifestyle of even the wealthy of Calvin's day was indeed primitive. Yet Calvin in his time saw the danger of being overly preoccupied with this present life. If believers in the sixteenth century needed his admonitions, how much more do we?

In summary, for Calvin, the true Christian life includes much more than a mere code of conduct. Above all, it means conformity to Christ in every area of life. It includes holiness of life, self-denial with respect to God and to other people, patience in adversity, a clear view of the next world, and the right use of this present life. Calvin is direct and challenging, even uncomfortably so at times. At the same time, he is quite balanced and encouraging, for he realizes our continuing struggles with the flesh.

NOTES

[1] John Calvin, *Golden Booklet of the True Christian Life*, trans. Henry J. Van Andel (Grand Rapids: Baker, 1952), 44.

[2] John Calvin, *Institutes of the Christian Religion*, ed. John T. McNeill; trans. Ford Lewis Battles; Library of Christian Classics, XX–XXI (Philadelphia: Westminster John Knox, 1960), 3.6.1.

[3] Calvin, *Golden Booklet of the True Christian Life*, 18.

[4] Ibid., 19.

[5] Ibid., 20.

[6] Ibid., 21.

[7] Ibid., 22.

[8] Ibid., 21.

[9] Ibid., 23.

[10] Ibid., 26.

[11] Ibid.

[12] Ibid., 30.

[13] Ibid.

14 Ibid., 43.
15 Ibid., 32.
16 Ibid., 35.
17 Ibid., 37.
18 Ibid., 44.
19 Ibid., 47.
20 Ibid., 56.
21 Ibid., 70.
22 Ibid., 72.
23 Ibid., 83–84.
24 Ibid., 86.
25 Ibid., 87.

Chapter 19

THE COMMUNION
OF MEN WITH GOD

JOEL R. BEEKE

We cannot even open our mouths before God without danger unless the spirit instructs us in the right pattern of prayer. This privilege deserves to be more highly esteemed among us, since the only-begotten Son of God supplies words to our lips that free our minds from all wavering. [1]

—JOHN CALVIN

John Calvin, renowned preacher and theologian, was also a pastor who wanted his sheep to grow in the Christian life. His pastoral emphases are abundantly evident in his writing on prayer.

Calvin focused more on the practice of prayer than on its doctrine, which shows how practical his theology was.[2] For Calvin, prayer is the essence of the Christian life; it is a precious gift, not an academic problem.[3] He writes warmly and experientially[4] about prayer in his sermons and commentaries—especially on the book of Psalms—and in one of the longest chapters of his *Institutes of the Christian Religion* (3.20), which spans seventy pages in the McNeill-Battles edition.[5] Editor John T. McNeill notes, "This thoughtful and ample chapter, with its tone of devout warmth, takes its place in the forefront of historically celebrated discussions of prayer."[6]

In this chapter, I would like to look at Calvin's thoughts on prayer: what it is and how effective it is; its purposes and methods; its rules; its trinitarian foundation; and its relation to authentic piety. Throughout, we will notice that although he sets high standards for prayer, even acknowledging that praying rightly is a "peculiar gift,"[7] Calvin assures his readers that these standards are not his but God's, as taught in His Word. As such, these standards are not attainable by our sinful human natures,[8] but God is pleased to help His children pray (Rom. 8:26).

THE DEFINITION AND EFFECTIVENESS OF PRAYER

In the final edition of his *Institutes*, Calvin defines prayer as "the communion of men with God by which, having entered the heavenly sanctuary, they appeal to him in person concerning his promises in order to experience . . . that what they believed was not in vain."[9] Elsewhere, he writes that prayer is "a communication between God and us whereby we expound to him our desires, our joys, our sighs, in a word, all the thoughts of our hearts."[10]

Calvin considered prayer to be holy and familiar conversation with God, our heavenly Father; reverently speaking, it is family conversation, or even intimate covenantal conversation, in which the believer confides in God as a child confides in his father.[11] Prayer is "an emotion of the heart within, which is poured out and laid open before God."[12] In prayer, we both communicate and commune with our Father in heaven, feeling our transparency in His presence. Like Christ in Gethsemane, we cast our "desires, sighs, anxieties, fears, hopes, and joys into the lap of God."[13] In other words, through prayer, a Christian puts his "worries bit by bit on God."[14] We are "permitted to pour into God's bosom the difficulties which torment us, in order that he may loosen the knots which we cannot untie."[15] Prayer is the outpouring of the soul, the deepest root of piety, and the bedrock of assurance. It is the most important part of the Christian life, the lifeblood of every true believer.[16]

One fundamental aspect of Calvin's thought on prayer is that it was instituted not primarily for God but for man.[17] Prayer is a means given to man so that we might, by faith, "reach those riches which are laid up for us with the Heavenly Father."[18] Calvin says prayer allows the believer to appeal to the providence, predestination, omnipotence, and omniscience of God the Father. It calls down the Father's tender mercy and care for His children because, having prayed, we have a sense of peace that God knows all and that He "has both the will and the power to take the best care of us."[19]

The childlike outpouring of the soul before the heavenly Father involves entreaties and thanksgiving.[20] Proper requests include "those things which make for the extension of his [God's] glory and the setting forth of his name, and those benefits which conduce [serve] to our own advantage."[21] Proper thanksgivings "celebrate with due praise his [God's] benefits toward us, and credit to his generosity every good that comes to us."[22] Owing to our spiritual needs and poverty as well as God's liberality, "we must assiduously use both kinds of prayer."[23]

Two objections often surface about Calvin's understanding of prayer. The first is that when the believer obediently submits to God's will, he relinquishes his own will. To that objection, Calvin responds that through the act of submissive prayer, the believer invokes God's providence to act on his behalf. Thus, under the Spirit's guidance, man's will and God's will work together.

The second is that prayer seems superfluous in light of God's omniscience and omnipotence. To that objection, Calvin responds that God ordained prayer more for man as an exercise of piety than for Himself. Our prayers do not get in the way of providence because God, in His providence, ordains the means along with the end. What God "has determined to give of His own free will, even before He is asked, He promises to give all the same in response to our prayers."[24] Thus, prayer is the God-ordained way in which believers seek and receive what God has determined to do for them from eternity.[25]

Prayer does not change God or His decrees. We know this is true for three reasons. First, God is immutable; second, God's good pleasure governs everything; and third, God is in control of everything, including our prayers. If prayer could change God or His decrees, the human will would usurp from God at least part of the control of history, which would deny God's all-controlling grace and would destroy our faith.[26] Rather, "prayer is something we do with God's help on the basis of what God has done for us in eternal election."[27]

Nevertheless, prayer is still effective, for these two truths must never be forgotten: "first, that in His divine wisdom God anticipates our prayers; and second, that in His divine love God responds to them."[28] In other words, it is against God's nature not to hear and answer the prayers of His people. God desires to help us and not to disappoint us in His grace.[29]

Calvin's view of effective prayer is summarized by Bruce Ware: "While prayer never coerces God to act other than his infinite wisdom has willed, it nevertheless is one important and necessary condition which must be present for certain aspects of God's work to be carried out. Prayer, then, is not contrary to divine sovereignty but a divinely ordained instrument functioning within the sphere of God's sovereign wisdom and power in carrying out his will."[30] Ultimately, God's response to prayer is a "divine response to a divine initiative in the elect."[31] Prayer is effective because it is grounded in God and flows out of His sovereign, loving grace at work in us.

THE PURPOSES AND METHOD OF PRAYER

In Book 3, chapter 20 of the *Institutes*, Calvin notes that there are at least six purposes of prayer: (1) to fly to God with every need and gain from Him what is lacking in ourselves to live the Christian life; (2) to learn to desire wholeheartedly only what is right as we place all our petitions before God; (3) to prepare to receive God's benefits and responses to our petitions with humble gratitude; (4) to meditate on God's kindness to us as we receive what we have asked for; (5) to cultivate the proper spirit of delight for God's answers in prayer; and (6) to confirm God's faithful providence so that we may glorify Him and trust in His present help more readily as we witness Him regularly answering our prayers.[32] All of these purposes are designed to foster communion with God so that "the promises of God should have their way with us."[33]

These purposes are to be pursued in a biblically directed way. For Calvin, faith and prayer are inseparable. Faith nourishes and compels prayer, and prayer nourishes and confirms faith.[34] "The true test of faith lies in prayer," for "we cannot pray to God without faith."[35] Prayer that proceeds from faith is the only way to invoke God. "It is faith that obtains whatever is granted to prayer."[36]

The Bible teaches that prayer is the chief and perpetual exercise of faith, Calvin says.[37] Prayer cannot help but express the hope and joy that are inevitably attached to faith.[38] As Walter Stuermann writes: "One may say that prayer is a catalyst for faith, a condition under which the transaction between man and God progresses swiftly toward perfection. . . . It is the principal means by which the faithful are armed to do battle with Satan and by which they are enabled to enjoy a confidence, peace, and joy in spite of the warfare in which they are engaged."[39]

Prayer must be grounded in God's Word by faith. "Prayer rightly begun springs from faith, and faith, from hearing God's Word."[40] This means that the content of our prayers must be shaped, controlled, and restrained by Scripture. Bible-borne faith provides boldness and confidence in prayer. As Ware says, "This progression from the Word to faith to prayer is, for Calvin, the key to apprehending from God all that is necessary to live the Christian life."[41]

Such prayer leans on God's promises.[42] Calvin writes: "Let us learn that God in his promises is set before us as if he were a willing debtor."[43] God's promises supply fuel for prayer.[44] "We testify by prayer, that we hope to obtain from God the grace which he has promised. Thus anyone who has no faith in the promises, prays dissemblingly."[45] But through the intercession of Christ, prayer obtains what God promises by faith. "We dig up by prayer the treasures that were pointed out by the Lord's gospel [promises], and which our faith has gazed upon."[46]

The promises of God buttress our faith because God has bound Himself to fulfill them. Those covenant promises invite and allure us to prayer.[47] God would deny Himself and His covenant were He not to fulfill them.[48]

THE RULES OF PRAYER

For Calvin, prayer cannot be accomplished without discipline. He writes, "Unless we fix certain hours in the day for prayer, it easily slips from our memory."[49] He goes on to prescribe several rules to guide believers in offering effectual, fervent prayer.[50]

The first is *a heartfelt sense of reverence.* In prayer, we must be "disposed in mind and heart as befits those who enter conversation with God."[51] Our prayers should arise from "the bottom of our heart."[52] Calvin calls for a disciplined mind and heart, asserting that "the only persons who duly and properly gird themselves to pray are those who are so moved by God's majesty that, freed from earthly cares and affections, they come to it."[53]

The second rule is *a heartfelt sense of need and repentance.* We must "pray from a sincere sense of want and with penitence," maintaining "the disposition of a beggar."[54] Calvin does not mean that believers should pray for every whim that arises in their hearts, but that they must pray penitently in accord with God's will, keeping His glory in focus, yearning for every request "with sincere affection of heart, and at the same time desiring to obtain it from him."[55]

The third rule is *a heartfelt sense of humility and trust in God.* True prayer requires that "we yield all confidence in ourselves and humbly plead for pardon," trusting in God's mercy alone for blessings both spiritual and temporal,[56] always remembering that the smallest drop of faith is more powerful than unbelief.[57] Any other approach to God will only promote pride, which will be lethal: "If we claim for ourselves anything, even the least bit," we will be in grave danger of destroying ourselves in God's presence.[58]

The final rule is to have *a heartfelt sense of confident hope.*[59] The confidence that our prayers will be answered does not arise from ourselves, but through the Holy Spirit working in us. In believers' lives, faith and hope conquer fear so that we are able to "ask in faith, nothing wavering" (James 1:6, KJV). This means that true prayer is confident of success, owing to Christ and the covenant, "for the blood of our Lord Jesus Christ seals the pact which God has concluded with us."[60] Believers thus approach God boldly and cheerfully because such "confidence is necessary in true invocation . . . which becomes the key that opens to us the gate of the kingdom of heaven."[61]

These rules may seem overwhelming—even unattainable—in the face of a holy, omniscient God. Calvin acknowledges that our prayers are fraught with weakness and failure. "No one has ever carried this out with the uprightness that was due," he writes.[62] But God tolerates "even our stammering and pardons our ignorance," allowing us to gain familiarity with Him in prayer, though it be in "a babbling manner."[63] In short, we will never feel like worthy petitioners. Our checkered prayer life is often attacked by doubts,[64] but such struggles show us our ongoing need for prayer itself as a "lifting up of the spirit"[65] and continually drive us to Jesus Christ, who alone will "change the throne of dreadful glory into the throne of grace."[66] Calvin concludes that "Christ is the only way, and the one access, by which it is granted us to come to God."[67]

THE TRINITARIAN FOCUS OF PRAYER

Calvin stresses the Trinitarian aspect of prayer. Prayer originates with the Father, is made possible through the Son, and is worked out in the soul by the Spirit, through whom it returns via Christ to the Father. The triune God gives, hears, and answers prayer.

Prayer is given by the Father, who graciously invites us to pray through Christ and buttresses that invitation with His promises. Apart from Christ, it is "folly and rashness for mortals to presume to address

God."[68] They should rather wait for the Father's call that He implements through His Word, "for when he promises to be our Savior he shows that he will always be ready to receive us. He does not wait till we come seeking him; rather, he offers himself and exhorts us to pray to him—and in doing so, tests our faith."[69] He draws us to prayer by the very sweetness of His name, *Father.*

Calvin devotes considerable attention to the work of Christ in prayer.[70] In His walk on earth, Jesus counseled His disciples to ask anything in His name (John 16:23). Only by His name can we have access to the Father, Calvin says. God will hear our prayers for the sake of His Son when we pray in His name.[71] Calvin also gives a stern warning that if we do not approach God in the name of Jesus Christ, "no way and no access to God remain; nothing is left in his throne but wrath, judgment, and terror."[72]

Christ is the nexus between the believer and God, the junction where the believer's sinful prayers are purified "by sprinkled blood" and presented to the Father.[73] "Let us learn to wash our prayers with the blood of our Lord Jesus Christ," Calvin counsels.[74]

Christ is also our Intercessor in heaven. Calvin notes, "God can listen to no prayers without the intercession of Christ."[75] Christ's finished work and the "power of his death [avail] as an everlasting intercession in our behalf," he adds.[76] We come through Christ and with Christ to the Father, so that "Christ becomes the precentor who leads the prayers of his people."[77]

The Holy Spirit also plays a crucial role in the prayer life of believers, Calvin says. He is "our teacher in prayer, to tell us what is right and [to] temper our emotions."[78] He intercedes for us with groans that are unutterable (Rom. 8:26). Calvin explains that He "arouses in us assurance, desires, and sighs, to conceive which our natural powers could scarcely suffice."[79] He affects our hearts in such a way that these prayers "penetrate into heaven itself by their fervency."[80]

Calvin further addresses believers' response when the Spirit does not seem to be present in prayer. He says that this is no excuse to cease praying until they feel the Spirit come upon them; rather, they must importunately "demand that they be inflamed with the fiery darts of his Spirit so as to be rendered fit for prayer."[81] We should never cease to pray for the increase of the Spirit.[82]

PRAYER AS PART OF PIETY

Calvin's concept of piety (*pietas*) includes attitudes and actions that are directed to the adoration and service of God. Prayer is the principal and perpetual exercise of faith and the chief element of piety, Calvin says.[83] Prayer shows God's grace to the believer even as the believer offers praises to God and asks for His faithfulness. Herman Selderhuis says Calvin's commentary on the Psalms stresses that "prayer is not so much about moving God to a responsive action so much as it is given to bring a believer to greater confidence" in God, which, in turn, promotes a lifestyle of authentic piety.[84] Growth in piety requires prayer, for prayer diminishes self-love and multiplies dependence on God. Prayer unites God and man, not in substance, but in will and purpose. Like the Lord's Supper, prayer lifts the believer to Christ and renders glory to God.

That glory is the purpose of the first three petitions of the Lord's Prayer, as well as other petitions dealing with His creation. Since creation looks to God's glory for its preservation, the entire Lord's Prayer is directed to God's glory.[85] In the Lord's Prayer, which Calvin dwells on at length in the *Institutes*, Christ "supplies words to our lips."[86] However, because the Lord's Prayer is a model for us, we are bound by its pattern, not its words. Our words may be "utterly different, yet the sense ought not to vary."[87] Fundamentally, the Lord's Prayer shows us how all our prayers must be controlled, formed, and inspired by the Word of God.[88] Only the Word can provide holy boldness in prayer, "which rightly accords with fear, reverence, and solicitude."[89] I. John Hesselink says Calvin's writing on the Lord's Prayer teaches four things about prayer: (1) it revolves around the reconciling work of

Christ, (2) it is corporate in nature, (3) it unveils the nature of God's kingdom, and (4) it involves our daily physical needs.[90]

We must be disciplined and steadfast in prayer, for prayer keeps us in fellowship with Christ. Without His intercessions, our prayers would be rejected.[91] Thus, prayer is the channel between God and man. It is how the Christian expresses his praise and adoration of God, and asks for God's help in submissive piety.[92]

There is also a corporate element of piety in prayer. Since Christ's ascension, the church has had "a surer advocate,"[93] Calvin says. Christ is not just an individual advocate but a corporate advocate, one to whom the church can apply for strength and comfort. Consequently, Calvin counsels us "to direct all intercessions of the whole church to that sole intercession" of Christ.[94]

Furthermore, Christ has entered into the heavens before the saints, "and thus the mutual prayers for one another of all members yet laboring on earth rise to the Head."[95] The corporate church and the individual believer pray for one another through and in Christ's name. So one of the best ways we can love one another as believers is to pray for each other. Our prayers should include the universal church and all mankind, even generations unborn.[96] In intercessory prayer, we forgo our propensity for selfishness and "clothe ourselves with a public character," sharing with Christ in His intercession.[97]

Prayer expresses piety both privately and corporately,[98] but effective private prayer is the prerequisite of effective corporate praying, Calvin says.[99] Individual piety must be learned and nurtured so that the church's corporate piety can grow. Calvin refers to the Old Testament temple as bearing the God-given title of "house of prayer," which indicates that "the chief part of his [God's] worship lies in the office of prayer."[100] By corporate prayer, the "unity of the faith" is nurtured so that "the prayers of the church are never ineffectual."[101]

In his commentary on the book of Psalms, Calvin focuses on singing as a part of prayer that helps lift the heart up to God. The psalms constitute a prayer book, for they are "an anatomy of all the parts of the soul."[102] In the commentary's preface, Calvin says the psalms are particularly helpful in making believers aware of their need, and they also tell where to find the "remedies for their cure."[103] Whether sung individually or corporately, the psalms teach us to place our trust in God and to find remission of our sins in Jesus Christ.[104]

The singing of psalms gives access to God and freedom "to lay open before him our infirmities."[105] Calvin includes singing as a way to "exercise the mind in thinking of God and keep it attentive."[106] Singing allows believers to glorify God together and it allows "all men mutually, each one from his brother [to] receive the confession of faith and be invited and prompted by his example."[107] Singing greatly aids prayer, not only because it glorifies God, but because it promotes corporate piety toward God.

PERSEVERING FOR PRECIOUS COMMUNION IN PRAYER

Throughout his writings, Calvin offers a theology of prayer. He presents the throne room of God as glorious, holy, and sovereign, while also accessible, desirable, and precious in and through Christ. Given the rich blessings accessible to us through prayer, those who refuse to pray "neglect a treasure, buried and hidden in the earth, after it had been pointed out"[108] to them. They also commit idolatry by defrauding God, since prayerlessness is a blatant denial that "God is the author of every good thing."[109]

We must persevere in pursuing precious access to God in prayer, Calvin concludes.[110] Discouragements may abound and almost overwhelm us: "Our warfare is unceasing and various assaults arise daily." But that gives all the more reason to discipline ourselves to persevere in prayer, even if "we must repeat the same supplications not twice or three times only, but as often as we need, a hundred and a thousand times."[111] Ceasing to pray when God does not answer us quickly is the surest mark that we have never become believers.[112]

Calvin counsels believers not only to better methods of prayer, but to a deeper devotion and a surer access to the triune God who has given the gift of prayer. He modeled this prayer life by accompanying every public act with prayer, by providing forms of prayer,[113] and by appointing days of prayer for a variety of occasions—as well as privately in his own life.[114] These merge well in the last prayer he records in his commentary on Ezekiel, which, because of failing health, he was not able to complete:

> Grant, Almighty God, since we have already entered in hope upon the threshold of our eternal inheritance, and know that there is a certain mansion for us in heaven after Christ has been received there, who is our head, and the first-fruits of our salvation: Grant, I say, that we may proceed more and more in the course of thy holy calling until at length we reach the goal, and so enjoy that eternal glory of which thou affordest us a taste in this world, by the same Christ our Lord. Amen.[115]

Ultimately, for Calvin, prayer is a heavenly act, a holy and precious communing with the triune God in His glorious throne room, grounded in an assured eschatological hope.[116]

"Lord, teach us to pray" (Luke 11:1).

NOTES

[1] John Calvin, *Institutes of the Christian Religion*, ed. John T. McNeill; trans. Ford Lewis Battles; Library of Christian Classics, XX–XXI (Philadelphia: Westminster John Knox, 1960), 3.20.34.

[2] Wilhelm Niesel, *The Theology of Calvin*, trans. Harold Knight (London: Lutterworth, 1956), 156.

[3] Charles Partee, "Prayer as the Practice of Predestination," in *Calvinus Servus Christi*, ed. Wilhelm H. Neuser (Budapest: Pressabteilung des Raday-Kollegiums, 1988), 246.

[4] Robert Douglas Loggie stresses that it is particularly Calvin's discussion of prayer that contributes to the experiential flavor of Book 3 of his *Institutes of the Christian Religion* ("Chief Exercise of Faith—An Exposition of Calvin's Doctrine of Prayer," *The Hartford Quarterly*, 5, 2 [1965]: 67).

5 Only Calvin's chapter on faith is longer in the original *Institutes*.

6 Calvin, *Institutes of the Christian Religion*, 2:850n1.

7 Ibid., 3.20.5.

8 John Calvin, *Commentaries of Calvin* (Grand Rapids: Eerdmans, 1948–1950), on Jer. 29:12. (Hereafter, *Commentary*)

9 Calvin, *Institutes of the Christian Religion*, 3.20.2.

10 John Calvin, *Instruction in Faith*, trans. Paul T. Fuhrmann (Philadelphia: Westminster, 1949), 57.

11 *Commentary* on Psalm 10:13; cf. Herman J. Selderhuis, *Calvin's Theology of the Psalms* (Grand Rapids: Baker, 2007), 219.

12 Calvin, *Institutes of the Christian Religion*, 3.20.29; cf. Ronald S. Wallace, *Calvin's Doctrine of the Christian Life* (London: Oliver and Boyd, 1959), 281–282.

13 *Commentary* on Psalm 89:38–39.

14 *Commentary* on Psalm 86:6.

15 *Commentary* on Genesis 18:25.

16 *Commentary* on Psalm 14:4.

17 Calvin, *Institutes of the Christian Religion*, 3.20.3.

18 Ibid.

19 Ibid., 3.20.2.

20 Calvin, *Instruction in Faith*, 58–59.

21 Calvin, *Institutes of the Christian Religion*, 3.30.28.

22 Ibid.

23 Calvin, *Instruction in Faith*, 58–59; Wallace, *Calvin's Doctrine of the Christian Life*, 284–286.

24 *Commentary* on Matthew 6:8.

25 Partee, "Prayer as the Practice of Predestination," 254; cf. David Crump, *Knocking on Heaven's Door: A New Testament Theology of Petitionary Prayer* (Grand Rapids: Baker Academic, 2006), 297.

26 Calvin, *Institutes of the Christian Religion*, 1.17.12; 3.20.43; Partee, "Prayer as the Practice of Predestination," 252.

27 Ibid., 254.

28 *Commentary* on Psalm 119:38.

29 *Commentary* on Psalm 65:2; Selderhuis, *Calvin's Theology of the Psalms*, 225.

30 Bruce A. Ware, "The Role of Prayer and the Word in the Christian Life According to John Calvin," *Studia Biblica et Theologica* 12 (1982): 90. Cited in David Calhoun, "Prayer: 'The Chief Exercise of Faith,'" in *A Theological Guide to Calvin's Institutes: Essays and Analysis*, ed. David W. Hall (Phillipsburg, N.J.: P&R, 2008).

31 Partee, "Prayer as the Practice of Predestination," 255.

32 Calvin, *Institutes of the Christian Religion*, 3.20.3.

33 Cited in Niesel, *The Theology of Calvin*, 157.

34 *Commentary* on Zephaniah 3:7; Acts 8:22.

35 *Commentary* on Matthew 21:21; Romans 8:26.

36 Calvin, *Institutes of the Christian Religion*, 3.20.11.

37 *Commentary* on Matthew 21:21.

38 *Commentary* on Psalm 91:15.

39 Walter Earl Stuermann, *A Critical Study of Calvin's Concept of Faith* (Tulsa, Okla.: Edwards Brothers, 1952), 303, 313–314.

40 Calvin, *Institutes of the Christian Religion*, 3.20.27.

41 Ware, "The Role of Prayer and the Word," 88.

42 *Commentary* on Psalm 85:5.

43 *Commentary* on Psalm 119:58.

44 Ronald S. Wallace, *Calvin, Geneva, and the Reformation* (Eugene, Ore.: Wipf & Stock, 1998), 211.

45 *Commentary* on James 1:6.

46 Calvin, *Institutes of the Christian Religion*, 3.20.2.

47 *Commentary* on Psalm 50:14; 36:13; cited in Selderhuis, *Calvin's Theology of the Psalms*, 220.

48 For covenantal prayer in Calvin, see Peter Lillback, *The Binding of God: Calvin's Role in the Development of Covenant Theology* (Grand Rapids: Baker, 2001), 267–269.

49 *Commentary* on Daniel 6:10.

50 Calvin, *Institutes of the Christian Religion*, 3.20.4–16.

51 Ibid., 3.20.4–5.

52 John Calvin, *Sermons on the Epistle to the Ephesians* (Edinburgh: Banner of Truth Trust, 1973), 679.

53 Calvin, *Institutes of the Christian Religion*, 3.20.5.

54 Ibid., 3.20.6–7.

55 Ibid., 3.20.6; cf. Wallace, *Calvin's Doctrine of the Christian Life*, 280–281.

56 Calvin, *Institutes of the Christian Religion*, 3.20.8–10.

57 Ibid., 3.2.17.

58 Ibid., 3.20.8.

59 Ibid, 3.20.11–14.

60 Cited in Niesel, *The Theology of Calvin*, 153.

61 *Commentary* on Ephesians 3:12. For a helpful explanation of Calvin's four rules of prayer, see Don Garlington, "Calvin's Doctrine of Prayer," *The Banner of Truth*, no. 323–324 (Aug.–Sept. 1990): 45–50, and Stephen Matteucci, "A Strong Tower for Weary People: Calvin's Teaching on Prayer," *The Founders Journal* (Summer 2007): 21–23.

62 Calvin, *Institutes of the Christian Religion*, 3.20.16.

63 Ibid.; John Calvin, *Commentary on the Book of Psalms*, trans. James Anderson (Edinburgh: Calvin Translation Society, 1845; repr. Grand Rapids: Baker, 2003), 2:171.

64 *Commentary* on Matthew 21:21.

65 Calvin, *Institutes of the Christian Religion*, 3.20.1, 5, 16; cf. Joel R. Beeke, *The Quest for Full*

Assurance: The Legacy of Calvin and His Successors (Edinburgh: Banner of Truth Trust, 1999), 49.

[66] Calvin, *Institutes of the Christian Religion*, 3.20.17.

[67] Ibid., 3.20.19.

[68] John Calvin, sermon on 1 Timothy 2:8 in *Grace and Its Fruits: Selections from John Calvin on the Pastoral Epistles*, ed. Joseph Hill (Darlington, England: Evangelical Press, 2000), 259–260, cited in I. John Hesselink, introduction to John Calvin, *On Prayer: Conversation with God* (Louisville, Ky.: Westminster John Knox, 2006), 4.

[69] Ibid.

[70] E.g., Calvin, *Institutes of the Christian Religion*, 3.20.17–20.

[71] Ibid., 3.20.17.

[72] Ibid., 3.20.19.

[73] Ibid., 3.20.18.

[74] John Calvin, *Sermons on Election and Reprobation*, trans. John Fields (Audubon, N.J.: Old Paths, 1996), 210.

[75] *Commentary* on Exodus 29:38.

[76] Calvin, *Institutes of the Christian Religion*, 3.20.20.

[77] T. H. L. Parker, *Calvin: An Introduction to His Thought* (Louisville: Westminster John Knox Press, 1995), 110.

[78] Calvin, *Institutes of the Christian Religion*, 3.20.5.

[79] Ibid.

[80] *Commentary* on Romans 8:26.

[81] Geneva Catechism, Q. 245, Reid trans., 131, cited in Hesselink, *On Prayer: Conversation with God*, 10.

[82] *Commentary* on Acts 1:14; cf. Wallace, *Calvin's Doctrine of the Christian Life*, 286–287.

[83] See Loggie, "Chief Exercise of Faith," 65–81; H. W. Maurer, "An Examination of Form and Content in John Calvin's Prayers" (Ph.D. dissertation, Edinburgh, 1960); and Joel R. Beeke, *Puritan Reformed Spirituality* (Darlington, England: Evangelical Press, 2006), 1–33.

[84] Selderhuis, *Calvin's Theology of the Psalms*, 224–226.

[85] Calvin, *Institutes of the Christian Religion*, 3.20.11.

[86] Ibid., 3.20.34; cf. 3.20.34–39.

[87] Ibid., 3.20.49.

[88] Joel R. Beeke, "Calvin on Piety," *The Cambridge Companion to John Calvin*, ed. Donald K. McKim (Cambridge: Cambridge University Press, 2004), 125–152.

[89] Calvin, *Institutes of the Christian Religion*, 3.20.14; Wallace, *Calvin's Doctrine of the Christian Life*, 276–279.

[90] Hesselink, *On Prayer: Conversations with God*, 26–30.

[91] *Commentary* on Hebrews 7:26.

[92] Lionel Greve, "Freedom and Discipline in the Theology of John Calvin, William Perkins, and John Wesley: An Examination of the Origin and Nature of Pietism" (Ph.D. dissertation,

The Hartford Seminary Foundation, 1976), 143–144. For how Calvin's emphasis on prayer impacted the Reformed tradition, see Diane Karay Tripp, "Daily Prayer in the Reformed Tradition: An Initial Survey," *Studia Liturgica* 21 (1991): 76–107, 190–219.

[93] Calvin, *Institutes of the Christian Religion*, 3.20.18.

[94] Ibid., 3.20.19.

[95] Ibid., 3.20.20.

[96] *Commentary* on Psalm 90:16.

[97] *Commentary* on Psalm 79:6.

[98] Cf. Thomas A. Lambert, "Preaching, Praying, and Policing the Reform in Sixteenth Century Geneva" (Ph.D. dissertation, University of Wisconsin-Madison, 1998), 393–480.

[99] Calvin, *Institutes of the Christian Religion*, 3.20.29.

[100] Ibid.

[101] Ibid.

[102] Calvin, author's preface in *Commentary on the Psalms*, 1:xxxvii.

[103] Ibid.

[104] Ibid., 1:xxxix; cf. Ross J. Miller, "Calvin's Understanding of Psalm-Singing as a Means of Grace" and "Music and the Spirit: Psalm-Singing in Calvin's Liturgy," in *Calvin Studies VI* (Colloquium on Calvin Studies at Davidson College, 1992), 35–58.

[105] *Commentary on the Psalms*, 1:xxxviii.

[106] Calvin, *Institutes of the Christian Religion*, 3.20.31.

[107] Ibid.

[108] Ibid., 3.20.1.

[109] Ibid., 3.20.14.

[110] Ibid., 3.20.51–52.

[111] Cited in Hesselink, *On Prayer: Conversations with God*, 19.

[112] *Commentary* on Psalm 22:4; Wallace, *Calvin, Geneva, and the Reformation*, 214.

[113] John Calvin, *Treatises on the Sacraments of the Church of Geneva, Forms of Prayer, and Confessions of Faith*, trans. by Henry Beveridge (repr. Grand Rapids: Reformation Heritage Books, 2002); Charles E. Edwards, *Expositions and Prayers from Calvin* (Philadelphia: Presbyterian Board of Publication, 1897); Clyde Manschreck, ed., *Prayers of the Reformers* (Philadelphia: Muhlenberg Press, 1958); and W. de Greef, *The Writings of John Calvin: An Introductory Guide* (Grand Rapids: Baker, 1989), 126–131.

[114] Elsie McKee, *John Calvin: Writings on Pastoral Piety* (New York: Paulist Press, 2001), 29, 167ff.

[115] *Commentary* on Ezekiel 20:44.

[116] Wallace, *Calvin, Geneva, and the Reformation*, 214.

INDEX OF SCRIPTURE

INDEX OF SUBJECTS AND NAMES

About Reformation Trust

As part of Ligonier Ministries, Reformation Trust Publishing was established in 2006 to produce books that are true to the historic Christian faith and the doctrines recovered during the Protestant Reformation of the sixteenth century.

Early titles from Reformation Trust have delved into the doctrines of God's sovereign grace and examined issues such as worship and evangelism. The authors whose names adorn the covers of Reformation Trust titles are gifted evangelical pastors, scholars, and leaders, men and women who are adept at rightly handling the Word of God, such as Dr. R. C. Sproul, Dr. Joel R. Beeke, Dr. Sinclair B. Ferguson, Dr. Michael A. G. Haykin, Mrs. Susan Hunt, Dr. Steven J. Lawson, Rev. Burk Parsons, Rev. Richard D. Phillips, Dr. R. C. Sproul Jr., and Rev. Jason J. Stellman.

Dr. Sproul, founder and chairman of Ligonier Ministries, has articulated the vision behind the name of this publishing house: "*Reformation* defines the theological perspective we're committed to propagating at Ligonier Ministries—that recovery of biblical Christianity in the sixteenth century. We want to produce materials that are consistent and faithful to that tradition. *Trust* involves a kind of fidelity and the idea of a legacy. We seek to perpetuate a tradition, but not a tradition of men. Our legacy, our trust, is to be faithful to that tradition."

Believing that an enduring message deserves an enduring medium, Reformation Trust is committed to publishing books of real value, using high-quality materials and processes. These books will be an investment that will last. We hope you will find that the heritage, the quality, and the authors behind Reformation Trust make this a publishing imprint you can rely on to strengthen your Christian walk. For more information and to learn about existing and new titles, please visit **www.reformationtrust.com**.

IR

Reformation Trust
PUBLISHING

ABOUT LIGONIER MINISTRIES

More than thirty-eight years ago, as it is today, the world was filled with challenges to biblical faith. Christians who sought to be equipped to answer these challenges had few options short of going to seminary. Dr. R. C. Sproul saw the need to offer an accessible, practical bridge of learning for the growing Christian, and Ligonier Ministries was born.

Ligonier Ministries is an international Christian educational organization established in 1971 to equip Christians to articulate what they believe and why they believe it. Our foremost desire is to "awaken as many people as possible to the holiness of God by proclaiming, teaching, and defending His holiness in all its fullness." Our vision is to propagate the Reformed faith to the church throughout the world.

To this end Ligonier endeavors to provide solid, trusted teaching that helps bridge the educational gap between Sunday school and seminary. By making Christian education materials available, Ligonier hopes to encourage Christian laypeople to be transformed by the renewing of their minds so that they will be equipped to serve the church and glorify God (Rom. 12:2).

Committed to training Christ's disciples—both pastors and lay people—to live in the Word and live out the gospel, Ligonier launched the Ligonier Academy of Biblical and Theological Studies in 2009. Knowing that reformation in the church is not only possible but also promised by the Lord, we hope that through this effort Ligonier Ministries will be of continued service to Christ and His church.

Ligonier also produces the *Renewing Your Mind* radio broadcasts, *The Reformation Study Bible* (ESV), *Tabletalk* devotional magazine, books true to the historic Christian faith through Reformation Trust Publishing, numerous teaching series, sacred music, and national and regional conferences. We have an extensive catalog with more than three thousand unique resources. To learn more about Ligonier, please visit **www.ligonier.org**.

LIGONIER MINISTRIES

Renew your Mind.